The
Central Banks

THE
CENTRAL BANKS

*The International
and European Directions*

William Frazer

Westport, Connecticut
London

Library of Congress Cataloging-in-Publication Data

Frazer, William.
    The central banks : the international and European directions / by
William Frazer.
      p. cm.
    Includes bibliographical references and index.
    ISBN 0–275–94732–7 (alk. paper)
    1. Monetary policy—European Economic Community countries.
2. Monetary policy—United States. 3. Banks and banking, Central—
European Economic Community countries. 4. Banks and banking,
Central—United States. 5. Keynesian economics. 6. International
finance. I. Title.
HG930.5.F75 1994
332.1'1'094—dc20   93–23491

British Library Cataloguing in Publication Data is available.

Library of Congress Catalog Card Number: 93–23491
ISBN: 0–275–94732–7

First published in 1994

Praeger Publishers, 88 Post Road West, Westport, CT 06881
An imprint of Greenwood Publishing Group, Inc.

Printed in the United States of America

The paper used in this book complies with the
Permanent Paper Standard issued by the National
Information Standards Organization (Z39.48–1984).

10 9 8 7 6 5 4 3 2 1

To

Chinkie, Monte, the people in London (Roger Alford, Tim Congdon, Charles Goodhart, Lord Joseph, Paul Mayhew, and C. T. Taylor), and the American nationals in London (Eugene Crook and Charles Wellborn)

Contents

Part I. Introduction

Part II. Operations, Mechanisms, and the State

Part III. Central Banking

Illustrations

FIGURES

TABLES

Preface

This work, referred to by the short title *The Central Banks,* is an extension of the theoretic/alternative systems approach I treat with respect to Keynes, the Keynesians (including some with a post-Keynesian flair), and Friedman (Frazer 1994a). Although the present work can be read independently of the theoretic/alternative systems, the latter is extended to the institutions that must implement monetary and closely related policies. The alternatives find their substance in and are influenced by the traditions, approaches to operations, and practices of the central banks. In part, this is because of the encompassing nature of monetary matters and the analytical system I associate with Friedman, and in part, it is, as I demonstrate, because the fiscal and tax policies of government are intimately entwined in one way or another with monetary policy.

To set an empirical tone and give perspective to the matters at hand, selected policy experiments on the part of the United States are reviewed early, along with parts of the alternatives at issue. I emphasize the major interconnections between the money- and credit-creating potential of central banks and the fiscal/deficit potential of government. The principal central banks I consider include, in the order of their evolution, the Bank of England, the Federal Reserve, and the Bundesbank.

Continuing effort at some historical perspective, recognizing the encompassing nature of monetary matters, and moving to the open economy with currencies, exchange rates, and balances of payments, I take up exchange-rate, reserve, and capital-flows mechanisms. Phases of the post-World War II years are sketched in reference to the International Monetary Fund, the early prospect of a super central bank, some bank operations, the closing of the gold window, freedom and sovereignty, the rise of private markets and private capital in the post-World War II context, the European Monetary System, and runs on currencies. The central banks and their roles come forward.

Later I deal with questions about the implications of theoretic/analytical alternatives of *The Legacy of Keynes and Friedman* (Frazer 1994a; hereafter referred to as *The Legacy*) for new institutions of a money and markets nature. However, the alternatives are not Keynes's economics and Friedman's so much as they are bodies of analysis emanating most distinctly from Keynes and Friedman. They are Keynesian/post-Keynesian, on the one hand, and a Friedman system, on the other. Although Friedman never set forth in a single effort the total analytical system I offer, *The Legacy* sets forth such a system, which is not essential to, but complementary to, what is presented here. In documenting early the roots of Friedman's work and his reactions against the Keynesians and their era of greatest influence to date (Frazer 1988), I note two regimes and set forth their extension to the worldly affairs of central banking. They have been encapsulated under the labels "i-regime" and "M regime," and moves toward the latter have been referred to as a "U-Turn," with reference to both ideas and the implementation of ideas at a political level.

As pointed out here, an impact of Friedman's monetarist ideas at the level of the instruments approach to policy occurred at the Federal Reserve, the Bank of England, and the Deutsche Bundesbank in the mid 1970s. The three peculiarly at approximately the same time literately moved to set targets for money aggregates, although policy changes toward the control of inflation by monetarist means were slow to come in the United States and the United Kingdom. At the center of the control approaches was a most novel idea, albeit well rooted in the Friedman system of analysis.

The idea is that monetary policy can be used to control inflation and that tax policy can be used in opposition to it to ensure faster or slower economic growth (Frazer 1988, 259). The main elements of analysis here are twofold: (1) that inflation is everywhere a monetary phenomenon and (2) that tax policy can be used to provide incentives for saving and thereby faster economic growth, in the private sector. Perhaps not surprisingly, the idea was not lost on Alan Greenspan, the Reagan appointee and monetarist/Ayn-Rand philosopher at the Federal Reserve, early in President Bill Clinton's administration. Against a backdrop of deficit reduction and tax matters on the latter president's agenda, Greenspan indicated support for deficit-reduction measures with emphasis primarily on expenditure cuts (1993a; 1993b). The view was that the Federal Reserve could move toward keeping total spending on a full-employment track (up to a non-inflationary unemployment rate), even as expenditure and/or tax increases occurred.

In reflection of the all-encompassing, monetary-inflationary-expectations matters, Greenspan summoned up the prospect that the bond market would lower the interest rate on the thirty-year, bell-weather bonds of the U.S. government. The interpretation from *The Legacy*, or a bond-market spokesperson's view, was that the debt-reducing tax package had potential for reducing the inflationary, monetary accommodation prospect, and/or for moving the U.S. economy into recession (an interest-lowering prospect in itself).

Early in his sojourn into central banking affairs, Milton Friedman emphasized that he offered an alternative to fiscal and interest-rate-oriented policies, as traditionally viewed. Particularly, he did so when confronting the Bank of England's Sir Gordon Richardson on monetary controls in 1980 (Frazer 1988, 557). Although Keynes noted quite emphatically in his *General Theory* (1936, 141-142) that the central bank controlled the long-term bond rate by the direct means of raising and lowering interest rates in effect, and although Friedman had a different tact, I was a long time in coming to the view of the long-term bond rate as a surrogate for monetary policy in money and credit aggregates terms (Sections 2.2 and 2.3 here).

As I confront here, there were numerous difficulties in the United States and the United Kingdom in targeting money aggregates as means of exerting control over inflation and non-inflationary economic growth. I ask why and I ask other questions too; namely, Why was Keynes so adamant in his view of the central bank's control of interest rates? Why was Friedman so insistent that central banks could control the money aggregates, confront the closely related changes in the income velocity of money, and control price levels in doing so? Perhaps, most astonishingly of all, I inquire why the Deutsche Bundesbank was so much more successful than the others in controlling inflation, even in the oil-shock years of the mid and late 1970s.

Indeed, by the end of the 1970s following the United States's closing of the gold window, the movement toward the partial floating of exchange rates, and the early rise in the importance of foreign exchange dealers, I note the move toward a European Monetary System. And I then inquire about the success of the Deutsche Bundesbank in providing a "hard," highly regarded currency.

Against the foregoing backdrop, I offer the implications for the central banks. There are two main hypothesis concerning bank operations and academic works (H_{CB} and H_{TW}; see Section 1.1) and some others relating to the present work as a whole.

Moreover, in bringing attention to the Bank of England, the Federal Reserve, and the Bundesbank, I note the operating procedures and approaches of these principal central banks, point to the evolution of central banking, and note principal dates in the emergence of the principal banks. Whereas the common view envisions central banks as similar institutions, I note differences and different connections to economic theory.

Giving special note to the U-Turn moves toward an open-economy economics and giving attention to central banks, I revive the old gold-flows mechanism and reappraise the roles of the central banks, exchange rate mechanisms, and the foreign exchange markets with respect to it. These appraisals are in the light of the interests of Keynes, the Keynesians, Friedman, and the emergence of a European Monetary System.

Noting the prospects for a new central bank for Europe and a single currency for selected member states, as well as citing hypotheses, I inquire about the implications of alternative theoretic views and uses of statistical methods for the operating procedures and prospects for such a bank and a common currency. Attention is given to problems with respect to the European Community, the central role of the Bundesbank, and the sovereignty issue found in Milton Friedman's work and Margaret Thatcher's historical role in the United Kingdom.

Even though I deal explicitly with these aforementioned matters, the reported lessons need not be lost for Poland, the provinces of the former Soviet Union, and other former socialist states that seek to achieve a functioning above-ground, market economy. To be sure, the proper functioning of the monetary part of a market economy is essential to both the functioning of the real goods markets and the freedom Margaret Thatcher sought for her society.

Acknowledgments

A number of my interests started to coalesce in the early and late 1980s and led to *The Central Banks*. First was an early interest in J. M. Keynes's works, money matters, and the Bank of England, which in one way or another led to my assignment at the Federal Reserve Bank of New York to report on the Sterling money market in 1956-57. This interest in London then lapsed for a time as socialist government steadily gained in the United Kingdom and as Milton Friedman started to make his moves in the monetary area in the United States and to offer antidotal means for dealing with the rise of Keynesian governments, inflationary developments, and ultimately the simultaneous occurrence of both inflation and recession in the United States and the United Kingdom.

So, in the broad scheme of things, my interest was renewed as Friedman's ideas gained attention in London, as he entered into his work with Schwartz on *Monetary Trends in the United States and the United Kingdom* (1982), and as he gained Margaret Thatcher's attention. The renewed interest, the events, and research on *Power and Ideas* (including Milton Friedman and the Big U-Turn) then led me to London in the early 1980s and to an academic assignment there in the school year 1989-90, at a time of monumental events with monetary, economic, and political implications. The events included extended controversy over the Delors Report on monetary union (Report 1989), the breaching of the Berlin Wall, and rumblings of German unification and the breakup of the Soviet Union.

My first reaction was a draft manuscript titled *A European Monetary System* which I circulated in London and submitted to Praeger Publishers. It dealt with money matters, Thatcher's reactions, and what appeared in the manuscript as the sovereignty issue. That manuscript now appears as *The Central Banks*. Although based in part on *The Legacy* (Frazer 1994a), this work has benefitted from contacts in London during the 1989-92 period and with Milton Friedman in the United States. Among those in London, special mention should be given to Lord Joseph, the Thatcher confidant, Paul M. Mayhew of National Westminster's World Current Trading Center at the time, Tim Congdon of Lombard Street Research Ltd., C. T. Taylor of the Bank of England, and Roger Alford and C.E.A. Goodhart of the London School of Economics.

Part I

Introduction

As variously stated, *The Legacy* deals with theories about money, and markets broadly viewed to include money, financial, real goods, and foreign exchange markets (Frazer 1994a). The theories and the extension of them broadly viewed, however, depend on central banks to which I presently turn for their implementation, in one way or another. Indeed, this world is not easily compartmentalized to fit the artificial classification schemes supplied by the United States's *Journal of Economic Literature*.

As a consequence of this frailty of economic science, I begin with a package of interrelated theoretic constructs, central bank arrangements, econometric prospects, evolutionary changes, and alternative approaches to the attainment of economic goals.

Chapter 1 states some hypotheses and then discusses the central banks and variations of economic theory. The main policy-connected variations relevant to the central banking matters at hand are the Keynes/Keynesian variation (on occasion with post-Keynesian flairs) and a Friedman variation.

These variations appear and reappear in connection with the various orientations of the central banks I considered, namely, in the order of their evolution, the Bank of England, the Federal Reserve, and the Deutsche Bundesbank. Some introductory, theoretically connected distinctions between them appear in Chapter 2, although the three appear and reappear throughout the book.

Chapter 1

Introduction

1.1 INTRODUCTION

The Central Banks centers mainly about two sets of hypotheses. The five comprising set one are:

H_{CB}. *The central banks.* Traditions, operating procedures, and accounting controls influence the choice of economic theory on which government bases its central banking and financial markets policies. (Note: The choice of a theory on which to implement policy may have not only political overtones but dependence on accounting arrangements, for accounting control purposes, and on past practices and traditions [including constitutional and statutory matters].)

H_{TW}. *The theoretical works.* Underlying the theoretical works, such as Keynes's *General Theory* and Friedman and Schwartz's *Monetary Trends,* are implied views of central banking arrangements, policy approaches, and the means of intervention into the money market.

H_{FE}. *Fashionable econometrics.* The 1970s and 1980s sample periods—for which I analyze data represent the same universe.

$H_{i(long)}$. *The long-term bond rate.* "The rate of interest" is raised or lowered *directly* via the central bank and thus independently of the inflation/deflation rates (also, inflationary/deflationary expectations rates).

$H_{UT/FE}$. *The U-Turn prospects.* The seventies and eighties policy regimes are indistinguishable. (This is such as to leave open the traditional prospects whereby inflation rates, interest rates, and exchange rates can be manipulated by government, as if they were independent of one another.)

Additional hypotheses, comprising set two, concern the "Big U-Turn," in reference to the changes in policy and inflationary trends as the United States, the United Kingdom, and the Federal Republic of Germany moved from the 1970s to the 1980s. Extending the U-Turn concept, to the member countries of the European Monetary System (EMS) and to non-member countries, I note that the EMS came into being in 1979, just as the U-Turn changes from the 1970s to the 1980s were occurring. It did so in part with German leadership, and with initial prospects for symmetry, as to power and participation, but with what is seen later as Bundesbank dominance. A coincidence of the timing for the EMS and the U-Turn changes is associated mainly with the United States, and the United Kingdom. However, the appearance of the Bundesbank as a "strong" Fed/Friedman/monetary institution, and its role in the Federal Republic of Germany (FRG), and the FRG's role in the EMS led some economists to see the EMS as a positive force for disinflation.

Combining these notions, and drawing on Fratianni and von Hagan (1990, 93-95), the hypotheses comprising set two are:

H_{FTL}. *Follow the leader (FTL)*. Following Bundesbank and German leadership, the EMS-member countries find credibility for inflation-control commitments by virtue of membership in the EMS.

H_{PA}. *Policy autonomy (PA)*. EMS-member countries are attracted to the democratic, flexible arrangements offered by the EMS for voting, the prospects for realigning exchange rates, and hence by autonomy in the policy sphere.

$H_{U\text{-}Turn}$. *The U-Turn*. The main non-Asian, Western trading countries of the 1970s and 1980s were led for the most part by Keynesian ideas in the 1970s and—following crises in the United Kingdom and the United States, and to some extent elsewhere—monetary/disciplinary and markets-oriented ideas for much of the 1980s.

A third, one-hypothesis set that can be added is:

H_{SE}. *Shared United States, United Kingdom experiences*. The United Kingdom and the United States have in common the same determinants of the money demand functions (Friedman and Schwarts 1982, Section 5.4; hereinafter discussed and cited as FS). (Note that a major result of the findings giving rise to this statement from *Monetary Trends* is that no conditions special to one of the countries needs to be brought into discussion as far as the empirical findings are concerned.)

This shared-experiences hypotheses was very much supported by FS's *Monetary Trends* (1982), and it gains additional, marginal support from the analyses of data in Figures 2-1a, 2-1b, 2-1c, 2-2a, 2-2b, and 2-2c. However, there are three problems concerning the perspective I take with respect to the shared-experience hypothesis. They are (1) It should not be taken as extending to countries with widely different cultures, practices, and states of development. (2) Controversy arises over FS's uses of statistical methods (FS 1991), and it may well do so in regard to the use in Figures 2-1 and 2-2. What I have is continuation of the differences between the respective Keynesian/Friedman approaches. (3) The shared-experiences hypothesis should not be taken to mean that the central banks are on an equal footing when it comes to implementing a money/credit aggregates approach to the stabilization of income and the control of inflation. As variously asserted, the Bundesbank appears at a higher stage in the evolution of central banking.

With reference to the first set of hypotheses, I have accepted H_{CB} of set one, noted some evidence for H_{TW}, and rejected H_{FE}, $H_{i(long)}$, and $H_{UT/FE}$ of that set. The rejections are in fact partly supportive of H_{U-Turn} from the second set of hypotheses. In addition, Fratianni and von Hagen (1990) show inflation-rate data for the Federal Republic of Germany and six other EMS countries, and for nine non-member countries. They report that inflation for the EMS and non-EMS countries—and for the United States and the United Kingdom separately—reached peaks in 1980. Inflation rates then dramatically declined for the groups involved and for the United States and the United Kingdom separately. In addition, most of the countries experienced peak inflation rates in 1980, most moved toward considerably lower rates through 1987, and as inflation rates declined, the standard deviations for the inflation rates in the EMS and non-EMS countries also declined.

These results support the H_{FTL} (or follow-the-mark) and H_{U-Turn} (or shared-ideas) hypotheses of set two, and offer no evidence that countries were autonomous in following monetary and inflation-rate goals. Fratianni and von Hagan conclude that the first hypothesis from set two is impossible to test separately from the shared-ideas one because the observations to support the two are equivalent, but rather we see that the results do not lead to rejecting H_{FTL}. Fratianni and von Hagen provide some weight for the German dominance thesis by pointing to the FRG's role in "the group of five" major countries and to the fact that the Germans did not impose on the EMS a strategy of pegging to the dollar.

1.2 THE CENTRAL BANKS

In the order of their evolution, the central banks I considered are the Bank of England, the Federal Reserve, and the Bundesbank. For the present purpose, the striking features of the Bank of England are its inherent reliance on "the bank" (minimum lending, or Sterling money market) rate and responsibility for the U.K. government's public sector borrowing requirements (PSBR), certainly since nationalization in 1946. Its traditions concerning accounting controls and reserves are mostly just traditions and appear quite different from those of the United States.

Although the Federal Reserve was founded in 1913, and drew on the tradition of a "bank rate" (or discount rate in the Fed's case),[1] the major instruments for controlling bank reserves were written into the Federal Reserve Act via the Banking Acts of 1933 and 1935 (Frazer and Yohe 1966, 156-166; hereafter FY). The most remarkable of these was open market operations of a very special sort (FY 1966, 164-166).

Under the Federal Reserve Act, reserves were fixed by law, accounted for, and defined quite simply as consisting of deposits on the part of member banks at the Federal Reserve Banks, although there have been later variations in definition.

For the special purpose of the analytical system I associate with Milton Friedman (Frazer 1994a), however, I use the bank reserve equation (FY 1966, Chapter 9). An accounting identity, it accounts for the principal sources of bank reserves (including gold and international monetary reserves, Federal Reserve credit, currency drains, and less significant variables). This accounting identity connects directly to the reserves of non-central, deposit-creating banks via money and credit multipliers (FY 1966, Chapter 3).

1.2a The Bundesbank

The Deutsche Bundesbank dates from 1957. Perhaps not surprisingly in the light of allied influence and the United States's dominance during and for a time after World War II, it took on a federalist structure, somewhat like the Federal Reserve. Even so, it is more on an equal footing with the executive and legislative branches than with the Federal Reserve (Bundesbank 1989; Kennedy 1991) and, as a minor detail and contrary to policy at the Bank of England, the direct purchase of government securities is prohibited.

Appearing late in the evolution of central banks, it adopted instruments somewhat similar to those at the Federal Reserve for controlling money and credit aggregates. For the present purpose, note that the two most important ones, in the order of importance, are (1) open market operations and (2) the lombard and discount rates. In close relation to the discount rate, the lombard rate applies to loans from the Bundesbank "to bridge temporary liquidity needs on the part of credit institutions" and to repurchase agreements. The lombard rate especially serves as a ceiling for money market rates, since the extensions of funds for meeting minimum reserve requirements via this route are unlimited except for the cost of funds.[2]

More important to an aggressive policy than the discount and lombard rates, however, is the Bundesbank's overall use of its instruments and liquidity management as a means for attaining growth rates for a broad M3 measure for the money stock. This achievement comes about by way of a "complex transmission mechanism" (Bundesbank 1989, 104), which I see as relating to the Friedman system and time frames since the mid 1970s.

Even statements in the original Bundesbank Act suggest an inherent compatibility with a "quantity theory of money" based economics. Most notably, "The Deutsche Bundesbank regulates the quantity of money in circulation and of credit supplied to the economy, using the monetary powers conferred on it by this Act, with the aim of safeguarding the currency." Further, the Bundesbank text states:

> According to the Bundesbank Act and the central bank's own understanding of its role, the basic aim and direction of monetary policy are unequivocal: in the interaction of all the entities responsible for economic policy, the Deutsche Bundesbank has the particular task of safeguarding the currency by regulating the quantity of money in circulation and of credit supplied to the economy. By keeping purchasing power stable and the money supply under control, the central bank in the market economy at the same time creates the monetary conditions for maintaining a high level of employment over the longer term with adequate economic growth. (Bundesbank 1989, 81)

1.2b Issues Regarding the Bundesbank

For the present, I summarize only a little concerning the Bundesbank. However, there are some issues that need to be brought out. Most notably, although on the forefront of liquidity management (Bundesbank 1989, 67-69), the lombard rate is not the source of permanent growth in bank reserves. Rather, the open market operations (OMO) of a different dimension play that role, since short-term borrowing is directed toward easing temporary adjustments to liquidity.

Next, I distinguish between liquidity management via lombard and discount rates (say, i_s) and the long-term bond rates (say, i_L). I do so for a variety of reasons: (1) because these rates are often confused in the press and in economics, (2) because of notions associated with J. M. Keynes, and (3) because the two rates have (or have taken on) a different place in the scheme of things. The London and New York presses have, since the money targeting days of the early 1980s, published a lot about the central bank lowering (or raising) *the* interest rate, when in fact the reporting meant the discount or bank rates. In Keynes's work, the distinction may have been blurred a bit because of the "backwardation" view of the yield curve that he held. In that view, there was a predominant upward sweep in the relation between rates on short- to long-dated government securities (such as seen in Figure 1-1). And for him, a central bank action at the short end (say, Δi_s) was envisioned as being passed in the same direction to the long end of the treasury yield curve (say, Δi_L).

This mistaken view of interest-rate behavior even appears in Federal Reserve research pieces (e.g., Kahn and Jacobson 1989, 24; hereinafter KJ). KJ say, "For example, when the Bundesbank reduces monetary growth, interest rates . . . rise." Continuing, they say that "as a result, the growth of interest-sensitive spending . . . slows." And, moreover, they have the Bundesbank using the short-term rate (say, i_s) to manage liquidity and then using liquidity (reserve availability) to influence short-term rates (KJ 1989, 24, 26). As taken

Figure 1-1
A Bundesbank Effect

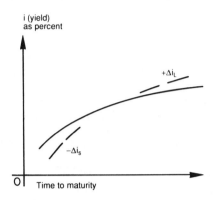

up below, KJ are wrong about the facts on the first two accounts and offer a mare's nest on the third count.

In any case, the Bundesbank itself and the governor of the Bank of England, for that matter, are clear about the short-term rates they control. The Bundesbank notes the use of the short rate in managing liquidity (Bundesbank 1989, 29-30, 32, 67-69, 82-83). Governor Eddie George's predecessor Leigh-Pemberton says, quite bluntly, it is the only rate the Bank of England controls. Further, the Bundesbank says that the rate on the long-dated bonds is the one of crucial importance to investors and that the Bank does not directly control it (Bundesbank 1989, 73, 83). Rather, Bundesbank officials see it as determined by the bond market and the economic and inflationary outlook of the active participants in that market.

Emphasis on this interpretation of long-term rate movements has been slower to appear in the U.S. media and on the part of the Federal Reserve's Chairman, but it did begin to appear in 1993 (Greenspan 1993a; Vogel and Wassel 1993; Vogel 1993).[3] Although such interpretations of the long-term rate behavior are discussed again later, Dr. Greenspan's comments are appropriate:

Long-term interest rates . . . fell in 1992 and in early 1993, as inflation expectations gradually moderated and optimism developed about a potential for genuine progress in reducing federal budget deficits. (Greenspan 1993a, 292)

At the first indication of an inflationary policy—monetary or fiscal—investors dump bonds, driving up long-term interest rates. (Greenspan 1993a, 294)

An overly expansionary monetary policy, or even its anticipation, is embedded fairly soon in higher inflation expectations and nominal bond yields. (Greenspan 1993a, 294)

[T]he effects of fiscal policy on the economy, in turn, will depend importantly on the credibility of long-run deficit reduction and the market reaction to any package. The lower long-term interest rates that resulted from a credible deficit-reduction plan would themselves have an immediate positive effect on the economy. (Greenspan 1993a, 301)

Fiscal policy similarly can contribute to sustainable and robust economic growth. The President's budget proposals have prompted anticipation in the markets that there will be genuine progress in the reduction of federal budget deficits. This anticipation has been the most important factor behind the very significant recent declines in intermediate- and long-term interest rates. (Greenspan 1993b, 302)

Finally, along these latter routes, is what is illustrated in Figure 1-1 and called the Bundesbank effect. The Bundesbank effect, goes thus: a lowering of the administered short rates ($-\Delta i_s$) may lead the bond market to actually set a higher rate ($+\Delta i_L$) when the lowering action is interpreted by the bond market's participants as an inflationary move ($\dot{P}^e$). Indeed, in discussing rates on long-term bonds, the Bundesbank says "the long-term rate is predominantly determined by market factors which the Bundesbank . . . can influence only indirectly, such as interest rate movements abroad and inflationary expectations [say, $i_L = i(\text{real}) + \dot{P}^e$]" (Bundesbank 1989, 73).

1.3 VARIATIONS OF THE ECONOMIC THEORY

The economic theory at hand draws on *The Legacy* (Frazer 1994a). The two outstanding figures in that work both reacted to the neoclassical economics represented by Alfred Marshall (1842-1924). J. M. Keynes did so first in his 1923 work when he gave attention to the Cambridge equation of exchange [M = k(...)Y, wherein he had the money stock (M) as some proportion [k (...)] of income (Y)] and he later did so in *The General Theory* (1936). His main points were (1) in the 1923 work that the demand for money [the factor k(...), k(...) = M/Y] was not constant as assumed at Cambridge at the time and (2) in the *General Theory*, that, in the presence of an increase in the demand for money, prices (P) did not adjust downward so much as did output (Q), and hence employment in the short run. As is known, the first led Keynes to his liquidity preference demand for money and to his special treatment of the definition of money.[4] This was in lieu of the treatment inherent in the classical dichotomy.[5] The second led to his treatment of consumption (or household demand) as a function of income (Y) rather than prices as in Marshall's demand functions, which is shown later.

From the positions taken by Keynes, the Keynesians (and/or Keynesians with a post-Keynesian flair) go one route and Friedman another. This division is such that a broad outline shows alternative theoretic approaches to the achievement of economic goals (Frazer 1994a, Section 1.2). As taken up in summary form below, the Keynesians adopt Keynes's two-asset, money-bond approach to liquidity preference, investment demand, and the place of the central banks. It ends with a position in which money does not matter much (also, a Keynesian dichotomy)[6] and with special views about the central bank's position. Most notably, it is a twofold position, one of raising and lowering interest rates (without fruitful distinction between the short- and long-term rates, i_s and i_L) and one of controlling both the supply and demand for money balances via interest rates and fiscal policy (defined as a budget deficit).

At a theoretic level the Keynesian system can be identified with the Hansen/Hicks investment/saving-liquidity/money (IS-LM) model (shown later in Figure 1-3) and shown to have a special inherent, separation-of-effects, statistical approach. This I identify with the following: (1) a heavy use of separating effects by artificial means (ceteris paribus and the assumption of independence in key, interrelated variables); (2) a statistical approach of adding variables and equations to account for unexplained variation in a key variable such as gross national or domestic product[7]; (3) issues surrounding the endogeneity and/or exogeneity of the variables and forces at work (also related to the causation issue), and the fiscal policy connection to the control of the money stock, both discussed in Chapter 3; (4) old, often revived, notions about a trade-off between the acceptance of inflation for a reduction in unemployment (Frazer 1994a, Section 6.2; KJ 1989, 27-34); and (5) efforts to explain inflation by market-structures/nonmonetary means (Frazer 1994a, Sections 3.2e, 6.3).

In contrast to the Keynesians, Friedman proceeds as follows: namely he, (1) connects to a restatement of Marshall's demand curve (Frazer 1994a, Section 1.3); (2) offers theoretic constructions with time frames adopted via the National Bureau of Economic Research (NBER) connections to Wesley Mitchell, Arthur Burns, and Simon Kuznets (Frazer 1994a, Sections 1.4, 4.2b, 4.2c); (3) redirects Keynes's liquidity preference and consumption function blocks (Frazer 1994a, Sections 2.2, 2.4, 5.3); and (4) introduces "psychological time" into his approach. Taking into account the main roles of time, a summary comprises:

1. Keynes's short run (a period over which the psychological state remains unchanged);

2. The permanent components (or trends) in the time series, for example denoted Y_P for permanent (or even quasi-permanent) income;

3. The components for transitory (or cyclical) change in the time series, for example $|Y - Y_p|$ for transitory income; and

4. Psychological time (as defined later).

The transitory components in the time series are also those commonly referred to in reference to the state of business conditions (e.g., as in *Business Conditions Digest*). The phases of business conditions are those designated as expansion and recession phases. They are market peaks and troughs (Frazer

1994a, Section 1.4), which are determined by the NBER's committee for the dating of turning points (also appearing in *Business Conditions Digest*).

1.4 THE KEYNES/KEYNESIAN VARIATION

In taking up the positions with respect to Keynes, I proceed first with Keynes and the Keynesians (including some with a post-Keynesian flair) and then with Keynes and Friedman. After doing the latter, the variations of the economic theory are extended in Chapter 2 to the roles assigned to the central banks.

Restatements of the Keynes/Keynesian constructions extend to liquidity preference, investment demand, and the IS-LM model.

1.4a Liquidity Preference

The liquidity preference restatement leads to an essentially Keynesian rationale for the liquidity preference curve in Figure 1-2. It envisions the asymptote to the curve (the vertical, broken line at aY) as fixed (ceteris paribus like), attributes to the central bank a capacity to raise and lower "the rate of interest" (actually meaning the long-term bond rate, for Keynes at least), and proceeds with the idea of assets consisting of a stock of money balances (M) and a stock of bonds that pay the rate of interest (i_L). As the central bank

Figure 1-2
The Liquidity Preference Curve and the LM Curve: The Static State

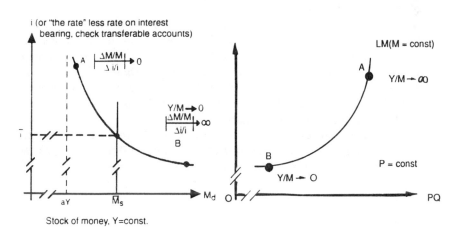

a.   b.

raises the rate of interest, it provides the asset holders with an inducement to hold more bonds and to extinguish some of the existing money stock (possibly by repaying bank loans) in the process of getting more heavily into bonds by way of the concept referred to as the opportunity cost of holding money balances.[8] With the income fixed (the asymptote, at aY), the rise in the interest rate means a rise in the income velocity of money [Y/M, or the inverse of the Cambridge k, in $M=k(...)Y$]. At a very high interest rate, velocity increases dramatically as at point A in Figure 1-2. As rates are lowered all of the reverse follows at point B (velocity approaches zero).

Such parallel movements in the interest rate and the velocity of money were widely observed before high rates of inflation set in during the mid 1960s (Frazer 1967b, Chapter 5 mainly). The pre-mid 1960s movements were denoted

$$\ln Y/M = a + b \ln i \tag{1}$$

and may be so denoted in reference to Figure 1-2a. Symbolic of Keynesian and Bank-of-England views of controlling money balances, the last equation can be rewritten

$$\ln M = a_0 + a_1 \ln i + a_2 \ln Y \tag{2}$$

Imposing some amount for the money stock in Figure 1-2a (albeit a not so controlled variable in the Keynesian perspective) yields the interest rate. Indeed, in an essentially British, will-o'-the-wisp view, the money stock is so unimportant to the real goods economy that the economic agents will adjust to whatever stock exists for the expenditure on current output. If the stock is low in relation to the output, the agents simply increase the turnover of it. The reverse attains if the stock is larger.

Stressing first the interest rate as the policy variable and taking the money stock as given (fixed, and non-extinguishable) we obtain the Keynesian LM curve (shown as Figure 1-2b). It is a reflection of the liquidity preference curve, with the points A and B in the a and b parts of Figure 1-2 showing the same conditions. Moreover, of the price (P) and output (Q) components for income (Y = PQ), the price level is held constant and a rise in the interest rate parallels a rise in real output and employment.

A closely related block to the analysis surrounding Figure 1-2a is attained by both recognizing an extended list of assets and treating those other than the money stock (M) as a bond. The classes appear thus:

	(Column 1)		(Column 2)		(Column 3)
I	Fixed, contractual claim assets (so-called monetary assets)	(1)	Money balances	(1)	Money
		(2)	Noncash liquid assets such as government bonds	(2)	Bonds (for purpose of central banks control); Keynes's treatment of real capital
II	Residual claim assets (so-called non-monetary assets)	(1)	Common stocks		
		(2)	Plant and equipment (or real goods generally)		

Column 1 contains assets classified by whether a fixed claim against future income (as in a contract) or a claim against the part of income left over after fixed claims are met. Column 2 shows the assets in terms of ordinary classifications (money, bonds, etc.), and column 3 shows the classes Keynes imposed in turning to the money-bond model of Figure 1-2a and the treatment of real capital as a bond.

1.4b   Keynes/Keynesian Investment Demand

Going the latter route leads to Keynes's *General Theory* and the concepts of the capital value of additions to real capital (note, CV of ΔK) and the cost (or supply price) of the additions (Frazer 1994a, Section 4.4a):

$$\text{Capital value of } \Delta K = \frac{R_1}{(1+i)^1} + \frac{R_2}{(1+i)^2} + \frac{R_3}{(1+i)^3} + \ldots + \frac{R_n}{(1+i)^n}$$

$$\text{Cost of } \Delta K = -\frac{R_1}{(1+r)^1} + \frac{R_2}{(1+r)^2} + \ldots + \frac{R_n}{(1+r)^n}$$

The Rs represents net returns per annum after all costs are met, except those for obtaining the financing for the capital outlays. They are the respective streams of Rs expected with respect to the future, although they are treated for the interest rate, policy-control purpose as fixed streams (as in bond contracts).

Given the Rs and the central bank's presumed control over the rate of interest, as in Figure 1-2a, the central bank is also viewed as controlling the capital value of additions to real capital (ΔK). In the cost (or supply-price) instance, the costs are given, as in the case of obtaining a contract for the purchase of plant and equipment. This is such that values for the Rs and the cost are known (if expected), and consequently the unknown r is also known. Keynes called the unknown r the marginal efficiency of capital (m.e.c.), but it can also be viewed as the rate of return on capital.

Having made these helpful (if artificial) distinctions, I have the notion of central bank intervention to control capital spending via the control of the rate of interest (i_L). For a reduction in the rate of interest ($-\Delta i_L$), the intervention is:

$$\text{Capital value} > \text{cost}$$

$$\text{rate of return} > \text{rate of interest}$$

Hence, an inducement for additional capital spending (I, where $I = \Delta K$) by firms and the suggested link between the long-term interest rate and investment, $-\Delta i_L \rightarrow \Delta I$.

The additions to capital may increase, with the prospect that the stream of Rs and the cost will increase. However, in anticipation of the disposal of enlarged production, the Rs are expected to rise less than the cost of new capital (cost of ΔK) for generating them. In the static context of reasoning, this means the rate of return (r) declines. Hence, the curve in Figure 1-3a (the m.e.c. curve, so-called by Keynes), which declines as investment increases, results. Imposing "the" interest rate in Figure 1-3a, the flow of investment is determined (or partly so).

1.4c The IS-LM, Keynesian Summary

Taking up the equations usually offered with the Keynes/Keynesian, total-expenditure/income block (Frazer 1994a, Section 4.2), yields one equation for total spending (Y_d) on consumption (as a function of income, C[Y]) and investment (I) and a second equation for the income received (Y), which goes for consumption and saving. In the second, saving is defined as that part of income not spent on consumption. The two equations are

$$Y_d = C(Y) + I \tag{1}$$

$$Y = C(Y) + S(Y) \tag{2}$$

With the slopes for the lines given by assumption ($0 < dC/dY < 1$), in one case, and by definition [$S(Y) = Y - C(Y)$, $dY/dY = 1$], in the other, the lines intersect at a point (Y, Y_d) and a solution exists. Approximating the consumption function with a simple linear equation,

Figure 1-3
Investment Demand and the IS-LM Construction

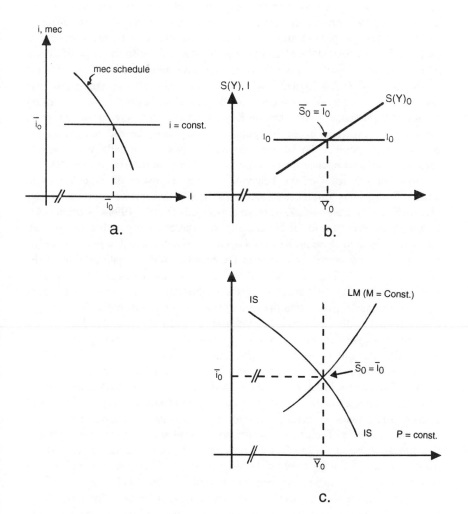

$$C = a + bY, \quad 0 < b < 1 \tag{3}$$

the solution is

$$\bar{Y} = \left(\frac{1}{1 - b}\right)(a + I) \tag{4}$$

Further, the equations and the accoutrements to them ensure that the lines for Equations (1) and (2) intersect and that saving and investment are equal [S(Y) = I], as shown in Figure 1-3b.

In spite of the simplicity, very behavioral notions are present in the basic model. The groups engaged in the respective activities of consumption (and hence saving too), on the one hand, and investment, on the other, are different behavioral groups, plus saving flows into investment (S → I), and non-central banks and other financial institutions appear intermediate to the flow of saving into investment. Further, the behavioral notions extend to what Keynes called "a fundamental psychological law" (1936, 96). As for investment, it was "autonomous" (or even exogenous) in the sense of being outside the usual economic calculus. Even though Keynes treated the stream of Rs from additions to capital as fixed for policy prescriptions, he did not do so for behavioral purposes. To be sure, investment was potentially very volatile because of its dependence on expectations (denoted as the streams of Rs).

However—in spite of the behavior and the exposure of expectations to outside, exogenous influences—Keynes's simple system was closed up and extended in very elaborate, Keynesian dimensions (Frazer 1994a, Section 6.4). I do not presently turn to the big models with these numerous dimensions, but I do note efforts to close up Keynes's open-ended system and to place interest-rate changes and monetary policy in the results. Indeed, taking note of the m.e.c. schedule in Figure 1-3a, and the saving investment equality in Figure 1-3b, an early effort at summarizing the Keynesian system appears as Figure 1-3c. There an IS curve with the m.e.c. curve's properties appears to provide a construction with the combined properties of Figure 1-2a and 1-3a.

From a Keynesian monetary-policy point of view, increasing the money stock shifts the LM curve to the right, and the interest rate from Figure 1-2a declines to give rise to movement along the m.e.c. schedule, and hence the IS curve. The causal linkage appears as $\Delta M \rightarrow -\Delta i \rightarrow \Delta I$ (or ΔY), despite the presence of several facts. Notably, the policy emphasis is really on the rate of interest (and not simply inverse movement between money growth and interest rates); and the rate of interest is the price for credit and not the money balances that appear in Figure 1-2a. The price for holding money balances consists of the opportunities foregone by not holding bonds or other assets as well as any allowance for an inflation-rate penalty on holding money balances.

The matters are complicated, and not simply by returns foregone when holding money balances. There may even be omitted variables, from Keynesian and even divergent points of view. The following material attributes special roles to central banks and introduces special time frames, structural changes underlying the formation of inflationary expectations, and episodic change and psychological time (as defined shortly).

1.5 THE FRIEDMAN VARIATION

Early steps in the emergence of the analytical system associated with Friedman included a restatement of the Marshallian demand curve; the move toward the treatment of the money and credit matters in money-stock terms for policy purposes and away from interest-rate, credit-conditions terms for policy purposes; a recasting of analysis in dynamic, time-rate-of-change terms; and, in part thereby, the attainment of statements of motion in lieu of statements of position, such as appeared in most of price theory and with Keynes's consumption function.   These time-rate-of-change and motion-and-position statements first started to appear in the monetary and consumption function works, where time frames came via NBER connections, and where the distinction between permanent and transitory components came much earlier. In FS's *Monetary History* (1963), the money stock was a leading time rate of change. It impacted via the expenditure of income and at the same time on general business conditions.

The report was that the affects of accelerated growth in income were powerful, started immediately, and accumulated for a long time. A monetary guide to policy began to emerge via the Cambridge, cash-balances expression, $k(...) = M/Y$. It called for a growth in money balances that equaled the inflation-free growth in income, expressed in secular (or long-run) terms. More toward the stabilization of business conditions can be sought in the short term, but there was danger because of the power of accelerated and decelerated growth in the money stock. Even so, as the approach evolved, adjustments to the money stock growth could occur in the long run to offset shifts in the secular trend for income velocity. Historical examples of such a shifts include "the Great Depression in the United States and the stagnation in the United Kingdom from the mid-1920s until after World War II" Each produced "a temporary upward shift in the quantity of money demanded for given values of the other variables" (FS 1982, 625).

The time frames and data components for the income variable in the Friedman system are illustrated in Figure 1-4a. The trend line such as may be defined, is noted as the more permanent component, Y_P than the transitory one, $|Y - Y_P|$. The common growth equation, when fit to data, readily yields a growth rate ($\times$ 100 = percent growth) for income. Moreover, the trends that appear in the Friedman system are expected magnitudes that depict the expectations of the economic agents. As further illustrated in Figure 1-4b, agents look backward at past income history (say, to $-\infty$) and at a some present time (say, t_o) the past is extrapolated into the future, up to the time horizon (T). Another example of this, in terms of Figure 1-2a, appears when the money stock (M_s) variables grows at the same rate as nominal income (in the asymptote, aY) to yield a level trend line for the rate of interest. It appears in Figure 1-4c, and it is one of the expected rates in the money-demand relation (Equation [1], Section 1.4).

Figure 1-4
**Trends and Transitory Components, Expected Income and Interest, and
the Saving- and Consumption-to-Income Ratios**

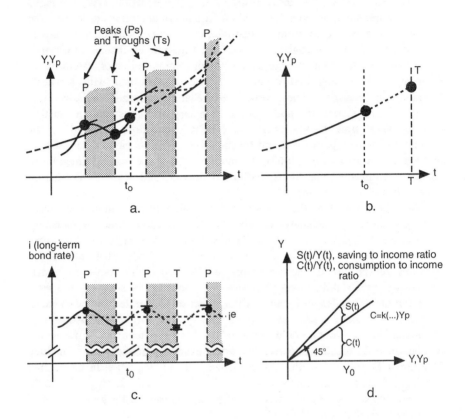

The permanent income illustrated in Figure 1-4b is what I call psychological time in a neutral environment (just a stable state for business conditions). Part c of Figure 1-4 shows changes in interest rates for a common pattern that appeared prior to the date at which the great peacetime inflation got under way in the United States. It shows interest rates declining during recession, as in the classic 1937-38 recession in the United States and the more recent 1990-91 recession with sluggish recovery. In the presence of these declining/recession rates, what I observed is an absence of faster growth in capital spending of the sort suggested by movements along the m.e.c. schedule in Figure 1-3a and its counterpart in Figure 1-3c.

What I offer instead of the smooth movement can be illustrated in reference to Figure 1-4c. The phenomenon surrounding it is in terms of *psychological time in a non-neutral state*. In that case, *agents look back in time at past* *recessions, take note of the interest rate behavior, and form judgements about the condition at t_0 in relation to the past and the future.* In regard to psychological time and t_0, questions are raised by those who bring new issues of bonds to the market, refinance debt, and so on at a time of declining interest rates. These are along the line of whether the conditions of business and interest rates have bottomed out and whether an expansion is more eminent than it was when the interest rate was at mid-recession level. The phenomenon under consideration is such that agents anticipate a future in the light of current information and information about past patterns. *Time in the mind of the beholder is not treated so much as calendar time but rather in looking back and analoging current states in terms of past comparable states.* The time frame becomes the historical states or episodes. There is an element of learning and of processing new information in the light of past experience. It takes on a Bayesian probabilistic quality (Frazer 1994a, Section 3.2g), which is depicted with the use of a statement of Bayes's theorem as

$$\underbrace{P\ (\theta_i \mid X)}_{\substack{\text{posterior} \\ \text{probability}}} \qquad \propto \qquad \underbrace{P(\theta_i)}_{\substack{\text{prior} \\ \text{probability}}} \qquad \qquad \underbrace{[P(X) \mid \theta_i]}_{\substack{\text{likelihood} \\ \text{function}}}$$

In words, the probability after gathering information (i.e., the posterior) is proportional to ($\propto$) the prior belief times the likelihood function (the function expressing the probability of observing a given sample as some parameter or given condition varies). In other words, the current probability function (the left hand member of the proportionality) is some combination of previous and new information.

1.5a The Marshallian Demand Curve

Friedman's restatement of the Marshallian demand curve contains three features of current interest: a sharp distinction between the ordinary and the compensated curves (shown in Figure 1-5); the simultaneous linkage of the central, price-theory equation of E. E. Slutsky to the latter distinction and to the terms of a price index (P); and the linking up of the demand curve to the economy as a whole (Frazer 1994a, Section 1.3). In the first two instances we have the curves shown in Figure 1-5 for the price (p_1) and the quantity of one commodity (q_1), and the Slutsky equation namely,

$$\underbrace{\frac{\partial q_1}{\partial p_1}}_{} \qquad = \qquad \underbrace{\left(\frac{\partial q_1}{\partial p_1}\right)_{u - \text{const.}}}_{} \qquad - \quad \underbrace{\partial q_1\left(\frac{\partial q_1}{\partial y}\right)_{\text{prices - const.}}}_{}$$

a. change in q_1 b. substitution   c. income effect
   with respect to p_1 effect

a. slope of the   b. slope of the   c. change in income
   ordinary demand   compensated   required to keep the
   curve   demand curve   individual on the
                                                          same level of utility

Viewing the terms of a price index as the products of weights (w_1, w_2, . . . , w_n) and the respective market prices (p_1, p_2, . . . , p_n) gives

$$\underbrace{P}_{\text{P = const.}} = \underbrace{w_1\bar{p}_1}_{\substack{\text{price change in}\\ \text{Figure 1-5}}} + \underbrace{w_2\bar{p}_2 + \ldots + w_n\bar{p}_n}_{\substack{\text{change in other prices required}\\ \text{to keep P const. (i.e., real income,}\\ \text{Y/P, unchanged)}}}$$

What Friedman showed was that the last term in the Slutsky equation (the c term) has a counterpart in an ordinary cost-of-living index (P). The change in income required to keep the individual on the same level of utility (on Friedman's compensated demand curve) is the same as changes required in real income (Y/P) to keep it constant when a price (P_1) changes.

All of this results in a means of measuring the compensation required to keep household utilities unchanged on the average and it leads to the price level (P) found in the Cambridge, quantity-theory expression, $M = k(\ldots)Y$. With

Figure 1-5
Friedman's Marshallian Demand Curve

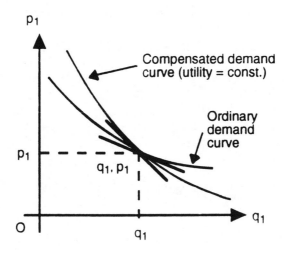

respect to it, $Y = PQ$, $Q = Y/P$, and $k(...) = (M/P)/(Y/P)$. Moreover, this last algebraic expression contains two of the crucial terms of Friedman's money demand function (FS 1982, 39),

$$M/P = f(Y/P, w; \ldots ; u) \tag{1}$$

Additional to the real money balances (M/P) and real income (Y/P) terms, w (also Wnh/W) is a symbol for liquidity and u is a collection of variables of secondary importance. The three dots in the equation represent the following expected rates of return on four classes of assets:

r_M^e the expected nominal rate of return on money;

r_B^e the expected nominal rate of return on fixed-valued securities, including changes in their prices;

r_E^e the expected nominal rate of return on equities, including expected changes in their prices; and

r_R^e the expected rate of return on physical or residual-claim assets in terms of any direct income they yield (or storage costs they impose), plus the expected rate of change of prices of goods and services [i.e., the expected inflation rate, $(1/P)$ $(dp/dt)^*$].

The demand function (Equation [1]) should not be read as suggesting an interest in the following: cycles and trends in real money balances, real income, or so-called real business cycles; and a regression of the left-hand member of the equation on the terms of the function $f(Y/P, w; \ldots ; u)$. Rather the form of the expression deals with a more technical question of the identification of a demand relation. Confronting it, the private sector of the economy determines the real money balances it wishes to hold via spending more or less of its money balances (i.e., by increasing or decreasing the income velocity of money). The central bank (or governmental authority) determines the stock of money in nominal terms. This occurs along lines introduced later with reference to the Bundesbank.

1.5b Liquidity Preference

In the rather dynamic orientation surrounding Figure 1-4 both the liquidity preference demand for money balances and Friedman's permanent-income consumption function, which carries with it some elements of interest to liquidity analysts and central bank enthusiasts, are encountered. In the first instance, the mathematical property of the liquidity preference curve in Figure 1-2a is retained and an expectations/psychological rationale for the curve itself is taken up. Of perhaps little interest to central bank enthusiasts, the curve is essentially that of an equilateral hyperbola with the asymptote aY. It is such that money growth [(1/M)(dM/dt) or $\dot{M}$] in the Friedman orientation impacts on income to impart the same growth rate on income [say (1/Y)(dY/dt) or $\dot{Y}$]. Qualifications are that there may be feedback from income to money growth and that under some central banking arrangements, the fiscal (or deficit) policy of some governments may even be the driving force in the analysis.

The added rationale for the shape of the curve in Figure 1-2a is illustrated in Figure 1-6. Here, the "agent" (a speculator or a bond trader) faces the limited choice and perceives present rates in relation to a normality toward which future rates will be pulled.

When "the rate" is above "the normal (or safe) rate," the probability favors a pull toward normality and the further it is above the normal rate the greater the probability of a return. At the latter point the agent's preference is for large holdings of bonds, in order to realize possible capital gains (as bond prices rise and interest rates fall), and smaller holdings of money balances. As "the rate" falls below the normal rate, the pull toward normality coincides with

Figure 1-6
The Demand for Money Balances: The Speculator/Bond-Trader Perspective

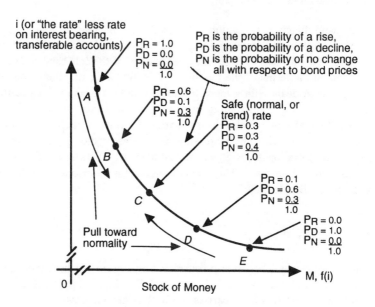

holdings of more money balances and fewer bonds in order to avoid capital losses as bond prices decline during the future pull toward higher rates. There is then an inverse variation between interest rates and the demand for money (given the safe or normal rate, such as encountered as the expected interest rate in Figure 1-4c).

From a neutral environment state (smooth trend paths and all), the growth of the money stock accelerates from 3 to 5 percent at a time when income growth is also 3 percent (as on the left-hand side of Figure 1-7). The secular-trend result is then a move away from the 3 percent path (denoted C) to the 5 percent path (denoted B). However, the real production remains on a 3 percent-rate path $[(1/Q)(dQ/dt) \times 100 = 3$ percent] and the increase in income to the 5 percent rate contains two percentage points for inflation $[(1/P)(dP/dt) \times 100 = 2$ percent].

Figure 1-7
Liquidity Preference with Overshooting

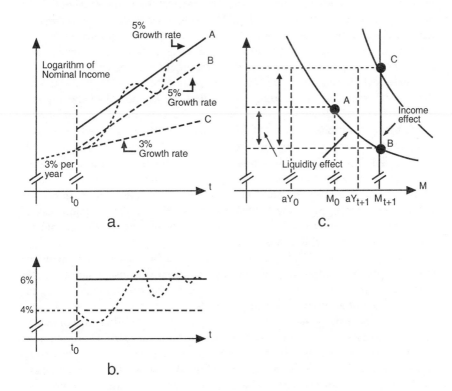

The bond-market participants come to anticipate the 2 percent inflation rate. Lenders will come to expect higher inflation rates. All of them wonder about the repayment of fixed income streams and the repayments of principal with balances of reduced purchasing powers. A twofold result follows: the interest rate shown on the bottom left of Figure 1-7 increases from the 4 percent path to the 6 percent path, and the penalty on holding cash balances shifts spending on production (Q) from path B to path A. As a part of the last shift, the income velocity of money (Y/M) is higher. The nominal interest rate (i) fully reflects the expected inflation rate ($\dot{P}^e$ = 2 percentage points) via i = i(real) + $\dot{P}^e$; but velocity responds only to the change in it, in that income, viewed as expenditure, rises by only a small additional amount in relation to the money stock. To be sure, as in fact occurred in terms of U.S. data from the mid 1960s through the 1970s, and in response to inflation, interest rates moved considerably above income velocity and away from the relation depicted in the equations surrounding Figure 1-2a. In the transition from the trends of Figure 1-7, in the transitory state as it were, interest rates declined initially and only subsequently start to rise as spending accelerated. Agents come to expect inflation, as overshooting occurs and the interest rate moves about the 6 percent/i^e line for a time. A liquidity effect appears in the downward movement, and then the income effect enters. In the liquidity preference illustration on the right-hand side of Figure 1-7, the first effect appears as a movement from point A to point B along the liquidity preference curve. The income effect appears as the distance from point B to point C. It comes after the money stock has, with some lag, shifted the asymptote to the liquidity preference curve. However, that is the view of events prior to the mid-1960s.

All of this was indeed a part of FS's *Monetary Trends* in which, Friedman and Schwartz were searching for a stable statistical relationship (Equation [1] in Section 1.5a). Most notably, this would be a relation with underlying lag times and parameter estimates unchanged. At a less sophisticated level, it would be like expecting the parameters (a_1 and a_2) of Equation (2) in Section 1.4a, to be unchanged as the United States and the United Kingdom moved from the early post-World War II years through the mid 1960s on into the decades of the 1970s and 1980s.

To be sure, FS would have preferred to celebrate the research that uncovered these foregoing patterns, but instead, they confronted a disappointment. As reported in *Monetary Trends* (1982, Section 10.8), the structure underlying the formation of inflationary expectations on the part of the market participants changed. The participants had started to pay more attention to money and credit aggregates, and news and policy actions concerning inflationary expectations. In other words, bond prices (and therefore interest rates) could adjust quite readily in response to new information along the lines of what I have called Bayesian learning. The lagged adjustments, illustrated in Figure 1-7, vanished for the most part. From the point of view of monetary science,

FS had lost the handle to the stable relationship they had searched for and reported.

So, I offer New York's revenge (Frazer 1994a, Section 2.4a), as where news of an inflationary sort emanates from the U.S. Capitol and appears almost immediately in higher interest rates rather than maintenance of the lower rates Washington's politicos may have hoped for. *New York's revenge is the idea that participants in the money and financial markets may learn and adjust very rapidly to the inflationary prospects we identify with Washington based political actions, inactions, and contemplated actions.* The adjustments on the inflation front may be such as to nullify even "well-intended" actions, as where the government moves to increase and broaden social programs, but is confronted instead with higher nominal long-term bond rates, higher mortgage payments, and reduced housing starts.

However, the reverse too can appear, and bond rates can decline as fast as they rose on a different sort of news. It may concern uses of monetary policy to control inflation, as in Ronald Reagan's early years in the White House and Margaret Thatcher's stay at Number 10 Downing Street (Frazer 1988, Chapters 15, 16). It may similarly have occurred in the early years of a later president who appeared to offer a believable promise to lower U.S. deficits and the prospect of their being monetized by the central bank (Vogel and Wassel 1993; Vogel 1993; Greenspan 1993a, 1993b). Whereas in the Reagan years monetary policy could be set in opposition to tax policy as a means of reducing inflation rates (and thereby interest rates), the tax policy under President Bill Clinton held the promise of reducing the inflationary effects of deficits, which always occur when central banks monetize government debt along lines reported in Chapter 3 for the Bank of England.

Of course, everything concerning intended actions and anticipated outcomes can not be held with great certitude, because much information can be regarded with a varying amount of confidence and officials and those who perform official acts differ as to reliability and credibility. Writing $i = i(\text{real}) + Pb[\dot{P}^e] \dot{P}^e$, where $Pb[\dot{P}^e]$ is the probability of the expected outcome, allows for this. In depicting the nominal rate, $i = i(\text{real}) + \dot{P}^e$, however, I will simply take for granted the probability of the expectation.

Discussing structural changes of the sort referred to here, Chairman Greenspan of the Federal Reserve comments on the United States's economic problems in 1992. He says:

Another less-discussed factor that contributed to the formulation of our recent monetary policy dates not from the 1980s but rather from the 1970s—inflation and inflation expectations. Over the past decade or so, the importance of the interactions of monetary policy with these expectations has become increasingly apparent. The effects of policy on the economy critically depend on how market participants react to Federal Reserve actions as well as on expectations of our future actions. These expectations—and thus the credibility of monetary policy—are influenced not only by the statements and behavior of the Federal Reserve but by those of the Congress and the Administration as well.

Through the first two decades of the post-World-War II period, this interaction was patently less important. (Greenspan 1993a, 293)

Although monetary science appears to have lost out with the changes in the structure behind inflationary expectations, it may have gained in other respects. Instead, this economics of reporting how the world works has two features, as presently approached. One feature (the scientific one) is the elusive search for a stable statistical relation, which Friedman perused so diligently. The second feature is to describe the workings in the most accurate way, even when abstraction enters. Where repetition fails to appear in one instance it may appear in another (Frazer 1994a, Chapter 9). For the present, I simply confront two types of changes in the time series that must be sorted out; namely, changes of a possible repetitive sort (such as are sought in science) and changes of an episodic nature. What I confront are numerous events of a sort that occur outside of the usual economic calculus and that move key time series about. Friedman passed along the skeleton of an open-ended analytical system, which has a role for episodic, non-repetitive changes. These are confronted in the search for regularity and repetition.

1.5c The Consumption Function

Milton Friedman framed his consumption function in terms of the permanent income path noted in Figure 1-4b (Frazer 1994a, Section 5.3):

$$C = k(. . .)Y_p$$

It was a remarkable achievement in that its statements reconciled two known sets of observations; namely, results obtained from consumption and income data for households at a given time, which provided evidence in support of Keynes's function, and results from Simon Kuznets's national income studies (Frazer 1988, 99), which more or less appeared after Keynes's statement of his function (1936, 96). The Kuznets studies, in fact, pointed to more of a constancy of the saving-to-income ratio for the United States (S/Y, and thus also C/Y in view of Equation [2] in Section 1.4c) in terms of the long-run time paths (Figures 1-4a and 1-4b).

Via such routes, I extend the list of the great ratios (Frazer 1994a, Section 3.3b) to include

$$C_p = k[i(\text{real}), Wnh/W, u]Y_p$$

Hence, another of the variable factors of proportionality [i.e., k(. . .)] is obtained. In this case, the factor k(...) can vary with two measures of interest to central bank enthusiasts and a collection of other forces (u) that can also rotate the consumption function/ratio line of Figure 1-4d upward or downward. The first measure of interest, of course, is the real rate of interest [i(real)]. The other is a rather obscure measure of liquidity consisting of the ratio of non-human wealth (cash, bonds, stocks, plant and equipment, and so on) to total wealth.

The total extends to the inclusion of "human capital" (the job training, education, and specialized skills of the work force). It is present when I write broadly of wealth (W) as the interest-rate discounted value of income (Frazer 1994a, Section 3.3). The greater the liquid part of wealth, the higher the Wnh-to-W ratio and the more likely the consumption function line of Figure 1-5d will rotate in response to a shock to the ratio. The instance has been associated with Margaret Thatcher's privatization of government-owned companies in the second half of the 1980s, along lines discussed later.

Viewed overall, very dynamic analysis surrounds the function in such a way as to facilitate a reorientation of Keynes's economics. For one thing, the mechanics of an adaptive expectations model can be extended to capture the dependence of permanent income (Figure 1-4b) on past income values. By way of this, algebraic operations can lead to a restatement of the simpler Keynes/Keynesian function ($C = a + bY$). It is such that the intercept parameter (a) is made to depend on permanent income from the last period [a $= f(Y_{p, t-1}, \ldots)$].

Next, imposing this simple function back into the Keynesian income expenditure plane (Figure 1-4d), along with the Friedman function, results in part a of Figure 1-8. Parameter a (and hence total spending)—shown on the vertical axis—is set in motion by past values for the growth path for income (Figure 1-5b). To begin with, the total spending line (C + I) intersects the 45-degree (dY/dY) line at point A and the Keynes consumption function at point B (both at income value Y_0). Growth could have proceeded from there, such that the initial points A and B were sent to the right by the growth of income.

Now, an increase in saving (demonstrated later in Figure 1-9)—and hence the saving-to-income ratio and the real rate of interest—means faster economic growth (an upward rotation of the income path in Figure 1-4b). The increase in the ratio (say via the real rate) rotates the Friedman function [$C = k(...)Y_p$] downward (as shown in Figure 1-8a). The downward rotation goes with faster growth and, overall, consumption at income one (Y_1) is greater than consumption at income zero (Y_0).

As with liquidity preference and overshooting (Figure 1-7), the main features of the Keynes/Keynesian analysis are reversed. In the earlier figure, accelerated money growth meant higher interest rates [via $i = i(real) + \dot{P}^e$] rather than lower rates. Now, greater saving out of income (Δ S/Y) means higher income rather than lower income. As could be shown in Figure 1-8b

Figure 1-8
The Dynamic Consumption Function

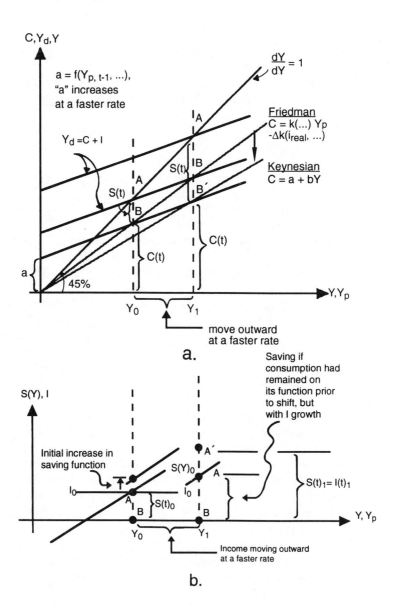

a.

b.

Figure 1-8 (continued)

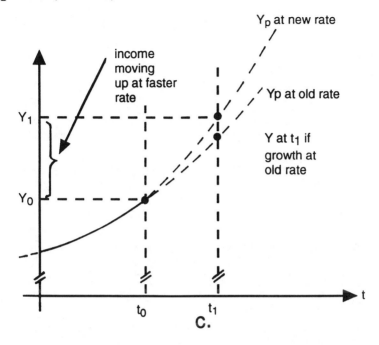

(an up date of Figure 1-3b), an upward shift in saving as a function of income [from $S(Y)_0$ to $S(Y)_1$] would at an earlier time be interpreted to mean less spending on consumption and lower level of income. This would occur at a lower point of intersection for the saving function $S(Y)$ and the constant/autonomous investment line. So, here is what Professor Samuelson called the paradox of thrift in the Keynesian context.[9] Most notably, in that context efforts by households to save out of current income were self-defeating in that income would decline and there would be little income from which to save.

Now, instead of the paradox, investment spending is a part of total spending and grows with it. The funds still flow from saving into investment, as Keynes and Keynesians implied, but two additional positions of some importance enter. One is the growth orientation toward money and credit aggregates, where accelerated money growth impacts total spending (Figure 1-7). To be sure, some central banks have the power to control bank reserves and the other money and credit aggregates, exclusive of a dependance on borrowers to approach the non-central banks for loans (Frazer 1994a, Section 4.3). As reported in Section 1.2, monetary policy can be seen in various combinations with tax policy, where its power is realized.

1.5d The Real Rate of Interest

The other important position regards, an interplay of the following: "the nominal rate of interest" (i_L), its possible dependence on inflationary prospects ($\dot{P}^e$), the dimension offered as psychological time, and the real rate of interest [i(real)]. This real rate is not exactly at the direct control of central banks, even less so than the nominal rate (i_L).

For the purpose of analysis, the real rate is that at which goods today are exchanged for goods one year hence. Figure 1-9 illustrates its dependence on saving, viewed as the act of foregoing the consumption of present income (P) in exchange for a greater future income (F).

Although not presently discussed in detail, the analysis is that of maximization subject to constraint. The idea is that of a preference for some combination of present and future income [Y_0 as opposed to $Y(1 + t)$, where the t component of the time preference, $1 + t$, is in effect a real rate of interest]. The constraint is defined by a line depicting some combination of what is possible today (Y_0) as opposed to that income times the one-year, real rate of return [$Y_0 (1 + r)$].

The satisfaction (or utility) functions U_1 and U_2 are shown in both parts of Figure 1-9. They are preferred combinations of present and future income yielding different levels of satisfaction with the possible combinations. In this regard, U_2 is one level and set of combinations, U_3 is another, and $U_3 > U_2$.

The constraint line is the downward-sloping line with terminal points at Y_0 on the horizontal axis and $Y_0(1 + r)$ on the vertical axis. The highest level of satisfaction, subject to this constraint, is at the point where the constraint line

Figure 1-9
A Change in the Real Rate of Interest

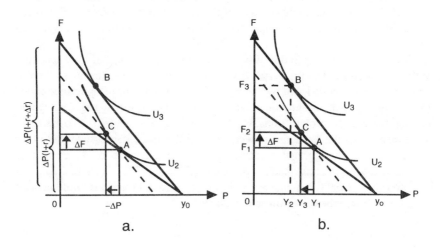

a.   b.

is tangent to the curve U_2 (U_2 = const.). At this point the slopes of the constraint line and that the U_2 = constant line are equal [i.e., $(1 + r) = (1 + t)$]. Raising the real rate of interest (i.e., increasing saving; foregoing present consumption) raises the possible future income $[Y_0 1 + (r + \Delta r)]$ and moves the point of tangency to a higher level of satisfaction at point B. However, this is income one-year hence and with income growth and I inquire only about the current, base-time substitution between present and future income. To separate it, a line parallel to the last constraint position and tangent to the initial satisfaction line, U_2, is sought. Thus, it ends at point C.

Referring back to the Slutsky equation (in Section 1.5a), when a price changes (say, now the real price of credit) there are two effects. As indicated, they are the income effect (in this case, from higher interest) and the substitution effects (in this case, the substitution of some consumption today for extra saving). Proceeding with a restatement of Figure 1-9a as Figure 1-9b, note the total move from point A to point B, as measured on the vertical axis (geometric distance $\overline{F_1F_3}$) in response to the reduction in present consumption on the horizontal axis (geometric distance $\overline{Y_2Y_1}$). In this way

$$\underbrace{\frac{\overline{F_1F_3}}{\overline{Y_2Y_1}}}_{} \quad = \quad \underbrace{\frac{\overline{F_1F_2}}{\overline{Y_1Y_3}}}_{} \quad + \quad \underbrace{\frac{\overline{F_2F_3}}{\overline{Y_3Y_2}}}_{}$$

change in future income with respect to change in present	substitution effect from higher real rate	income effect from higher real rate

Certainly this is a long way to go to arrive at a conclusion, *which is that central banks have no direct control over the real rate of interest, which in fact depends on saving and income growth.* The savings part enters into economic growth, to be sure, but that part is more a matter of tax policy than monetary policy and of technology giving rise to growth in income per unit of labor input. As powerful as the effects of monetary policy are, it would also appear that monetary policy has no direct effect on "the rate of interest" (i_L). Rather, I see this as being left to the bond market in a market economy, that is, the bond rate (i_L) is left to the forces impacting most immediately on the bond traders and their perceptions of the political and monetary forces (deficits, debt monetization, expected inflation [deflation], and general economic performance).

NOTES

1. Actually each regional bank of the Federal Reserve System could set its own discount rate, but the practice became one of following the New York bank for the most part. Via this practice, I speak of one rate. The rate was never envisioned as working along purely incentive (or disincentive) lines, as a means of achieving faster or slower growth in bank reserves. Rather, it was part of the central bank's function as lender of last resort. The discount window was available to meet the temporary liquidity needs of banks, as it met seasonal and other drains on bank reserves, partly at times in response to seasonal and other needs for bank credit and currency.

2. Compare note 1 regarding the discount and lombard rates.

3. These statements are very much at odds with those that came from U.S.'s secretary of the treasury Nicholas Brady in the last years of the Bush administration and from U.S.'s vice president Albert Gore on CNN international news on Easter weekend 1993. Writing on Brady, the *Wall Street Journal* (25 September 1992, A8) referred to him as an Ahah chasing "lower interest rates" around the globe. But Brady's credibility with financial markets was said to be somewhere south of the Italian government's.

4. Viewing the definition of money in terms of its functions, Keynes added to the medium of exchange function the standard and store of value functions. As the reader may recall, the latter concerned speculation of two sorts and various motives for holding those assets that serve as money.

Each function was linked to motives for holding money. The complex arrangement is sketched in Figure 1-10. As indicated by moving down the first of the four columns, money is defined as a medium of exchange, a standard of value (i.e., simply the unit of account), and a store of value. This last function of money made the crucial difference, as it encompassed the speculative and precautionary demands for money. Although Keynes had dealt with the speculative demand for money in relation to price-level changes in 1923, in his most famous work the speculative demand for money was confined to speculation in bonds and the choice between holding money balances and bonds.

As Milton Friedman adopted the definition of money stated here, he did a number of additional things: (1) he went back to Keynes's treatment of the demand for money in 1923, where Keynes had first started dealing with speculative demand in relation to price level changes and the Cambridge equation $M = k(. . .) Y$; (2) he related the Cambridge equation to the liquidity preference construction; (3) he broadened the classes of assets held to four; and (4) he related all of this to his special use of time frames, which is pointed to later in the chapter. In doing all of these things, expectations about bond prices and inflation (or deflation) were no longer constant for policy execution purposes. Motion was added to the analysis. Thus across the lower part of Figure 1-10 are the store of values function of money extended to the two classes of speculation, and to the speculative and precautionary motives for holding money, which J. M. Keynes first introduced into economics.

5. The "classical dichotomy" is the separation of the theory of money (M) from the production (Q). In terms of the Cambridge expression, $M = k(. . .) PQ$, the factor $k (. . .)$ is truly constant and all more or less of the money stock can do is to influence the price level (P). The demand for money, the inverse of the $k(. . .)$ factor, has nothing to do with production.

Figure 1-10
The Functions of Money, Money Demand, and the Motives for Holding Money

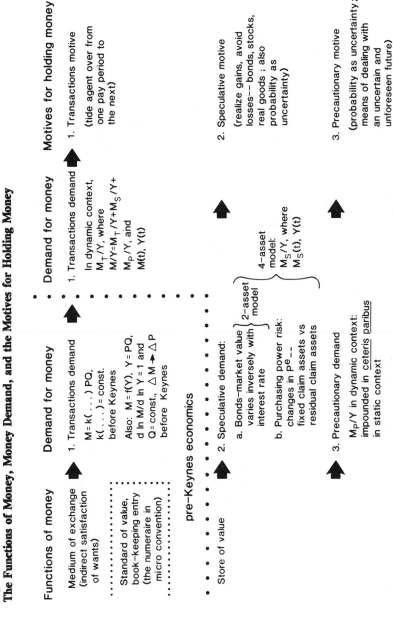

Functions of money

Medium of exchange
(indirect satisfaction
of wants)

Standard of value,
book-keeping entry
(the numeraire in
micro convention)

Store of value

Demand for money

1. Transactions demand

   $M = k(\ldots) PQ$,
   $k(\ldots) = $ const.
   before Keynes

   Also: $M = f(Y)$, $Y = PQ$,
   $d \ln M/d \ln Y = 1$ and
   $Q = $ const., $\triangle M \rightarrow \triangle P$
   before Keynes

2. Speculative demand:

   a. Bonds-market value
      varies inversely with
      interest rate $\}$ 2-asset
      model

   b. Purchasing power risk:
      changes in P^e –
      fixed claim assets vs
      residual claim assets

   4-asset model:

3. Precautionary demand

   M_P/Y in dynamic context:
   impounded in ceteris paribus
   in static context

pre-Keynes economics

Demand for money

1. Transactions demand

   In dynamic context,
   M_T/Y, where
   $M/Y = M_T/Y + M_S/Y +$
   M_P/Y, and
   $M(t)$, $Y(t)$

   M_S/Y, where
   $M_S(t)$, $Y(t)$

Motives for holding money

1. Transactions motive

   (tide agent over from
   one pay period to
   the next)

2. Speculative motive

   (realize gains, avoid
   losses-- bonds, stocks,
   real goods ; also
   probability as
   uncertainty)

3. Precautionary motive

   (probability as uncertainty;
   means of dealing with
   an uncertain and
   unforeseen future)

Keynes/Friedman monetary economics of the 20th century

The stock of money was held only for transactions purposes (as shown in the upper-left part of Figure 1-10 and changes in it went entirely into the price level (increasing the money stock twofold simply doubled the price level). What Keynes did was to extend the definition of money, and thereby the analysis of the role it played, to include its being held for speculative and precautionary reasons also.

6. The Keynesian dichotomy distinguishes between (1) the determination of output and (2) the prices entering into a price index. The first is determined by aggregate demand, and the second by costs and not by monetary means.

7. Gross national produce (GNP) represents the total expenditures for consumption, government, and private investment in real capital as well as foreign expenditures for the net exports of goods and services (a minus when imports exceed exports). Gross domestic produce (GDP) is GNP after adjusting for purchases abroad.

Citing GDP has become more fashionable in the United States since the opening up of trade in the 1980s (see, e.g., Greenspan 1993a, 296, 300). Countries such as the United Kingdom have tended to note GDP all along to call attention to their large export sector.

8. A common term in economics, "opportunity cost" is the benefit foregone from choosing one alternative over another. It arises in a variety of ways, including in the money and bond model in relation to Equation (2) of Section 1.4a, and in relation to Federal Reserve efforts to use interest rates to predict the money stock (see, e.g., Higgins 1992; Greenspan 1993a, 287-298).

9. The paradox has a much earlier history in economics and gets stated in different ways.

Chapter 2

The Central Banks and the Respective Governments

2.1 INTRODUCTION

In the United States and the United Kingdom attention in the immediate post-World War II years was focused on the effects on unemployment resulting from the elimination of wartime spending on the military. Prospects were envisioned of a return to the perceived problems of the 1930s, in the U.S. case, and to the interwar period more generally, in the U.K. case. The perceptions included the stagnation of private sector spending, as may follow from what Keynes called the declining marginal propensity to consume, and socialist's views of the evolution of market economies toward unemployment.

In the United States, the reactions took the prospect of subordinating the Federal Reserve to the Treasury with the view to ensuring low interest rates on the government's debt and an underwriting of debt refinancing. It resulted in a first case of the phenomenon which later became known as "chasing interest rates" (Frazer 1988, 212-213, 237-238, 297-298, 448-449, 545, 567, 652-653, 746, 809). The unintended effects of the policy of trying to peg rates at a low level were fairly sustained open-market purchases of government securities along lines taken up in Chapter 3. As also discussed there, this results in the expansion of the reserves of commercial banks and hence accelerated growth in bank credit and the money stock with predictable effects. The problem became inflation and not the feared return to a depression.

In the United Kingdom, the immediate reaction to the perceptions of the past and to the end of World War II were the nationalization of the Bank of England and the wave of the nationalization of industry that Clement Atlee's labor government brought about. The effects of subordinating the central bank to the Treasury, were more permanent in the U.K. than in the specific U.S. case just cited.

Meanwhile, in the Federal Republic of Germany, attention was less clearly focused on ideological choices initially than in the United States and the United Kingdom. Military occupation was the order of the day, the banking system of the future was only in the process of being put in place, and the Federal Republic of Germany experienced a destructive, hyperinflation of the currency, such as Germany had experienced following World War I. In preparation for a currency reform, which came in 1948, at a time of military government, a central banking structure was set up along the lines of the Federal Reserve in the United States (Bundesbank 1989, 4).

From the start of this allies-dominated central banking, banking was independent of the government. Moreover, banking gained autonomy by way of actions on the part of the allies in 1951. Under laws that had been put in place, however, the Federal Republic of Germany's government was to establish its own central bank, which it did in 1957, under the Bundesbank Act (Bundesbank 1989, 110-135).

Hence the result was the Deutsche Bundesbank, which is very similar to the Federal Reserve with respect to instruments and structure with two possibly major exceptions. The first is that the Bundesbank is more on an equal footing with the legislative branch of the Federal Republic of Germany government, under the law, than the Federal Reserve is under U.S. law. The second major exception is that the Bundesbank Act reflects very quantity-theoretic ideas, which are discussed in Chapter 3. Most notably the act says that the Bundesbank "regulates the quantity of money in circulation" and that, in using this power, it has "the aim of safeguarding the currency [meaning the money stock]."

This orientation could have come from ideas circulating in the early 1920s, such as those found in Keynes's *Tract on Monetary Reform* (1923), and possibly in Hjalmar Schacht's small book (1964). What existed, in any case, were ideas that can be readily associated with the Cambridge cash-balance expression, $M = k(. . .)Y$, and elements of the quantity theory of money. Even so, under what judge Robert Bork called "the rule of reason" (Frazer 1988, 318-319), the Bundesbank Act itself left much open for economic reasoning. Because this parallels the Bundesbank's history, there is even more that can readily be identified with the emergence of quantity/theoretic ideas in the United States. For one thing, the Bundesbank moved toward a very direct targeting of a money aggregate in the mid 1970s (first central bank money [CBM], and then deutsche marks M3). Moreover, in confronting the link between money growth ($\dot{M}$) and spending ($\dot{Y}$) and inflation (P), the Bundesbank gives due attention to the velocity ratio (Y/M) or its inverse (1989, 18, 65, 98).[1]

This latter move toward targeting came in the same period as the United States and United Kingdom moves to target money aggregates. Also, despite the targeting of a money aggregate and the stringent anti-inflation stances of the Bundesbank, it, like the other central banks, did not move toward the more severe control of inflation by money aggregate means until the U-Turn I associate with the changes from the 1970s to the 1980s (hypothesis $H_{U\text{-}Turn}$).

2.1a Autonomous Moves toward Targeting

Although Federal Reserve economists Kahn and Jacobson describe the Bundesbank's steps toward targeting as if they were autonomous (KJ 1989, 19-23), note that there is too much coincidence between the moves by the three central banks for any one of them to be credited with that sort of behavior. Rather than autonomous behavior with respect to the timing of the moves toward monetary targeting in the mid 1970s, I see the Bundesbank, the Federal Reserve and the Bank of England responding to the ideas that Friedman set on course. Further, KJ make much of the uses of the interest rates (which I label i_S and i_L in Chapter 1) to control spending (KJ 1989, 24, à la Keynesian lines, $\Delta\dot{M}\rightarrow\Delta i\rightarrow\Delta Y$), which Friedman and the Bundesbank avoid.

Instead of KJ's emphasis, the Bundesbank uses short-term rates in the performance of defensive operations and/or the management of liquidity. This combination of defensive and long-term strategies is described by Eizenga (1987, 7), where he discusses the 1979 move from targeting a specific growth rate for the aggregate of choice to setting of upper and lower bounds on the money aggregates growth rate by the Bundesbank. Continuing, he describes the change as enhancing flexibility for responding to unforeseen developments "in the areas of economic activity, prices, and exchange rates." Eizenga says it is important for the monetary policy based on the monetary targeting to be viewed as flexible in the "medium term" and as safeguarding monetary stability in the long term. The Bundesbank itself (1989, 106) indicates that by managing liquidity in a more responsive way through "securities repurchase agreements," it actually reduces the need for the discount mechanisms to serve as a "buffer function." The bank says, "The result is that monetary expansion takes place at a pace which is compatible with the achievement of the monetary target [over the rather longer term]."

Indeed, open market operations enter the management of liquidity with the view of controlling the money aggregate of choice and not that of controlling interest rates. The Bundesbank itself takes note of market interest rates (1989, 83), as I do and will on numerous occasions, but it views them as weak links in the control of spending and inflation, and notes that the long-term rates "are likely to change spontaneously with fluctuations in the price climate, without any actions by the central bank." Here the bank alludes to the earlier discussed interest-rate/inflation relation; namely, $i = i(\text{real}) + \dot{P}^e$.

2.1b Monetary Policy

It would be ideal to have an indicator of monetary policy in money aggregate and income-velocity terms, such as is found in *Friedman's rule*. It would reflect the acceleration and deceleration present in any change in the direction of policy and the measure would coincide with the quarters of the years for which data are analyzed. Closely related to ideas discussed earlier is the rule that *the central bank should allow the money stock to grow at the same rate as that expected in the time trend (Figure 1-4b) for real output (Q = Y/P), but with allowance for secular shifts in the velocity ratio.*[2]

So the desirable measure would consist of the product for a change in money growth ($\pm\Delta\dot{M}$) and the income velocity of money (Y/M). In such a case, the change in growth would provide the direction of the policy and the velocity ratio would indicate the amount of work done by the additions or diminutions to money growth. However, such an ideal measure of policy is elusive for a variety of reasons, including the changes in asset classification that are included in a given money-stock measure, errors in the income data, imperfect means of achieving money-stock targets on a quarter-to-quarter basis, the need to allow for changes of an episodic nature, such as oil price shocks of 1973-74 and 1979; and so on.

Among the three central banks dealt with here, the Bundesbank has been the most successful in hitting its targets. I attribute this to the will to achieve the targets, skill in employing its approach for achieving them, the reduced volatility that occurs as a result of the Bank's success, and to the mark's smaller role as an off-shore currency. Even here, however, the approach has centered on a fairly loose combination of targeting on an annual basis, reexaminations of the progress at six-month intervals, and allowances for velocity changes (Bundesbank 1989, 95-109; KJ 1989, 23-27).

So, drawing on the notion that the traders and other active participants in the bond markets have become quite sensitive to the monetary policy prospects for inflation and deflation since the mid-1960s in the United States and the United Kingdom (FS 1982, 478, 558-573), I offer a surrogate for the ideal measure. For the United States, the United Kingdom, and the Federal Republic of Germany, the surrogates are the respective bond rates. Traders and other market participants are seen as adjusting for inflationary prospects, the closely related debt-monetization prospects, the credibility of the past positions of the policy authorities, and so on. Via this route, rising bond rates are seen as a reflection of prospects for monetary accommodation of wage and price changes, possible deficit financing by governments (with the added possibility of debt monetization), controls over the allocation of services regardless of the supply side of the pricing mechanism, and so on. Declining rates are seen as a reverse set of prospects.

Viewing the decade of the 1970s as one in which monetary policy was accommodative for the most part and the early 1980s as a period of policy reversal (the U-Turn thesis), the monetary indicators for the Federal Reserve, the Bank of England, and the Bundesbank appear as described in Section 2.2. What is observed for the 1970s is significantly upward sloping trends for the United States and the United Kingdom and a mildly downward trend for the Federal Republic of Germany. As to the ranking for the decade, the Bank of England was the most accommodative of the inflationary impacts of government policies, oil-cartel shocks of the early to mid 1970s and the late 1970s, and other episodes. In some detail, the Bundesbank experienced the same shocks as the United States and the United Kingdom but allowed them to affect the market perceptions of policy less.

Following the early 1980s turns in policy (the U-Turn hypothesis), the three central banks all moved to reduce inflation until after the mid 1980s. The United States moved to allow the dollar to fall in the foreign exchange markets in lieu of further deflationary effort. However, once again, the Bundesbank, moved much farther than the United States and United Kingdom toward the control of inflation.

In terms of what in fact, happened to the inflation rates in these three countries, the U.K. rates were dramatically higher in the 1970s than the U.S. rates, and the U.S. rates were dramatically higher than the FRG rates. Then, following changes early in the 1980s, the inflation rates all declined. They did so to the lowest level in the Federal Republic of Germany, to the next lowest levels in the United States, and to the least lowest level in the United Kingdom.

Looking at upward trends for the United States and United Kingdom in the 1970s, and the significant downward trends in the early 1980s, leads to the conclusion that the 1970s and 1980s were simply decades of different policy experiments. The samples of interest-rate and inflation-rate data are from different universes, which means that fashionable regression results spanning the two decades as one sample period would be meaningless in the ordinary interpretation (the fashionable econometrics hypothesis). The series discussed in Section 2.2 are simply shared responses to shared experiences on the part of the Federal Reserve and the Bank of England in the 1970s. All three of the countries and their respective central banks shared experiences and responses in the 1980s.

It would be difficult to make the case that the three countries and their respective central banks were behaving autonomously (the policy-automony hypothesis). Nevertheless, if there was some degree of autonomous behavior, it should likely be assigned to the Bundesbank (hypothesis H_{FTL}).

2.2 THE POLICY INDICATOR, THE SURROGATES, AND FOSTERING AND CONTROLLING INFLATION

The ideal indicator would consist of the change in money growth ($\pm \Delta \dot{M}$) and the income velocity of money (Y/M), along the lines already introduced. As we discussed, the change in growth provides the direction of policy and the velocity ratio indicates the amount of work the change performs. Taking the product of money growth and velocity, and multiplying by 100 to get growth in percentage terms, monetary accommodation and discipline appear as:

$$\Delta\dot{M} \ (Y/M) \times 100 > 0 \ \ \text{(accommodation)}$$

$$-\Delta\dot{M} \ (Y/M) \times 100 < 0 \ \ \text{(discipline)}$$

The idea of accommodation is that the monetary authority accommodates other things, such as government financing of deficits and wage increases that appear as higher priced goods and services and that on the average exceed the growth in productivity. Discipline, of course, is just the reverse of accommodation. In that case, authority is moving to deny government any special accommodation and to reduce inflationary price changes, and so on. Monetary neutrality with respect to prices, wages, and production and the real goods economy is attained when the indicator approximates a zero value for a sustained period of time.

The fear that bond market and other participants in market economies associate with the prospect of the accommodation of government deficits concerns the *monetization of debt*. It is the *conversion of government debt into* credit creation and *monetary growth*, which is discussed in Chapter 3 along with Keynesian causation, the Bank of England, and Lord Kaldor. The process of debt monetization is sometimes referred to as seigniorage, meaning "the right of the crown." In times when the crown no longer rules, the term "seigniorage" simply refers to the right of some governments to take some share (or tax) in a form of revenue that comes by way of some inflationary or other process regarding money and benefits to the state.[3] Within the European Community, the central banks of Italy and Spain as well as the Bank of England have been associated with such means of obtaining government revenue.

Accommodative policy was very much the tenor of a Keynesian era (Frazer 1988, Chapter 8) which ended with Margaret Thatcher in Britain and Ronald Reagan in the United States. At a crucial time in the 1970s, in the United States, the central bank's chairman Arthur Burns took on the powerful role of the micro manager of the macro economy and took the view that it was not the intent of the U.S. Congress to relegate to the Federal Reserve the power to nullify the intentions of Congress with respect to deficit financing (Frazer 1988, Chapter 8). In other words, Burns led the Fed into an accommodative mode, which continued into 1980 with his Carter-appointed successors William Miller and Paul Volcker (Frazer 1988, 648-651).

Partly underlying the accommodative mode was what Sir John Hicks called Keynes's labor standard (Frazer 1994a, Sections 2.3b, 7.3). It was such that government and even total spending could be brought about to reduce unemployment without prices rising and with nominal wages growing no faster than production. However, the prospect was not to be realized, as is shown shortly (in Figure 2-2). Instead, the United States and the United Kingdom confronted inflationary conditions, partly as a result of the monetary accommodation of oil shocks in the early and late 1970s. That decade included the simultaneous occurrence of inflation and recession during the 1973-75 and 1980 recessions.

As a response to new antidotal ideas of a monetary sort in Friedman's work and to the crises states of record peacetime inflation and the inflationary recession phenomenon, a U-Turn in the policy orientation of the governments came about in the United States and the United Kingdom (H_{U-Turn}). And, to be sure, the prospects did not escape the officials at the Bundesbank. Although the Bundesbank proceeds quite successfully with monetary targeting, there are problems connected with the use of the ideal indicator in relation to what was actually occurring. The special U.S. and data problems may include: vacillation at the Federal Reserve in the 1970s over the Federal Reserve's independence and over commitment to the targeting of money aggregates (Frazer 1988, chap. 8); the tendency in the United States for the money-stock series M1 to be over stated in the early 1980s when new classes of accounts were included in it (Frazer 1988, 654-659); the vulnerability of dollar-denominated paper notes to shifts in their use as in cases of the underground and off-shore economies and as currency in Eastern European countries; and especially just plain errors in the money stock and GNP data, to which the indicator would be highly sensitive.

Even though the Bundesbank's approach to targeting occupies some of Chapter 3, it is rather ad hoc in relation to the ideal indicator. As would be the cases for the United States and the United Kingdom, the aggregates of choice were targeted with varying degrees of success after the mid 1970s, and in the 1980s the ranges were set with the view to reducing and containing inflation. Furthermore, the income velocity ratios (or the inverse of M/Y) trended upward in the 1970s and then leveled off or turned down for most of the 1980s. The combination of changes in money growth and the velocity ratios should yield what I expected for the ideal indicator, but they do not for the possible reasons stated earlier.

Instead of the indicators as policy measures, I offer surrogates for the United States, the United Kingdom and the Federal Republic of Germany. These consist of long-term bond rates, and I take the position that bond traders in the financial markets may determine the thrust of policies concerning inflationary/deflationary (accommodation/discipline) prospects better than economists, government clerks, and policy people can measure them.

These U.S., U.K., and FRG surrogates are shown in Figure 2-1, and the inflation rate counterparts for each of the respective countries are shown in Figure 2-2. The surrogate for U.S. policy shows a rather dramatic U-Turn in the early 1980s. This continues until somewhat after the mid 1980s, when (as

Figure 2-1a
Yield (Percent per Annum, Quarterly Data) on Thirty-Year, U.S.
Government Bonds: A Surrogate for the Monetary Indicator, $\pm\Delta\dot{M}(Y/M)$
× 100

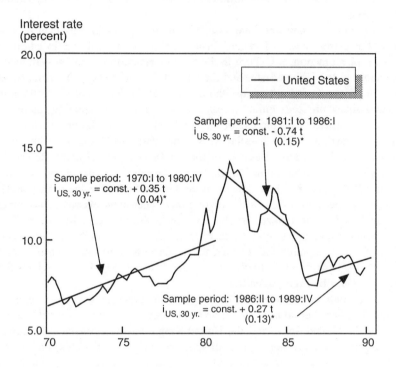

Interest rate
(percent)

Sample period: 1981:I to 1986:I
$i_{US, 30\ yr.} = const. - 0.74\ t$
                          $(0.15)^*$

Sample period: 1970:I to 1980:IV
$i_{US, 30\ yr.} = const. + 0.35\ t$
                          $(0.04)^*$

Sample period: 1986:II to 1989:IV
$i_{US, 30\ yr.} = const. + 0.27\ t$
                          $(0.13)^*$

United States

*The regression coefficients are significantly different from zero at the 1 percent level of
significance. The standard error of the estimate is in parentheses in the present and subsequent
cases.

Notes: The series on thirty-year, U.S. bonds is available only for the period since 1977.
         Consequently, to obtain data for the entire period 1970:I to 1991:III, I used 30-year yields from
         1977:II to 1991:III and those on the 10 year series for the same period to construct a forecasted
         series for 1970:I to 1977:II. It is $i_{30\text{-}year} = 0.81 + 0.92\ i_{10\text{-}year}$ with correlation coefficient
         squared of 0.99 (whether adjusted or unadjusted).

This was simply to obtain a complete series for the classic 30-year bond rate. Other series on
bonds (those for the 10-year government bonds, and the AAA and BAA rated bonds) provided
the same patterns of change, as expected. Also, the data were smoothed using a four-quarter
moving average.

Source: Board of Governors of the Federal Reserve System

Figure 2-1b
Yield (Percent per Annum, Quarterly Data) on Twenty-Year U.K.
Government Bonds: A Surrogate for the Monetary Indicator

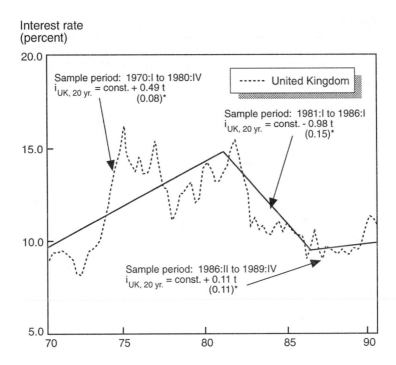

*Significantly different from zero at the 1 percent level of significance.

Source: Bank of England

depicted in Chapter 4) the United States adopted a James Baker led policy to allow the dollar to decline in the foreign exchange markets rather than to bear more aggressively on the control of inflation by monetary means. In the surrogates case, policy accommodation calls forth higher interest rates and discipline calls forth lower interest rates [both by way of the interest rate relation, $i = i(\text{real}) + \dot{P}^e$]. This occurs along the lines referred to earlier in reference to New York's revenge and Alan Greenspan. In any event, for a time, the policy to reduce inflation was substantial and, further (referring to the inflation rate data in Figure 2-2), U.S. inflation rates declined significantly.

Figure 2-1c
Yield (Percent per Annum, Quarterly Data) on Ten-Year, FRG Bonds: A
Surrogate for the Monetary Indicator

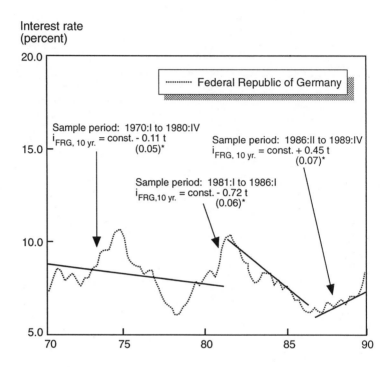

*Significantly different from zero at the 1 percent level of significance.

Source: Deutsche Bundesbank

The U.K. data for the surrogate show virtually the same trends and U-Turn pointed to in the U.S. case, although the U.K. inflation rate had much farther to decline than the U.S. rate. Also, as in the U.S. data for the surrogate, a change in the trend is seen after the mid 1980s. As arises much later in the discussion of the U.K. case, I attribute this last development to the Thatcher government's efforts at privatizing government-owned enterprises and to the Bank of England's failure to forecast and offset the effects of private-sector liquidity from stock ownership on household spending.

Figure 2-1d
U.S., U.K., and FRG Yields

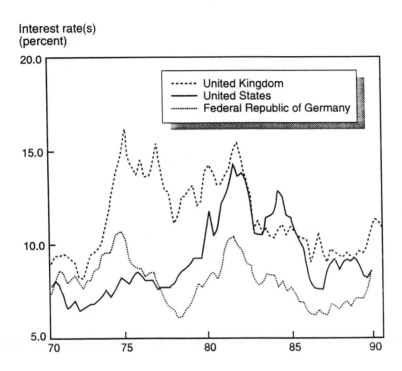

Looking still further east to the Federal Republic of Germany and the Deutsche Bundesbank, a slightly downward trend is seen in the surrogate for the 1970s and a sharp downward trend through the mid 1980s. In other words, the Bundesbank followed a policy of much greater monetary discipline in the oil-shock/Keynesian years of the 1970s, than either the United States or the United Kingdom, despite the Federal Republic of Germany's total dependence on imported oil. And it still went through the turn in direction, despite the mildness of its inflation in the 1970s.

The final point about the results in Figures 2-1 and 2-2, discussed further in Section 2.5, is that the 1970s and the trends through the mid 1980s are obtained from different universes. The significant upward trends in the 1970s for the United States and the United Kingdom and the sharp, significant,

Figure 2-2a

The U.S. Inflation Rate (Percent per Annum), the 1970s and the 1980s (Quarterly Data)

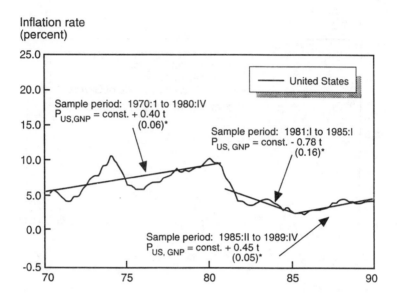

*Significantly different from zero at the 1 percent level of significance.

Note: The GNP deflator is used to compute the inflation rate.

Source: Board of Governors of the Federal Reserve System

downward trends afterward for the United States, the United Kingdom, and the Federal Republic of Germany mean that the respective trends are significantly different from each other. The additional interpretations I give to these trends are that they reflect primary, pervasive, monetary/political influences; that the latter reflect outside forces rather than the internal workings of an economic system; and that, as a consequence, the statistical results render inapplicable the ordinary uses of econometric methods in for the market economies. In other words, the results constitute a rejection of the fashionable econometrics hypotheses H_{FE} and its corollary hypothesis $H_{UT/FE}$. Via this route, much is obtained by way of interpretation with little by way of statistical results.

Figure 2-2b

The U.K. Inflation Rate (Percent per Annum), the 1970s and the 1980s (Quarterly Data)

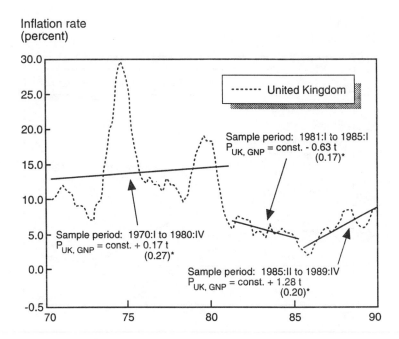

*The regression coefficient is significantly different from zero at the 1 percent level.

Note: The GNP deflator is used to compute the inflation rate. All data are seasonally adjusted or smoothed with a fourth-quarter moving average.

Source: Bank of England

2.3 THE RULE AND THE INDICATOR: AN OVERVIEW

Taking note of analytical, observational, and data complexities in relating Friedman's policy-guidance rule to the policy indicator (monetary accommodation, and all), enables further consideration of the relationship between the rule and the indicator. First, in the rule, the leading time rate of change in the money stock impacts income (and thereby general business

Figure 2-2c
The FRG Inflation Rate (Percent per Annum), the 1970s and the 1980s
(Quarterly Data)

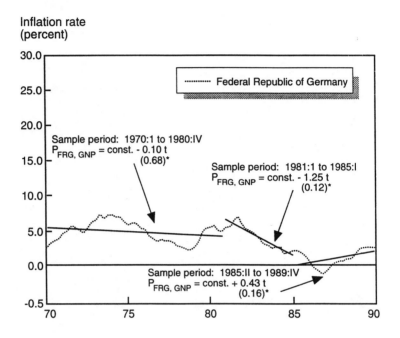

*The regression coefficient is significantly different from zero at the 1 percent level of significance.

Source: Deutsche Bundesbank

conditions, see Figure 1-4). Second, long-run shifts in the velocity ratio (Y/M) may be allowed for because they indicate a change in the extent of the effects of money growth on income. In the rule context, Friedman limits this allowance because the effects of accelerated (decelerated) growth start immediately and accumulate for a long time, although shifts in velocity may in fact occur in the short run. They simply are not allowed in the context of the rule, because in Friedman's view policy reactions to them may be even more destabilizing. Nevertheless, the Bundesbank appears to confront short-run shifts successfully.

Moreover, seeking the direction of policy and its effects (as to whether accommodative, and so on), does not necessarily entail the restrictions imposed

Figure 2-2d
The U.S., U.K., and FRG Inflation Rates

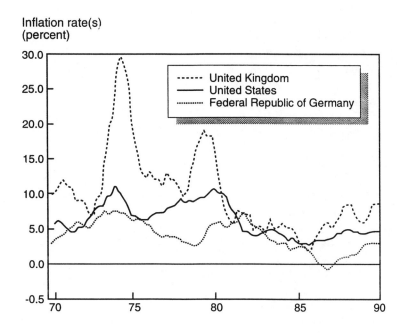

by the rule. So, I seek at least the concept of a measure of redirection, whether upward or downward ($\pm\Delta\dot{M}$), which may also indicate effects, exclusive of efforts to abstract from day-to-day and even quarter-to-quarter changes.

The concept, offered in Section 2.1b, calls attention to two well-known sets of observations—that of the somewhat parallel, quarter-to-quarter movements in the money stock and income growth rates (most recently reported for the 1970s and 1980s decades by Schwartz 1990) and that of upward and downward movements in the velocity ratio for the respective decades (described later in Figure 5-2). However, there are complications for each of the separate sets of facts and consequently for combined statements of them. In the first set are measurement errors and statistical problems arising from the changes in the composition of the dollars M1 and M2 measures and from whether accounts draw interest or not. In the period since 1960s, FS have first relied on a measure for dollars M2, then a new M1 series, and then a different dollars M2 series. In addition, as seen later (in Figures 3-1 and 3-3), velocity too has changed in relation to interest rates.

Although the concept for accommodation and so on brings forward measurement error and statistical problems, it does suit the use of "the [nominal] rate of interest" as a surrogate for the policy because I establish a direct tie to the assessments of the traders in the bond market as to whether policy is inflation/accommodative, disinflation/disciplinary, and anticipatory in both cases.   Indeed, these anticipatory instances provide the prospect of inflation that may be associated with the monetization of public debt by the central bank along the lines of accommodative policy (say, bank support of the public sector's borrowing).

In effect, in reaction to the described data and statistical problems, Friedman exerts efforts to achieve smoothness in the analyses of data and policy via three routes: (1) that of using broader measures in selecting the money aggregate of choice (dollars M2 rather than M1); (2) that of "filtering" the data, as it were, by focusing on the trend (or long run) rather than the day-to-day changes in the money and bond markets and in the perceptions of the traders in those markets; and (3) in general, that of focusing on Friedman's particular time frames and the movements in quarter-to-quarter changes in dollars M2 and nominal GNP, such as found in Schwartz (1990).

So, in giving perspective to the data and analytical problems, the monetary indicator is seen partly in conceptual terms. One may ask about the purpose to stating it in those terms. The answer is, namely, to obtain a refined statement of the measurement that can be sought; to call attention to the data and other problems that are present when consideration strays away from special features of the Friedman approach to policy and the uses of statistical methods; and to bring in the long-term bond rates I associate with New York's revenge and the like.

2.4 THE ZERO INFLATION RATE GOAL AND THE UNEMPLOYMENT RATE

The prevailing focus of attention in the United States and the United Kingdom was on unemployment rates and surely not inflation rates in the early post-World War II years, as indicated earlier. As this occupation with the unemployment prospects continued in the United States, the following are on its domestic side:

1. higher unemployment rates in each successive recovery phase of the business cycle (FY 1966, 581-582);

2. operation twist as an attempt to deal with gold outflows and unemployment in the early 1960s;

3. monetary accommodation of inflation rates in the 1970s; and

4. the U-Turn toward reduction of inflation rates.

The period embracing the second and third domestic developments has been called a Keynesian era (Frazer 1988, Chapter 8).

Parallel to the four domestic developments and related to them, the following developments occurred on the international side:

1. the closing of the U.S. gold window, when the United States could no longer support the dollar tie to gold and continue with the inflationary policy;

2. a growth of private-sector foreign exchange operations following the freeing up of exchange rates;

3. the founding of the EMS in 1979, partly as a German/French reaction to unstable exchange rates against the dollar; and

4. the Delors Report's plan as a feature of monetary developments in the European Community (EC).

By the spring of 1989, the EC's Delors Report had set out goals for a supercentral bank, a common money-supply for EMS-member countries, and a zero inflation rate goal. In the same year the Berlin Wall was breached, and in the following year, the two Germanies were integrated economically and politically as command economies in the former Soviet Union and Eastern Europe continued to fall apart.

Without traversing these developments in any detail, these notions bear on the unemployment rate, in the light of the following:

1. developments in the United States and the United Kingdom;

2. upward trends in the unemployment rates in the United States, the United Kingdom, and the Federal Republic of Germany in the decades of the 1970s and the 1980s;

3. views expressed by Federal Reserve economists Kahn and Jacobson, to the effect that German unemployment suffers in the presence of monetary efforts to reduce and contain inflation (KJ 1989, 27-34); and

4. the zero-inflation goal favored by the Bundesbank.

2.4a The U.S. and U.K. Developments

Emerging from World War II, U.S. and U.K. economics was dominated by views about the ominous effects from the elimination of wartime/military spending, the stagnation of private-sector spending, and the evolution of the market economy toward unemployment.[4] Among U.S. and U.K. Keynesians, targets for the unemployment rates were set quite low by comparison with later experience, and A.W. Phillips of the London School of Economics offered in 1958 what came to be called the Phillips curve (Frazer 1994a, Section 7.2). Based on rather limited observations of the interwar period, it posited an inverse movement between inflation and unemployment rates and, indeed, reinforced views that the acceptance of a positive inflation rate would result in a reduced unemployment rate.

By 1968, Milton Friedman posited the "natural" (i.e., non-inflationary) rate of unemployment, questioned the Phillips curve trade-off of inflation for reduced unemployment, and soon began to take up other views of the inflation rate and unemployment. Most notably, by the time of *Monetary Trends*, the United States and the United Kingdom had experienced record peacetime inflations and some history of the simultaneous occurrence of both recession and unemployment. With Schwartz, in *Monetary Trends*, Friedman reformulated the Phillips curve relation (FS 1982, 213-214) in terms of a direct relation between the price index and the output/capacity-output ratio and in some measure abstract from the short run. FS said (1982, Chapter 9), they expected a positive relation (Figure 2-3a), as called for by the Phillips curve, but what they found after combining the data for the pre-World War I and post-World War II years was an inverse relation between the price index and the output/capacity-output ratio (Figure 2-3b).

Mentioning a possible short-run effect of a stimulative monetary policy, Ayn Rand philosopher Greenspan (1993a, 294) says it "can prompt a short run acceleration of activity." But then he says, "the experience of the 1970s provided convincing evidence that there is no lasting tradeoff between inflation and unemployment; in the long run, higher inflation buys no increase in employment."

This Friedman relation in Figure 2-3b would be roughly as expected from movements suggested by two separate prospects. One is movement relating prices to output, as suggested by the demand curve (Figure 1-5). The other is the gold-flows mechanism, which is discussed in Chapter 4. It appears with fixed (or occasionally fixed) exchange rates and variable price levels for the respective countries (say, P_{US} and P_{UK}). Here balances of trade favor the exports of the country with the most improvement in the relative price level $[-\Delta(P_{US}/P_{UK})$ for the United States, and $+ \Delta (P_{US}/P_{UK})$ for the United Kingdom]. Clearly, in an open-economy world, such as the United States and the United Kingdom moved further toward in the 1980s, trade and capital flows favor countries with the more disciplined prices (including wages as a special price) and the more productive work forces.

Figure 2-3
The Price-Q/Q_capacity Relation

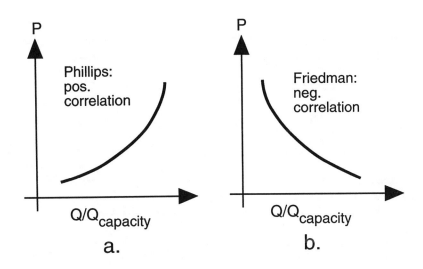

a.   b.

2.4b The Trends and the German Case

Without belaboring the foregoing, post-World War II trends toward higher unemployment rates in the United States and the United Kingdom and the opening up of trade between the industrialized, market economies, some perspective is called for. In that of the system I point to, a threefold conclusion stands out; namely, the move from the 1970s to the 1980s was toward the emergence of market economies, and away from those envisioned in the United States and the United Kingdom on the part of economists for the most part in the early post-World War II years; markets require stable monetary arrangements and a monetary umbrella for voluntary association in the markets; and viable market economies (monetary control and all) are accompanied by higher unemployment rates than command economies.

Some old ideas are included, of course. Market economies in the open trade context take on a momentum of their own, generate rapid change, and provide stress and growth in production as a part of being open. Karl Popper, the Mont Pelerin Society's philosopher (Frazer 1988, 172-173, 336-337), put the matter of neutralizing the stress thus: "Personal relationships of a new kind can arise where they can be freely entered into, instead of being determined by the accidents of birth; and with this, a new individualism arises."

The sources of unemployment arising in a market economy have been variously enumerated as the movement from one job to another, the search for employment, the mismatching of job requirements and job skills, suitability for employment in other respects, and the failure of prices and wages to adjust downward adequately in the presence of an inadequate demand for the product and job skills. This especially occurs in the opening-up phase of high-wage countries as employment moves toward lower wage markets and payment according to the value of the marginal product of labor and capital (Frazer 1994a, Section 3.2c). In more established market economies, the dynamics of the Friedman consumption function may offer some solace. Most notably, the unemployed are not permanently unemployed. There is upward and downward special mobility (Frazer 1988, Chapter 13). But there is more.

The large context reveals more of a managed (forced) and hesitating compliance with the rules of a market economy. It is seen in the Federal Republic of Germany, in the EC, in the United States, and at the meetings of the group of five (the G-5). The scenario is as follows. Achieving a central bank for the EMS, a single currency, and zero inflation would have been easy, except for political impediments to yielding control and the presumed need for educating economists and the public about markets and institutions, where the forces of a market economy call for institutional changes. First, there are, as in the latter instances, moves toward market economies that call forth higher unemployment rates, but then these may be even compounded by notions of social justice as governments confront them by raising minimum wages, increasing the costs of discharging improductive workers and of hiring permanent additions to the work force. In a country-specific case, KJ (1989, 27-35) describe the efforts by the Bundesbank to move toward lower inflation rates at a time when the Federal Republic of Germany increased the cost of discharging workers so as to put upward pressure on prices. Then, as a consequence, the unemployment rate increased.[5]

Such political dominance regarding the transition from the 1970s to the 1980s and to market economies may be the result, along with what can best be called a managed-market/managed-finance system. There is reluctance on the part of the political body to entirely yield control to the markets.

The ideological dimension to unemployment gains even further perspective from the observation that unemployment in the Federal Republic of Germany was running over 8 percent prior to German unification, and unemployment in the socialist German Democratic Republic, prior to German unification, was 0 percent. As Marx was very much aware—through he did not state it correctly—the monetary/market economy has unenviable unemployment numbers. Governments of the market economies may of course offer some programs and supports for reducing the "natural rate" of unemployment by other than monetary and fiscal policy means, but there are potential dangers to voluntary association in what government may offer in a market-economy context.

2.5 EXOGENOUS/ENDOGENOUS FORCES, THE SEPARATION OF EFFECTS, AND AN OVERVIEW

The Friedman approach to analyses of time series (of the sort introduced in Figures 2-1 and 2-2) proceeded as a contrast to the econometric fashion of the period over which Friedman analyzed data (Frazer 1984; 1988, 68-87, and chap. 18; and FS 1991). As Friedman proceeded from the leading time rate of change in the money stock—and what is discussed in Chapter 3 as "helicopter" money—he set off controversy over causation, which in fact appears with hindsight as only the tip of an iceberg.

At this tip, the policy variable (M) was external (exogenous) to the economic system in Friedman's analysis and internal (endogenous) in James Tobin's analysis. An early meaning associated with the closely related term "autonomous" had been whether the value for the variable in each period was statistically independent of the random disturbances in the stochastic model (say, regression equation) in all periods (Frazer 1973, Section 5.2), but as controversy over such meaning proceeded, the prospect arose that the result might simply be degrees of exogeneity (say fifty percentage points) and degrees of exogeneity (say, $[1.00 - 0.50] \times 100$, or fifty percentage points). That is to say, the variable was fully accounted for in terms of some part of its value being inside and some outside (Frazer 1993).

Below the tip of this iceberg was an even more fundamental prospect. It centered around the classes of information found in the time series itself. This, as it turns out, was at the base of the Friedman search for a stable statistical relation (i.e., one that held over time, from the sample to the forecast period, see, e.g., Figures 1-4a, 1-4b, and 1-4c). The classes of information, in this Friedman context, are the permanent and transitory components of the time series, on the one hand, and changes in the data series that are responses to episodes, on the other. These episodic impacts come from oil crises, an Iraqi invasion of Kuwait, an election outcome, and a change in the composition of a time series concerning included or excluded information.

Even farther below the tip of the iceberg, is the prospect that the structure underlying the formation of inflationary expectations may change, such as FS reported for the mid 1960s. So taken overall, this iceberg meant that the Friedman approach was very open ended in terms of outside forces impacting the data series, the economic outlook, and the processing of new information. In contrast, I have in the econometric fashion (as depicted by the fashionable econometrics hypotheses H_{FE} and its corollary $H_{UT/FE}$) the idea of a universe that remains free of outside influences as consideration proceeds from one sample period (say 1970s decade) to the next (say 1980s) and on beyond the sample period. The changes confronted are thought to spring from the internal workings of the economic system (i.e., to be endogenous). To the extent that outside forces operated in terms of policy control variables, they were (and are) assumed to be independent of one another. There is no other outside force making these variables interdependent and inseparable for policy purposes.

I symbolize this separation of effects as:

$$\text{GNP and/or GDP} = a_o + a_1\,i + a_2\,M_{US}/M_{UK} + a_3\,\$/\pounds + a_4\,\text{fiscal policy}$$
(or central bank support policy with respect
to it) + . . .   (1)

The idea here is that interest rate (i) effects, money-growth ($\dot{M}$) effects, exchange-rates ($\$/\pounds$) effects, and so on, can be manipulated by political agencies to put GNP on target as far as convention and economic policy are concerned. However, there is a problem with the uses of methods. It reduces to the prospect that a U.S. (or another country's) monetary policy may itself set off interdependence in the variables. That is, accelerated money growth may cause inflation, inflationary prospects, higher interest rates [via $i = i$(real) + $\dot{P}^e$], a declining dollar exchange rate [$\Delta(\$/\pounds)$, $\Delta(\$/D\text{-}M)$, etc.], and so on with respect to numerous other time series.

Now, I conclude that monetary policy itself may set off all these changes, even as Friedman warns of infinite regress (e.g., it is the money stock, but Friedman called attention to it, so it is the "power of ideas," due to Friedman, and so on). Where I begin here and end later is that the buck stops somewhere (exogenous, endogenous, or whatever). I say the "buck stops" with the official(s) responsible for the policy orientation. I see this as accommodative and Keynesian (as an ideological orientation) in the 1970s, and as moving toward monetary discipline and inflation containment in the early to mid 1980s. In other words, I return to hypothesis $H_{U\text{-}Turn}$ of set two in Chapter 1. The ideologically connected policy orientation (i.e., the ideas) are driving the numbers. This drive is such that the variables on the right-hand side of the preceding symbolic equation are all interrelated by the policy/ideology connection. In the case of Figures 2-1 and 2-2, different universes exist for the 1970s and the 1980s, broadly viewed. It is the accommodative/targeting duality and the Bundesbank's success at targeting as discussed.

If there is substance to this position, it constitutes a rejection of hypotheses H_{FE} and $H_{UT/FE}$, leaving $H_{U\text{-}Turn}$ of set two.

In brief, the analytical system I developed in *The Legacy* (Frazer 1994a) and take up with respect to central banks is a total, analytical system that also has its own unique uses of statistical methods. In this sense, and for its special policy-oriented purpose, it is at odds with some fashionable approaches and uses of techniques, which can include (1) the fashionable econometrics; (2) the multiple regression model with its implied separation of effects; (3) efforts to determine the endogeneity or exogeneity of policy connected time series (such as the interest rate, the government's deficit, and the money stock) in lieu of having the buck stop with the government in the case of the managed market economy; (4) microeconomics, when viewed as positive and/or neoclassical economics (Frazer 1994a, Chapter 3); (5) Keynesian macroeconomics; and (6) the New-Classical School's rational expectations (Frazer 1994a, Chapter 9, note 1). Instead I suggest in *The Legacy* (and therefore here) in lieu of the foregoing are (1) concern about the information contained in a single time series (transitory and trend components, and episodic impacts of a significant sort that move the series about (such as are introduced with respect to Figures 2-1 and 2-2); (2) the treatment of a few variables at a time with the awareness that I am operating with interdependent variables in a total, open economy system of analysis when time is present; (3) a system of analysis that elevates the economic/psychological behavior of agents as it relates to the role of money, psychological time, the formation of income and inflationary prospects, and so on; and (4) a managed financial system that is inseparable from the proper functioning of a market economy.

This alternative to convention is enormously open ended concerning study. A place is left for it. Even so, efforts to ignore the exogenous forces I point to and to combine the Friedman approach with the approaches (1) through (6) above are likely to encounter inconsistency and/or the separation-of-effects problem. From the introduction of Bayesian learning onward, the alternative I offer leads in special directions that should be of interest to social scientists and others concerned with monetary policy of an encompassing sort. The Bank of England's governor stated the position on the separation-of-effects matters when he said

Outside commentators on monetary developments sometimes create the impression that those responsible for operating monetary policy sit in front of a battery of switches and levers, each one of which will produce a precise and certain response in some area of the financial markets or directly in some more distant part of the economy. I can assure you that there is only one switch in my room, and that is the light switch. (Leigh-Pemberton 1987)

NOTES

1. In general, the symbol for income (Y) is used to mean gross national product, although there are contexts where GDP appears as the numerator of the velocity ratio (Greenspan 1993a, 296; and compare note 7 in Chapter 1). Interestingly, the Bundesbank (1989, 18) uses GNP in presenting the Cambridge k, or the inverse of the velocity ratio.

2. This time trend (Figure 1-4b) is what others have referred to as "sustainable growth" in reference to the economy. Alan Greenspan does so (1993a, 294) in reference to the U.S. economy and the Humphrey-Hawkins Full Employment and Balanced Growth Act of 1978.

Although the act was signed by President Carter in tumultuous times, Greenspan calls attention to it in reference to policy during his tenure at the Federal Reserve. He says:

This view of the capabilities of monetary policy is entirely consistent with the Humphrey-Hawkins Act. As you know, the act requires that the Federal Reserve "maintain long-run growth of the monetary and credit aggregates commensurate with the economy's long-run potential to increase production, so as to promote effectively the goals of maximum employment, stable prices, and moderate long-term interest rates."

The goal of moderate long-term interest rates is particularly relevant in the current circumstances. (Greenspan 1993a, 294)

The Humphrey-Hawkins Act superseded the U.S. Full Employment Act of 1946. It also set forth the economic goal of a 4 percent unemployment rate. For a review of the act in reference to Jimmy Carter, see Frazer (1980, vol. 1, 357, 380).

3. For more detailed and technical discussion of seigniorage, see Emerson et al. (1992, 120-123, 131-132, 185-186).

4. For discussion of the United States in this transitional period, see Frazer (1984, 57 and 68). Also, recall that the Employment Act of 1946 was a products of the transition from World War II (compare note 2, above).

5. KJ appear to adopt a Phillips curve trade-off of higher unemployment rates for reduced inflation rates (1989, 31-32), as they describe inflation and unemployment rates data. In fact, it is a rather clear position, until it gets complicated by the introduction of labor-market and political-institutional matters that are drawn on in the preceding. Furthermore, they fail to deal with the distinction between controlling the rate of unemployment up to the "natural rate" and controlling the natural rate itself by non-monetary means.

Part II

Operations, Mechanisms, and the State

The Keynesian i-regime, fiscal-policy oriented economies introduced under "liquidity preference" are extended along both domestic and international lines. Chapter 3 turns to hypotheses about bank traditions and procedures and the interest-rate/fiscal policy orientation. It is a part of some central bank organizations (most notably, the Bank of England) and notions about "fiscal policy" causation as a part of the money and credit creation process.

This overall alignment of banking organization and economic theory reached a fruitful state of discussion at the hands of the United Kingdom's Lord Kaldor and in his public-policy writings which extend to his book, *The Scourge of Monetarism* (1982). In his hands, the central bank is accommodative of government fiscal policy and any demand for bank loans that may arise. Seen as a part of Keynesian economics (or that economics with a post-Keynesian flair), inflation can arise as the central bank accommodates the government in its efforts to attain "full employment." It did so in the United Kingdom and in the United States in the 1970s, including as direct controls over prices were invoked in both countries.

An extended Keynesian/theoretic dimension is that price increases under the accommodative arrangements may occur as a result of imperfect and monopolistic market structures. This in turn, links in part to the positions of J. M. Keynes (Frazer 1994a, Sections 2.3, 7.3), whereby wages would remain tied to production in the presence of the management of the overall economy. Market-structures (or "market-power") theories of inflation are linked to Keynesian/theoretic economics (Frazer 1994a, Section 3.2).

In all of these, there are theoretic and polity connected positions that I see as constituting alternative analytical systems. Beginning in Chapter 1 with connections between Friedman's variant of Marshall's demand curve and the price index, special time frames enter the analysis and appear in the extensions and reorientation of money demand and the interest-rate-dominated version of the liquidity preference demand for money.

These reoriented positions also reappear in Chapter 3 in connection with U.S. history and historically related banking institutions. Perhaps surprising for some, the Friedman positions and closely related U.S. banking arrangements are connected to the rise of the Deutsche Bundesbank, founded in 1957. Independence from fiscal policy was given the Bundesbank and the means for achieving the goals of the Bundesbank Act were left open to economic interpretation, as indicated. The interpretation there, which carries the day, draws heavily on the economic ideas I identify.

The American historical roots to Friedman's banking view go back to congressional hearings and economic analyses concerning the 1937-38 recession in the United States, special accounting arrangements associated with the Federal Reserve, and the old gold-flows mechanism that prevailed over much of the period Friedman and Anna Schwartz wrote about in *A Monetary History of the United States*, 1867-1960 (1963). In connection with the accounting arrangements (namely, the bank reserve equation), fractional reserve banking, and bank credit in the form of both loans and investments, I encounter what the late Lord Kaldor called Friedman's "black box" and what Friedman called, on occasion, "helicopter money." Reviewing the content of "the box" in Section 3.3, I proceed to show bank operations in a very different light from those found at the Bank of England. Referring to the "black-box" operations, the expansion and growth of the economic system is independent of both interest rates and fiscal policy. There is no requirement that interest rates be low (or lowered) for bank reserves, bank credit, and the money stock to expand, as explained in various chapters. On the contrary, the central bank targets growth rates for money and credit aggregates along lines best epitomized by the Bundesbank.

Taking up the international side, Chapter 4 reviews a movement from automatic, rules-oriented arrangements to managed economic systems. The bank reserve equation and open-market operations of the sort discovered in New York in the 1920s and written into the U.S. banking acts of 1933 and 1935 enter the picture. Phases of post-World War II developments, with the United States at the center much of the time, are reviewed. Attention is given to the International Monetary Fund, its exchange rate mechanisms, and the closing of the gold window by the United States in the early 1970s. The exchange rate arrangements and notions about a super-central bank are traversed as attention turns to the European Monetary System and the deutsche mark as an anchor currency.

Much that is said about interest rates under the introduction to i regime/fiscal-policy economics reappears in an international context in chapter 4. Milton Friedman's attention to floating exchange rates and their link to the sovereignty issue—as encountered with respect to Margaret Thatcher and the U.K. entry into the EMS—appear, as does the view of the Friedman system as an alternative to that with attention to fiscal policy and interest rates. The polity of these alternatives works its way in the EMS, in both U.S. and other attitudes toward the Deutsche Bundesbank in the early 1990s, and the days of crisis encountered with respect to the United Kingdom, exchange rate arrangements, and the EMS in September 1992. Moreover, the days of crises provide an opportunity to review theoretic positions about bank rates, capital flows, and foreign exchange reserves.

Chapter 3

Bank Operations, Control Arrangements, and the State

3.1 INTRODUCTION

The fundamentalist/economic analysis and the distinct micro and macro tracks it set appear to have thrived in the academy as if they were unchallenged by Friedman's work. There are several possible reasons for maintaining the old distinctions and retaining the distinct analyses for money and production. They include: the congeniality inherent in maintaining numerous, if artificial distinctions in the subject matter; a latent awareness that monetary analysis carries with it some heavy methodological and ideological baggage, of the sort pointed to in *The Legacy* (Frazer 1994a, Sections 2.4c, 3.4); a residual of inadequate understanding of the alternative analytical system Friedman offered; and the severity of the challenge Friedman provided on any number of fronts. These reasons for maintaining the old distinctions extend to the previously noted time frames (Figure 1-4), to the place assigned to episodic change and the interdependence of time series, to the emphasis on prediction outside the sample period and/or for policy in another country, and to the presently noted control arrangements I associate with theory choice and central bank stances on public policy.

In any case, I adhere to the monetary revolution and to the ideological-interplay thesis associated with the Keynesian economics and the Friedman substitute for it as discussed in *The Legacy* (Frazer 1994a, part II). In doing so, I continue with the interest-rate and money-aggregate distinction and extend the focus to the 1930s, to the post-World War II directions and experiments in economic policy, and to later developments in the previously introduced causation controversy. As previously introduced, the question was whether $\Delta \dot{Y} \rightarrow \Delta \dot{M}$ and $\pm \Delta i \rightarrow \mp \Delta M$ (Equation [2] in Section 1.4a) or $\Delta \dot{M} \rightarrow \Delta \dot{Y} \rightarrow \Delta i$ (Section 1.5b). From the controversy's a priori beginnings with the American

Keynesian James Tobin, this chapter moves to the introduction of institutional arrangements along the lines of the United Kingdom's Lord (Nicholas) Kaldor.

In doing all of this, I further explore the United States's Federal Reserve, the United Kingdom's Bank of England, and the Federal Republic of Germany's and European Community's highly successful Bundesbank. Two subjects on the international front are anticipated—the place of the i-orientation's "bank rate" (or the so-called discount rate in the United States) and hypotheses and theory choices bearing on the prospects for a European monetary system.

3.1a The Bank Rate and the Friedman System

As taken up in Chapter 4, the i-orientation's "bank rate" plays international as well as domestic roles. It becomes extended, as does the Friedman system.

On the domestic side, and with respect to the fundamentalist view, a lower bank rate was thought to encourage a reduction in rates of interest generally, and a higher bank rate to cause the reverse. These movements of rates were thought to come about via the activities of money market banks in the case of the Bank of England and a change in the discount rate at a Federal Reserve Bank in the United States (all in relation to money market rates). The discount rate was thought to encourage a change in the reserves of commercial banks via borrowing by commercial banking institutions at the Reserve banks. As suggested earlier, the view was that of lowering or raising the structure of rates.

Internationally, in a quite early tradition of thought, which still lingers, a rise in the "bank rate" has been thought to attract gold to the vaults of banks (and, where gold no longer flows, an inflow of capital funds from abroad). However, as with other areas of conventional thought, this prospect has been altered by the connections between the nominal interest rates and the inflation rate $[i = i(real) + \dot{P}^e]$, by the idea of monetary targeting, by the idea of a form of price competition between two countries (say, P_{US} and P_{UK} for the U.S. and U.K. price levels), and by extended discussion in Chapter 4 of the separation of effects problem. Taking up these latter views in chapter 4, I introduce international dimensions with regard to freedom and markets that may appear as extensions of the domestic views.

3.1b The Hypotheses

The considered hypotheses, the central banks hypothesis (H_{CB}), the theoretical works hypothesis (H_{TW}), and the U-Turn hypothesis ($H_{U\text{-}Turn}$), are of interest for a number of reasons. One reason is that the central banks come on the scene at different times in response to different circumstances, and another is that they have different traditions and orientations toward the world that make a difference with regard to how they should be viewed. In contrast, the common view—often taken for granted—is that they all raise and lower interest rates à la the static liquidity preference and IS-LM constructions and exert the effects suggested by those constructions.

Also—looking beyond the United States—the Bank of England, London as a financial center, and the Bundesbank are of interest for a number of special reasons. First, J. M. Keynes emerged as a monetary economist with close ties to London. Second, Keynes's influence was widespread and extended to the United States. Third, the classic work known by the short title *Monetary Trends* (FS 1982) encompassed study of the United Kingdom. Fourth, Friedman's quantity-of-money/theoretic influence extended to the economists in the City of London, to Margaret Thatcher's political undertakings (Frazer 1988, Chapters 14, 15), and to monetary practices at the Deutsche Bundesbank. Fifth, the Bundesbank came to play a special role in the European Monetary System. And finally, the 1980s saw movement toward an open-economy world (trade, competition, and so on), currency blocks, and a world that became set on a new course at political and policy levels.

3.2 BUSINESS CONDITIONS, POLICY EXPERIMENTS, AND THE ROLE OF GOVERNMENT

After World War I there were the matters of the 1920s that I associate with Keynes and efforts to return to pre-World War I mechanisms with gold and the British pound at the center of international trade and the monetary arrangements (Frazer 1988, Chapter 11). However, the matters Keynes confronted and a host of others ensured the failure that appeared most visibly in the form of the U.S. stock market crash of 1929. It and the ensuing move into deep depression with inadequate leadership at the Federal Reserve, as power in the system shifted from New York to Washington, gave rise to waves and waves of bank failures in 1931, 1932, and 1933, as commercial banks were pushed into liquidation and failure with other predictable consequences (Frazer 1988, 417-425). To be sure, there were no government means, such as developed in the United States, for taking over failed institutions and guaranteeing deposit liabilities.

Early responses to the failures in the monetary sphere were legislation against the ownership of gold by American citizens, the banking acts of 1933 and 1935 (also written into the Federal Reserve Act), and the introduction of new "general" credit control instruments in the United States. The main ones were open market operations (OMO), of the special sort discussed later, and the power to vary the legal reserve requirements of the Federal Reserve's member banks. These extended the list of "general" credit control instruments to three: the discount rate, OMO, and changes in the legal reserve requirements.   As the latest new comer to central banking, the Deutsche Bundesbank not only adopted fixed reserve requirements and the latest control arrangements (Bundesbank 1989), it also moved toward the control of money and credit aggregates along the lines found in the Friedman approach.

The first control instrument, as mentioned, came from traditions and practices at the Bank of England. The second was discovered at the Federal Reserve's New York bank in the 1920s, but was not to be well understood in terms of its prospects and role in the United States for years. In addition, the Bank of England has no exact counterpart to this instrument, and I see it as very much a part of Friedman's approach, as it emerged with the concept of "helicopter money," which in turn is rooted in 1930s policies and, more important, later discussions of them in the United States.

The third instrument was indeed powerful for soaking up any excess bank liquidity, in the United States via an increase in requirements, or for providing it by a decrease, but it has been viewed as too powerful and, as it was used in 1937 and 1938 by the Federal Reserve's Board of Governors, the results came to be viewed as a comical tragedy. In any case, OMO can be used in opposition to changes in reserve requirements, which I see as somewhat redundant and, in fact, not especially relevant to the routine of monetary policy.

The discovery of OMO in the 1920s was quite different. Here the role of gold in bank vaults was truly further demystified and the managed financial system was ushered in by this instrument more than in any other way. No longer was the economic system left to the movements of gold, or even to the initiative of borrowers and their responses to low interest rates.

So, taking account of the policy instruments, I turn to five policy experiments and consider some statutes that reflect the changed role of government. The first three experiments mainly concern the United States and the new instruments, but experiments 4 and 5 were shared by the United States, the United Kingdom, and the Federal Republic of Germany. Some errors and some successes in the conduct of policy are revealed by these experiments. They bear on the respective analytical systems—the Keynesian/i-oriented system and the Friedman system.

The errors in the early experiments are seen as being fostered by policies based on the i-orientation, bearing two other subjects in mind. One of these is the conventions and practices reported for the Bank of England in Chapter 5. The second subject follows from the discussion of the Bank of England and the central bank hypothesis H_{CB}; entails sovereignty.

3.2a Experiment 1: The 1937-38 Recession

In the 1930s in the United States, interest rates were quite low. These appeared even as banks held excess reserves, which could be seen by the mid 1960s as a shift in the preference for liquidity on the part of banks to deal with an uncertain future. In contrast, however, the common interpretation was a part of the orientation I identify. In a static liquidity preference curve context, it was that of a downward move along the liquidity preference curve shown earlier in Figure 1-2a. It focused on bank loans and interest rates and to a further two-fold prospect, notably that (1) recession-induced reductions in interest rates, as in some sense of a movement along an investment demand curve (Figure 1-3a), did not induce the public to borrow from banks and (2) the presence of excess reserves at commercial banks signified the ineffectiveness of monetary or credit policy, viewed in terms of interest rates. The perception became associated with the metaphor "you cannot push on a string" (Frazer 1973, 230-242).

To paraphrase the metaphor, there was no means by which to expand the money stock if borrowers do not take the initiative to come to the bank. One could tighten credit ("pull on a string") but one could not just ease it to attract borrowers. More was required, which I see in terms of "psychological time."

Under these conditions and interpretation, a presence of excess reserves in the banking system due to gold inflows from abroad in the 1935 to 1937 period led the Board of Governors of the Federal Reserve System to double reserve requirements in a series of steps under the authority granted by the Banking Act of 1935. The effects were disastrous—the 1937-38 recession on top of general depression in the economy.

As already indicated, the later interpretation was that the banks themselves had undergone a shift toward a preference for liquidity and that the general public had too, under the shocking conditions of the time. This interpretation and the later emphasis Friedman gave to the money and credit aggregates meant that bank reserves should have been expanded even more rapidly to fulfill the needs for liquidity. In addition, recognizing new authority for the conduct of OMO, and not simply a use of "the bank rate," and recognizing the place of bank investments as a part of bank credit meant that OMO could be used to accelerate the reserves, and in sequence bank credit (as discussed later). This, in turn, would give rise to *"helicopter money,"* namely, *the growth in bank credit would carry through to the deposit liabilities of the banks and, in turn, the public's holding of cash balances would soon exceed the desired holdings. Spending on the current output of goods and services would soon result in more production and employment.*

However, this prospect was not to be seen at the time, and indeed, was not to be seen even by a few until well into the 1960s. In spite of vast amounts of empirical study and some recognition of the M-orientation in economics textbooks, in the print media and by London's central bankers, an appreciation of the analytical and operations role of helicopter money is still awaited. Why? Does the answer lie in the rejection of the shared experiences hypothesis H_{SE}, or in the acceptance of in the acceptance of hypothesis two, or even in the acceptance of both H_{CB} and H_{TW}?

3.2b Experiment 2: Pegged Rates

The anticipation of the end of World War II was accompanied in the United Kingdom and the United States by the fear that the economies would fall back into the deep depression from which they emerged in a response to the monetary accommodation of defense and war-related spending by government. In the United Kingdom, the reaction to the fear was the election of a Labor government and immediate moves to nationalize privately owned industries. In the United States, the response on the monetary front was to peg interest rates at quite low, pre-war levels (FY 1966, 574-576) and to pass the Employment Act of 1946 to provide assurance that the government's economic policies would be directed toward maximizing employment, production, and purchasing power (Santoni 1986; Slesinger 1968).

The low, pegged interest rates were set partly in fear that the Treasury's financing of the government debt necessitated doing so and partly in fear that low interest rates were called for to avoid a renewed depression. In any event, recovery proceeded for reasons not well understood at the time and inflation rather than deflation appeared as the economic problem. By the time of recovery from the 1948-49 recession there was considerably less fear of the transition to peacetime conditions. The Federal Reserve soon entered into public disagreement with the Treasury over the effort at pegging interest rates, and on March 4, 1951, issued a statement of accord concerning interest rates (FY 1966, 576-578).

What I see as a result of the pegged-rate experiment and Friedman's later research is a phenomenon called "the chasing of interest rates" (Frazer 1988, 237-238). In connection with the experiment, the chasing would appear as follows: the Fed attempts to maintain low-rates along the i-orientation line of Figure 1-2a, and in the attempt, it accelerates the growth of the money stock, which in turn contributes to higher prices and interest rates. In terms of Friedman's liquidity preference analysis, I see the phenomenon as being implied by the patterns inherent there for money growth, the income velocity of money, and the historical tendency for interest rates to behave procyclically.

In the money-growth/interest-rate context, the leading time rate of change in money growth accelerates before the trough in business conditions and continues for most of the expansion phase as interest rates rise, possibly as some anticipation of inflation on the part of market participants set in [$i = i(\text{real}) + \dot{P}^e$]. Approaching the peak in business conditions, the money stock decelerates as spending continues for a time, as if for a brief moment the policy decision was to raise rates. And then, continuing with deceleration, the interest rates decline, and do so even as the monetary authorities appear to be restricting money growth to raise interest rates. On the velocity-of-money front, the early accelerated growth in the money stock lowers the velocity ratio for a time, and then, as spending takes hold (actual M greater than desired), velocity and interest rates rise. They do so as an anticipation of the inflation also takes hold.

Overall, there is a cyclical pattern of parallel movements in the rate of interest and income velocity, as illustrated in Figure 3-1 for the 1951:II to 1965:IV period (after logarithmic transformation of the data).[1] After some lag in response to monetary acceleration and deceleration, inflationary expectations impact on both interest rates [$i = i(\text{real}) + \dot{P}^e$] and spending, as indicated by the velocity ratio. On the spending side, there is both a penalty on holding cash balances as prices rise (the move from path B to path A in Figure 1-7a) and a premium for enlarging the holdings of real capital in terms of the expected rate of return on real capital.

The well-ordered relationship depicted in Figure 3-1 has some compatibility with the Keynesian notions surrounding Figure 1-2a. Returning to them (Section 1.4a) results, have in actuality, in Equation (1) and the prospect for Equation (2), although the interpretation of Equation (1) and the results in Figure 3-1 are vastly different. To be sure Equation (2) contains the prospect of controlling the money stock along Keynesian lines (namely, via interest rates and fiscal policy), and is at odds with Friedman's substitute analysis, which is discussed shortly.

Figure 3-1
Upper and Lower Bounds for the True Regression Coefficient: The Rate of Interest and the Velocity Ratio, 1951:II through 1965:IV (with Logarithmic Transformations of the Data)

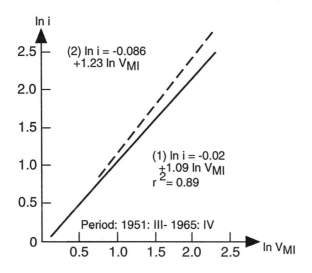

$$\text{(2) } \ln i = -0.086 + 1.23 \ln V_{MI}$$

$$\text{(1) } \ln i = -0.02 \pm 1.09 \ln V_{MI}$$
$$r^2 = 0.89$$

Period: 1951: III- 1965: IV

3.2c Experiment 3: Operation Twist

The years from 1952 to 1960 have been described as somewhat nondescript. There were mild recessions in 1952-53, 1957-58, and 1969-70, as mentioned in Frazer (1994a, Section 1.4a), but the U.S. economy performed fairly well in terms of economic growth and low unemployment rates, with the possible exception of gold and dollar outflows (FY 1966, Section 23.1). Confronting this and setting an agenda for the election in November 1960, J. F. Kennedy promoted a plan for faster economic growth. It set off what can be called "the Keynesian era" in the United States (Frazer 1988, 231-274).

There was inadvertent growth in money and credit aggregates for a time and then less inadvertent but no less rapid growth into the 1970s, which was a period of monetary accommodation. However, the more immediate experiment came in the early 1960s when leaders at the U.S. Treasury devised within the interest-rate orientation a response to the political claim of inadequate economic growth and the reality of deficits in the balance of international payments. In the first instance, the perception of slow growth called for low long-term rates (the Keynesian idea of a controlled low rate calling forth an expansion of bank loans and capital investment, i.e., $-\Delta i \to \Delta I$) and in the second—in the i-orientation discussed in Chapter 4—the i-orientation called for an increase in the short-term rate to slow the outflow of gold.

The structure of rates at any given time—on the almost sixty odd different issues of marketable Treasury debt instruments, which differ mainly with respect to maturity—gives rise to the Treasury yield curve, which is shown in Figure 3-2. The objective of the operation to raise short rates and lower long ones, becomes a matter of twisting the yield curve (FY 1966, Section 4.5), as illustrated in Figure 3-2.

Figure 3-2
Twisting the Treasury Yield Curve

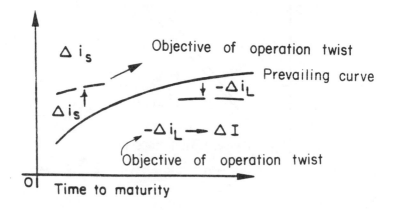

Under "operation twist," as it was called, the Federal Reserve was to twist the Treasury's yield curve within a short run period by raising short-term rates and lowering long-term rates via open-market sales in one segment of the market and by purchases in the other. The lowering of long-term rates was intended to attain the desired effects through capital-value/cost inequality (Figure 1-3a). Contrary to this prospect, however, is the factor of psychological time. In keeping with it, a reduction in interest rates—such as commonly occurs in recessions and related periods of sluggish growth—achieves stimulating effect by way of the perception that rates have "bottomed out." In this state, agents are looking back at prior recessions and asking whether a trough in business conditions and interest rates has been reached, all in lieu of responding as if declining rates moved along the m.e.c. curve of Figure 1-3a to call forth growth in capital spending.

Had operation twist been deemed successful, there would doubtless have been other times when the United States would have wanted to raise short-term rates to attract foreign funds and lower domestic rates to stimulate U.S. capital spending. In addition, it would have provided support for some theories of the term structure of interest rates, as they are known in reference to the yield curve.

I do not review these theories here, except for Keynes's theory of backwardation. It referred to the tendency for the curve to have a general upward sweep most of the time, as shown in Figure 3-2. In the early days of the Keynesian/i-orientation, a policy- or bank-rate induced shift in rates at one end of the curves was thought to shift the entire curve and indeed the long rate in the same direction. It was envisioned as being held to its shape, if not its position, through market/expectations forces. There were those who pointed to the curve as a forecast of future sequences of short-term rates and, incorrectly so (at least in terms of the actual content of the assumption of indifference), to the indifference on the part of those who owned the debt instruments as to whether to hold a sequence of short-dated instruments or simply long-term bonds. Of special significance in the short-run context in which the curve was viewed, the expectations were expected to impart a shape to the curve through a supply demand-quantity mechanism. Most notably, the lower rates at the short end of the curve were thought to be the result of a greater quantity of securities demanded at the short-dated end. The idea was that of a preference for liquidity over the earnings from higher-yielding assets.

What can, in fact, be seen is that the main holders of the debt instruments are groups of institutions with *preferred time-to-maturity holdings* (Terrell and Frazer, 1972).[2] These maturities coincide with a future need for funds. From the holder's position, there is a liquidity hedging hypothesis, namely, hedging against future changes in rates by holding securities with maturities that coincide with the need for future funds.

Except on rare occasions, as during operation twist, the U.S. Treasury has been known to tailor new issues of debt instruments to suit the market rather than to alter the short rates relative to the long. Given the foregoing ownership pattern, the U.S. Treasury's debt management policy, and the tendency for short rates to swing very widely over time, even as long rates appear more constrained, the behavior of the rates would be very consistent with the view that, in the short run, short-term rates simply adjust to reflect an extrapolative push of recent prospects into the near future and that long rates are more constrained by an expected return to normality (a long-term or trend condition, as in Figure 1-7b).

3.2d Experiment 4: Monetary Accommodation

On the economic front in the 1960s there were tax cuts and accelerated government spending, and for the two years following the 1964 cuts, the federal budget was balanced (Frazer 1988, 670-672). There are a variety of reasons, which Michael Evans (1983) pointed out—a brief pause in spending, monetary policy that could be expansive because inflation had been virtually contained, some offsetting tax increases, and even the fact that the low inflation rate pushed households to higher tax brackets.

However, the conditions that were to characterize the 1970s were on a course. Even by the mid to late 1960s, the historical patterns FS had pointed to in *Monetary Trends* were changing. As stated earlier in terms of New York's revenge and all, the structure underlying the formation of inflationary expectations changed; it appears as in Figure 3-3 when viewed in comparison with Figure 3-1.

In response to the expectations view and the inflationary trend in the United States, the interest rate drifted sharply upward. This occurred even as the velocity ratio moved only modestly upward to alter the prospect for a stable money demand relation in terms of the regressions,

$$\ln Y/M = a + b \ln i \qquad (1)$$

and vice versa, and

$$\ln M = a_0 + a_1 + a_1 \ln i + a_2 \ln Y \qquad (2)$$

Even so, what had been ushered in, one can say, was another experiment (an episode of government intervention) that needed to be taken into account in reassessing the search for a stable relation and in appraising the role of outside forces.[3]

Surprisingly, the particular pattern of governmental intervention in the United States was ushered in by Friedman's friend and associate Arthur F.Burns who had been appointed chairman of the Board of Governors (Frazer 1988, Chapter 8). Quite consciously, Burns pursued a monetary policy in

Figure 3-3
M1 Income Velocity and the Rate of Interest, 1959:I-1985:IV

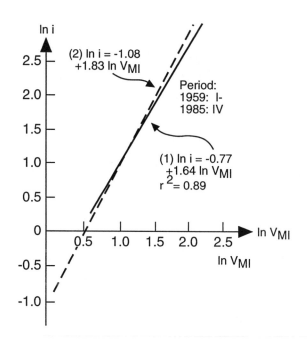

support of Congress' financing and even supported direct controls over prices in an attempt to contain them and at the same time reduce unemployment.

The ensuing 1973-75 recession moderated the inflation rate increases for a time, doomed the price controls, and Burns came to alter his policy stance. But by that time, Jimmy Carter was president, and in 1978 he replaced Burns with William Miller, who went about repeating the mistakes Burns had made.

Not only was Friedman's monetarist research getting international publicity to bring attention to the inflationary/monetary policies in the United Kingdom and the United States (Frazer 1988, Chapters 8, 14), but the Bank of England and the Bundesbank also made moves to target a monetary aggregate and the U.S. Congress was responding. A main piece of post-World War II legislation in the United States was House Concurrent Resolution 133 (later written into the Federal Reserve Act). It partly reflected monetary matters that had been before congressional committees from the later 1960s, and partly paralleled the 1974 Budget Act.[4] In the first case, it called on the Federal Reserve to report monetary policy to the Congress in terms of monetary aggregates rather than interest rates and to announce periodically the plans for policy over the coming year. The approach adopted under Arthur Burns's chairmanship called for

Figure 3-4
The U.S. Data for the M1 and M2 Money Stock Relative to Projected
One-Year Ranges, 1976, 1991, and 1992

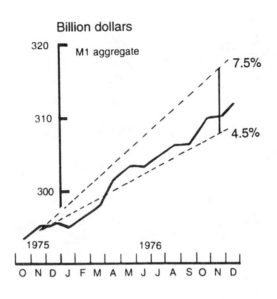

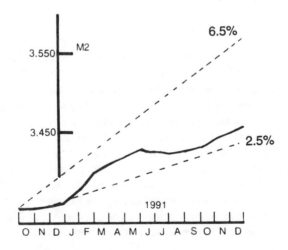

Figure 3-4 (continued)

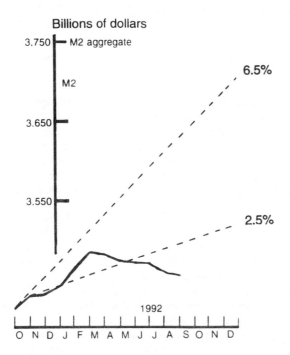

setting upper and lower bounds (expressed as growth rates) as illustrated for the money aggregate dollars M1 in Figure 3-4 for the year 1976.

By the early 1980s, there were obvious problems in targeting the United Kingdom's preferred money aggregate and the United States M1, as the respective governments moved toward decelerating the inflation rates. In the U.S. case, some deregulation of depository institutions led to the inclusion of new accounts in M1 (Frazer 1988, 654-659) and a later shift to M2 as the preferred aggregate for targeting and controlling inflation rates. In any case, a temporary surge of money growth in 1983 was later seen as indicative of an overstatement of monetary expansion, and, as Carlson and Samolyk also suggest (1992), the 1992 growth in M2 dollars may not portray the excess of tightness shown in Figure 3-4 for the year 1992.

The weakness of M2 growth in 1992 appeared, in the Fed chairman's words, "to have reflected rechanneled credit flows away from depository institutions, lessening their need to issue monetary liabilities." Elaborating on that position, Carlson and Samolyk point to structural change concerning the M2 aggregate. They see them in terms of a widening spread between yields on long- and short-dated instruments, regulatory constraints, and an unwillingness of depositories to compete for small time deposits by paying competitive yields. In that event, Carlson and Samolyk (1992) say that, "credit is channeled through non depository financial intermediaries (whose liabilities are not included in M2) rather than through banks and thrifts." They add that M2 growth "may be low relative to that of broader credit-market aggregates and nominal spending."

Chairman Greenspan later took up the same subject (including in reference to the ranges shown in the lower part of Figure 3-4):

These favorable outcomes [growth in real output, reduced inflation, reduced long-term interest rates, and diminishing inflationary expectations] occurred despite slow growth of the money and credit aggregates. The Federal Open Market Committee (FOMC) had established ranges of 2 1/2 to 6 1/2 percent for M2, 1 to 5 percent for M3, and 4 1/2 to 8 1/2 percent for domestic nonfinancial sector debt. Over the year, M2 actually rose 2 percent, M3 rose 1/2 percent, and debt 4 1/2 percent. Thus, both of the monetary aggregates finished the year about 1/2 percentage point below their ranges and debt just at its lower bound.

Interpreting this slow growth was one of the major challenges the Federal Reserve faced last year. You may recall that, in establishing the ranges in February and reviewing them in July, the committee took note of the substantial uncertainties regarding the relationships between income and money in 1992. Although the velocity of the broad monetary aggregates—the ratio of nominal GDP to the quantity of money—had not changed much in 1991, that result itself was surprising. In the past, when market interest rates declined, as they had in 1991, savers shifted funds into M2 because deposit rates usually did not fall as much as market rates, and this produced a decline in velocity in contrast to what occurred in 1991. As we moved into 1992, there appeared to be an appreciable likelihood that unusual weakness in M2 growth relative to spending would continue. But, in the absence of convincing evidence for increases in velocity, the FOMC elected to leave the ranges unchanged from the previous year and noted that it would need to be flexible in assessing the implications of monetary growth relative to the ranges. (Greenspan 1993a, 295-296)

Now, when this practice of targeting a money aggregate of choice was introduced in the United Kingdom and the United States in the mid-1970s, it was also adopted by the Deutsche Bundesbank in that period, and followed by it later with considerable success in both hitting targets and controlling inflation. For the United Kingdom the "targeting" practice has been hampered by traditions and practices (H_{CB}, I argue) and by reliance on the "bank rate" and fiscal policy to control the money aggregate (Equations [1] and [2] in Section 1.4a and Equations [1] and [2] in Section 3.2d). For the United States, there have been somewhat similar efforts to target money growth by relying on selected interest rates, as the Carlson/Samolyk and Greenspan discussions indicates, but that appears to be somewhat less necessary in the United States than in the United Kingdom because of the availability of more direct means of accounting for bank reserves and the special sort of open-market operations discussed in Section 3.3.

The Deutsche Bundesbank proceeds more directly to target its preferred aggregate and deals better deal with regulatory changes in doing so. It has confronted none of the particular U.S. and U.K. targeting problems (Bundesbank 1989). In addition, the notion of controlling the quantity of money in circulation as a means of achieving a sound currency is written into the legislative act that established the Bundesbank in 1957, and the Bundesbank appears to have proceeded with sophistication, considerable determination to achieve its goals, and with a German tradition in law that some emphasize (Kennedy 1991, Chapters 1-3).

3.2e Experiment 5: The "Big U-Turn" and Monetary Discipline

Although the fruits of Friedman's labor were highly visible in London as well as in the United States—and gained attention against the backdrop of high inflation and unemployment rates—there were only faltering steps to alter the conditions before the advent of Margaret Thatcher's government in the United Kingdom in 1979 and Ronald Reagan's presidency in the United States in 1981 (Frazer 1988, Chapters 15 and 16).[5] Both had established ties to Friedman's economics. Both were committed to taming inflation and lowering interest rates by monetary means, which were quite different from methods the previous post-World War II officials had offered. Both also faced some problems in the implementation of policies. For Thatcher, as anticipated by the central banks hypothesis H_{CB}, the accounting control arrangements and traditions surrounding policy implementation were poorly suited to the task, even though achievements were dramatic. For Reagan, the control and implementation problems were more cosmetic by comparison.

Even so, the early 1980s were a watershed in the implementation of ideas, in the execution of policy, and in ideological change that I have treated elsewhere in reference to Hotelling's line, the polarization of political parties, and Keynesian and Friedman views (Frazer 1988, 409-410, 614; 1994a, Section 3.4). By the end of the 1980s, Thatcher had led a way to a broader transitional move from collectivist and command states to the more market oriented prospects of the 1990s.

In Figure 3-5, Hotelling's line is used to classify technical economics topics as to whether they are centrist, the political left, or the political right. On the left of the line are the implied or stated uses of central powers to operate an economy, on the right appear implied or stated positions regarding the managed, market economy where voluntary association in terms of the Friedman system reigns. This deals with freedom to choose, sovereignty, and the like. To the center is what Professor Samuelson referred to as the "mixed economy," or what I see as fairly direct government intervention, as in Nixon's and Carter's imposition of price controls. Even beyond those, I can point to efforts to make the world

Figure 3-5
Hotelling's Line: The Classification of Economic Topics as to
Ideological Position

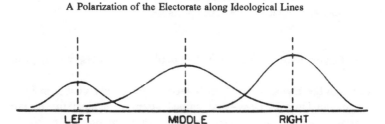

Thatcher and Reagan:
A Polarization of the Electorate along Ideological Lines

LEFT   MIDDLE   RIGHT

The collectivist state: detailed intervention by government; government mandated income distribution; state planning of production and distribution of income; direct controls over prices, credit, etc.; bartered foreign trade of goods with absence of hard currency	The Keynesian model: mildly effective incomes policy; government regulation of business; monetary accommo- dation; tariffs and manipulation of exchange rates to gain trade advantage	Monetary discipline: freedom; voluntary association; government provided infrastructure (formerly laissez faire); exchange rate mechanism and gold- (or currency-) flows mechanism such as Bank of England over- saw in last quarter of 19th century, or a full float in combination with monetary discipline on domestic side

conform to the econometric models, to regulatory aspects of economics and the theories of monopolistic and imperfect competition, and to efforts to alter the distribution of income. This excludes efforts to care for the needy, efforts to promote social mobility (say, along lines associated with Friedman's consumption function), and efforts to disperse power and enhance voluntary association and protection of minority positions.

Although treated elsewhere (Frazer 1994a; and 1994b), I return to views associated with Keynes and Friedman in other respects. These regard wages and production, where, in Keynes's case, wages were tied to production. This tie was expected to hold, even in the presence of inadequate demand, to ensure production at full employment. It was interpreted that—in the presence of a general shift toward liquidity on the part of the public—prices (and wages as a special price) would not adjust fast enough to ensure production at full employment. Hence, the terms "sticky prices" and "sticky wages." I accept this, indeed even as an explanation of occasional economic recession and sluggish growth (as in the United States in 1990-1992). Although the observed phenomenon is accepted, a response can still be expected on the part of the monetary authority to provide the liquidity via "helicopter money" and bring about recovery and less sluggish growth. However, the economic problem arises that some prior condition, in terms of potential inflation and debt, may preclude the monetary response. To be sure, this appears as part of Chairman Greenspan's explanation for relatively slow growth in money and credit aggregates (1993a).

The Keynes tie between wages and production takes even further interpretation along the line of what Sir John Hicks called Keynes's "labor standard." It was the idea that wages were a standard—somewhat fixed like a tie between gold and prices (the fixed dollar price of gold, e.g., before the floating of the dollar). Moreover, that idea appears in the Keynesian view of the management of total spending ... later.

Friedman, on the other hand, placed some store on wage and price adjustments, although in the slightly different time frames discussed in Section 2.4a and Figure 2-3, where it is shown that downward adjustments in prices (and wages as a special price) may indeed lead to more production and hence employment. As reported in *The Legacy* (Frazer 1994a) and elsewhere, productivity does increase in relation to wages in the presence of monetary discipline through much of the 1980s.

With allowance for slight difference in time frames, I reach two conclusions: first, in the presence of inadequate demand for goods and services, production adjusts more quickly than nominal wages in the shorter time frames and second, wages do adjust downward in the presence of monetary discipline. When the latter was tried in the United States and the United Kingdom in the 1980s, along with the use of tax policy, it worked.

3.3 CAUSATION (WHETHER $\Delta \dot{M} \rightarrow \Delta \dot{Y}$, OR VICE VERSA)

Following early statements by Milton Friedman about the leading time rate of change in the money stock, the American Keynesian James Tobin introduced an a priori, reverse-causation position. He had been a member of President Kennedy's Council of Economic Advisors in 1961-62, and presented his model later in 1967 (Frazer 1973, 126-129). To be sure, it is compatible with what is discussed shortly in Lord Kaldor's position.[6] In particular, as in Kaldor's explanation, the central bank keeps its discount window open to private banking institutions (i.e., it supplies reserves as a lender of last resort irrespective of any stabilizing function). Kaldor, however, proceeds (1) to have deficit spending by government (say, fiscal policy) as the main determinant of income and (2) to have the central bank accommodate the government's deficit financing so as to make the money stock dependent on income ($\dot{Y} \rightarrow \dot{M}$).

As this causation controversy got under way, it went through a statistical phase where elegant techniques were used,[7] but without much progress toward resolution of the differences of opinion. FS took up the matter in *Monetary Trends* (FS 1982, Section 12.5): "It is appropriate to regard the observed fluctuations in the two nominal magnitudes [money and income] as reflecting primarily an influence running from money to income." FS said that "the process is a two-way one, not unidirectional, so there undoubtedly has also been a feedback from income to money, yet the element that gives consistency to the century as a whole [1867-1975] is the influence from money to income." And later they said:

Everything depends on the purpose. In economic analysis, it may be appropriate to regard a variable as exogenous for some purposes and as endogenous for others. A simple example is the quantity of money. For the United States after World War I, we believe it is appropriate to regard the money stock as exogenous (i.e., determined by the monetary authorities) in an economic analysis of long-run money demand. We do not believe it would be equally appropriate to do so for week-to-week or month-to-month movements for which . . . "the money stock appears to be endogenously determined by the decisions of the private sector."[8]

However, Friedman himself never confronted experiments 4 and 5 in his theoretic/empirical work as I do, and, further, he never attempted to explain the content of what Kaldor called Friedman's "black box" (Frazer 1983). Indeed, this becomes the most enlightening phase of the causation controversy for several reasons. For one, the "black box" ties into the "helicopter" view of money, and bank operations and controls I readily identify more with the Federal Reserve and matters growing out of the 1930s in the United States as seen by Friedman. For another, Kaldor's views are easily aligned with the use of Equation (2) in Section 1.4, under experiment 4, and the positions taken by the Bank of England's Sir (later Lord) Gordon Richardson (Frazer 1988, 557-558) and his successor Governor Leigh-Pemberton. In opposition to the content of the "black box," they emphasized control arrangements whereby the Bank of England relies on interest rates and fiscal policy; hence hypotheses H_{CB} and H_{TW}. And, for still another thing, coming late to the central banking business and having roots in the period of allied occupation, the Deutsche Bundesbank took on the federalist structure, more of the arrangements found at the Federal Reserve than at the Bank of England, and initially moved with attention to the quantity of money rather than interest rates and fiscal policy.

So, each of the two substitute analytical systems has some latent set of institutional, accounting control, and operations procedures that are often simply taken for granted, as in the content of what Kaldor called Friedman's "black box." In the case of the United States' arrangements, it has both a pre-1930s central bank orientation (more along the lines of a "bank rate"), and the post-1930s possibility that I associate with Friedman. Said differently, *the Federal Reserve is capable of swinging two ways when it comes to the i-orientation and the M-orientation*, but, as will be emphasized, the Bundesbank harbors uniquely stronger monetarist potential than the Federal Reserve.

The Bank of England is especially restricted by its traditions and practices. By comparison with the Federal Reserve, it lacks a simple measure for bank reserves (R_o), a legal reserve requirements, the direct means of accounting for bank reserves (i.e., the bank reserve equation), and the prospect for a rather orderly system of money (M) and bank-credit (B_c) multipliers (FY 1966, 34-48). Lacking such orderly arrangements, the Bank of England's main informational/control link is via the interest rate and conditions in the Sterling money market. In addition, the Bank is directly responsible for supporting the financing of any deficits in the government's budgets. It adopts, along with the U.K. Treasury, a "funding" policy concerning the deficits (called the public sector borrowing requirement).

These accounting/control/operations matters gain in importance not simply because they light on causation, but because they show the different role for government, first in one analytical system and then in the other. Moreover, this role of government extends to matters bearing on the plans for a future European monetary system.

3.3a Causation (The Fourth Phase)

This last phase of the causation controversy concerns the money- and credit-creating mechanism found in fractional reserve banking arrangements and the concept of fiscal (or government debt) policy ushered into formal economics by J. M. Keynes. The fractional reserve banking arrangements—which are present in even partially market-oriented societies—has an interesting and long history, a parallel with the evolution of central banks (Goodhart 1988), and a place in the gold- (or specie-) flows mechanism. It is introduced shortly and discussed in Chapter 4.

Now I forego banking history and introduce the bank reserve equation found among the accounting control arrangements for the United States. Although it appears in the *Federal Reserve Bulletin* as an actual accounting identity, the concept can be used in more general analysis of how the world works. As such, the bank reserve equation is considered again in Chapter 5 with the exchange-rate and gold-flows mechanisms, and on later occasions. Although gold no longer plays its historical role in the vaults of banks, the mechanisms are alive.

J. M. Keynes's role in bringing about the conduct and concept of fiscal policy, as discussed shortly, was no doubt partly inadvertent. It was offered

by him in the place of an interest-rate oriented policy that could be seen as a
failure under conditions associated with the 1930s in the United States and
the United Kingdom and against a backdrop of an essentially flawed view of
monetary policy as working through interest rates. It was around in the
banking tradition of the 1920s and 1930s and was given formal analytical
standing by Keynes.

Dealing with this fourth phase of the causation issue, brings the
discussion closer to some very practical, policy-significant conclusions.
Along these lines, in the Friedman system we offer, monetary and fiscal
policy are substitute policies (not complementary and not reinforcing), and
his analytical approach combines with the accounting/control/operations
arrangement I outline. In particular, the non-complementing role for fiscal
policy in the Friedman system bears on three interrelated features of the
theoretic/empirical system. First, there is a dependence of fiscal policy on
monetary policy for its effects on total spending, even as the monetary
policy effects relate to the special time frames. Next, in the special time
frames, the monetary effects are powerful, occur with more or less lag
(depending on the structure underlying the formation of inflationary
expectations), and accumulate over time. And finally, Friedman's special
use of statistical methods (Frazer 1988, 68-87, Chapter 18; FS 1991) reveals
an awareness of the inability to separate the effects of interrelated variables
by the direct approach, usually referred to as "the fashionable econometric"
model.[9]

On the other hand, monetary policy is dependent on fiscal policy in
Kaldor's Keynesian approach. The former simply accommodates the fiscal
policy, which is thought to come about in the short run. Identifying Kaldor
with his British background, the Bank of England, and an approach to the
possibility to control both money demand and money supply through fiscal
policy and interest rates suggest a larger role for the separation of effects
problem.

3.3b The Bank Reserve Equation

The bank reserve equation can be found in terms of statistical accounts.
Algebraically, $R_o = G + R - C + $ residual. The symbols are R_o for
reserves of the private sector banks; G for bank reserves, which are a part
of international monetary reserves (most simply viewable as gold,
traditionally, or more recently paper gold and other monetary reserves; R
for Federal Reserve (or central bank) credit; C for the currency (paper note
and coin) holdings of the public; and "residual" for secondary accounts that
make up the accounting identity.

The central bank enters into the bank reserve equation in its capacity to
create reserves for institutions functioning as commercial banks. In the

United States, this has centered on two mechanisms: (1) the discount rates at the Federal Reserve Banks (viewable as a single rate, say discount rate, Federal Reserve Bank of New York) and (2) open market operations, which were discovered in the 1920s at the Federal Reserve Bank of New York.[10] In the context of U.S. central banking the "discount window," as it can be called, has been viewed as only a temporary source of reserves for commercial banking institutions intended to tide banks over during periods of strain on reserve positions.

The matter recurs regarding Kaldor where the central bank is called "a lender of last resort." A common function of central banks, Kaldor gives the role a special twist that gains meaning in the context of U.K. arrangements. These concern both earlier traditions and practices, as taken up later in Chapter 5, and the subordination of the Bank of England to the U.K. Treasury by very direct arrangements that have been in place since World War II. The combination of the two gives rise to two additional interrelated practices. One is the practice of having the Bank responsible for the financing of the public sector borrowing requirement (PSBR).

The second interrelated practice ocurred in the United Kingdom in the 1980s, after Margaret Thatcher attempted a Friedman/monetarist policy with some success (Frazer 1988, Chapter 14). In the absence of any clear systems of accounting control for bank reserves and of bank credit and multiplier relations, the Bank's policy people settled on an overly simple, Keynesian relation (Equation [2] of Section 1.4). Denoting the rather parallel movement in income velocity and the rate of interest in Figure 1-2, for example, results in

$$\ln Y/M = a + b \ln i$$

Then taking the logarithm of the velocity ratio and rearranging the terms of this equation,

$$\ln M = a_o + a_1 \ln i + a_2 \ln Y$$

In reference to thought processes of the Bank of England's policy people, I suggest they equated the money stock (or supply, M_s) with the quantity demanded (Equation [2] in Section 1.4 again) and took the view that the interest rate (i) and fiscal policy (the deficit spending component of Y) were the means of controlling the money stock. This means of approaching the implementation of policy, of course, contrasts with that of control via the bank reserve equation and the money and credit multipliers that arise with respect to fractional reserve banking. Furthermore, opting for the Keynesian approach does not preclude the workings in fact of all the other things (the reserves, R_0, the open market operations, OMO, bank credit, B_C, the multipliers, etc.). They are simply unavailable for control purposes or not preferred for political or ideological reasons.

Open market operations as the means of controlling money and credit aggregates appear as a major instrument for conducting monetary policy via a bank reserve equation arrangement in the United States (and not the U.K. context). They are genuinely a means of creating bank reserves of a permanent sort, and, indeed, of providing a base for growth in the money and credit aggregates, which I identify with "the macro commercial bank" discussed later. They will appear truly as what Keynes had in mind when he saw the loss of innocence about the automatic workings of gold in bank vaults and the fact that a managed financial system had crept into being.

Although things worked fairly well with gold and gold-flows for a long time, Friedman's concept of "helicopter money" is best illustrated in terms of OMO and the presence of bank credit in the form of bank holdings of securities (called "investments") as distinct from "loans." Friedman's view of "helicopter money" is entwined with his views of U.S. banking in the 1930s, as I have stated.

3.3c The Gold-Flows Mechanism

In much of the period 1867-1975, for which FS analyzed data (FS 1982), the world was on a gold or gold-exchange standard. In fact, for most of the nineteenth century and until the early 1930s, with World War I and its immediate aftermath aside, the world with London at its center was on a gold or gold-exchange standard that gains its significance in relation to the gold-flows mechanism. Under the classical form of the gold standard three rules held: (1) there is free coinage of gold; (2) the price of gold is fixed by law in terms of a country's monetary unit (e.g., the dollar in the United States and the pound (£) in the United Kingdom), and hence fixed relations between the units (e.g., $/£ = const.) for the most part; and (3) paper currency, coins, and bank deposits are freely convertible into gold under a gold-exchange standard. It comes about where some currency, such as the British pound in its day, is accepted as a key currency and hence as good as gold.[11]

Quite briefly, under the gold standard, countries trade goods and services and compete for sales in domestic and foreign markets where attention is focused on prices. The matter is viewable as if the respective countries have averages for their prices (or price indexes). As one country's relative position is favored [say, $-\Delta$ (P_{US} /P_{UK}) for a favored U.S. position], that country exports more and enjoys an inflow of monetary reserves (the symbol G in the bank reserve equation), as a rule.

There is a balancing out of reserves as the countries compete in terms of trade. The main point, however, is that the competition regulates prices and disperses power that may otherwise reside in government bureaus. Under the arrangement, moreover, a country with efficient productivity (including as enhanced by new capital goods) is rewarded with rising income and reduced unemployment. No grand scheme of state or international planning and direct control is required. Exchange rates are for the most part fixed under the classical gold-flows mechanisms (say, $/£ =$ const. within fixed limits), as stated, and adjustments to trade imbalances take place through price-level changes (e.g., P_{US} versus P_{UK}) or product prices (and the special part of product prices called wages). Faced with unemployment, a country's position can be improved by enhancing productivity and having prices and wages adjust downward relative to those of other countries.

Another way to achieve adjustments in trade positions (or more generally balance of international payments positions) is to have exchange rate changes (e.g., Δ $/£) rather than price changes (e.g., $- \Delta P_{US}/P_{UK}$), as taken up in Chapter 4. Whatever the case—exclusive of full floating that the world does not come to—some elements of economic efficiency and wage and price discipline (via relative prices, as under the gold-flows mechanism) enter from an international point of view.

This mechanism of monetary flows and price-level discipline, as it were, impacts on the domestic monetary mechanism (the G term in the bank reserve equation). Complexities aside, in principle the idea is of a stock of reserves being identical to factors such as international monetary reserves, credit extended by the central bank, with discount windows and open market operations as the principal sources.

These reserves, in turn, support liabilities of banking institutions (mainly, since the National Banking Act in the United States, deposit liabilities). These liabilities are in the form of bookkeeping entries, they are a part of the money supply, and paper and other currency can be freely exchanged for the deposit liabilities. Here is the idea of a money supply (the currency and the deposit liabilities) that can vary in its measures, depending on the assets included from the point of view of the economic "agent." Since reserves can be controlled, allowing for various factors, they have a link with the money supply, which in turn can be controlled, after allowances for shifts in the liquidity preference requirements for reserves, on the part of the banks themselves, and other factors such as changes in the ratio of the currency held by the public to deposit liabilities.

The bookkeeping entries on the liabilities side are a part of the money supply, as stated, and they may come about as bank credit expands in response to increases in bank reserves (mostly via open market operations, or historically gold inflows). The expansion of the money supply comes about via banks extending credit (loans), or purchasing securities. Both actions give rise to banks increasing deposit liabilities, as personal and business accounts are credited, coincidental with the depositing of checks or the crediting of accounts.

The banking institutions that are in turn dependent on the central bank have balance sheets that can be thought of as an aggregate balance for all of the banking, money-creating institutions comprising the national economy. On the asset side are mainly the reserves (R_o) and bank loans and investments (called "bank credit"), and on the liabilities side are mainly a component of the money supply. There are what can be called credit and money multipliers, to refer to the inverse of the fractional relations (i.e., the inverse of R_o to bank credit, and R_o to the deposit liabilities, respectively). These concepts are synonymous with the idea of a fractional reserve banking system.

The fractional reserve operation is illustrated in Figure 3-6 with reference to a simplified and consolidated balance sheet for the non-central bank part of the banking system. Under such a system, reserves (R_o) are some fraction of deposit liabilities (say, one-fifth of check transferable deposits) and a slightly smaller fraction of bank credit (say, one-fourth B_c). The deposit liabilities are identifiable in the United States as a main component of the money supply since the National Banking Act of 1863, and they are readily substitutable for currency considered as paper notes and coins.

Confronted with an increase in reserves, under the properly functioning fractional reserve system, banks have every inducement to expand bank credit in that it is the major source of income to the banks. The increase in reserves may come about because of deposits of currency (or gold coins at an earlier date) and/or because of the deposits of checks drawn on the Federal Reserve and used in purchase of commercial paper and/or government securities by the Federal Reserve.

As bank credit is extended via an increase in loans (or purchases of securities) the recipient of the credit rarely wants the credits to his/her deposit account to hold. They are soon transferred and the bank loan remains on the books. Questions remain about how fast the deposit liabilities get moved around and turned over (the matter of velocity, Y/M). These are discussed in

Figure 3-6
The Macro Non-Central Bank

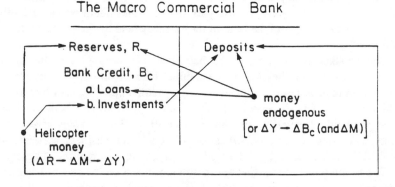

The Macro Commercial Bank

the subsequent chapters. Further, the process of reserve, bank credit, and deposit creation may go fast, slow, or in reverse.

The process of expansion may start in a financial center (say New York, to continue with open market operations) and spread throughout the banking system. There are two reinforcing mechanisms—those within the banking system and those within the larger financial system. Within the banking system, the reserves may get passed around through trading among banks in reserves (called in the United States trading in federal funds) and through other means, including the sale of securities, mortgages, or loans to other banks. In the larger financial system, a deposit balance for a New York securities dealer (the dealer who sold securities to the New York Fed), may get passed to the hinterland as the dealer replaces the inventory by the purchase of more securities from a firm in the hinterland. Financial markets adjust quite rapidly, even internationally, as seen in Chapter 4.

The point, nevertheless, is that important control is exerted through the fraction of reserves supplied by the central bank. This control may be for good, or for evil. It exists whatever the latter complexities. The general thrust of operations under the historical gold-type mechanism leads to a conclusion; namely, efforts via effective international competition to export goods (as symbolized by $-\Delta P_{US}/P_{UK}$) and to obtain gold (or monetary reserves) under fractional reserve banking arrangements raise nominal and/or real income within the time frame of the inflow, and possibly with some lag afterward.

Starting the sequence of events with a more favorable stance with respect to United States via-à-vis U.K. prices ($-\Delta P_{US}/P_{UK}$) would result in a more favorable balance of trade in the United States. The United States could face greater monetary growth without adverse balance of payments consequences. The money growth or inflow of monetary reserves (ΔR_{US}) could support the expansion of bank credit and the money stock (ΔM) and also contribute to the prospect of increased spending and increased income received ($\Delta \dot{Y}$). There would always be the threatening prospect of relatively higher U.S. prices ($\Delta P_{US}/P_{UK}$). Quite clearly, causation is from money to income ($\dot{M} \rightarrow \dot{Y}$).

3.3d Kaldor and Bank Credit

Now—with respect to the credit and money creation mechanisms, as just outlined—two closely related questions are raised by Kaldor's *The Scourge of Monetarism* (1982): one is about whether "new money comes into existence in consequence of, or as an aspect of, the extension of bank credit" and the other is about whether causation runs from the control of the money stock (M) to income (Y), or vice versa. Thinking in terms of money balances arising from "the extension of bank credit," as outlined above, Kaldor said without illustration the following: "If, as a result, more money comes into existence than the public . . . wishes to hold, the excess will be automatically *extinguished*—[1] either through debt repayment or [2] its conversion into interest-bearing assets."

At issue is a difference between money and credit and whether borrowers in fact seek to hold more money balances or simply seek loans with money balances arising as a part of the process. In the first case, an "agent" receiving credit in the form of a loan should not want to extinguish the credit immediately, and another receiving the money balances may wish to use them or repay a loan, but the latter act in the overall banking system does not extinguish the reserves that gave rise to the credit to begin with and it will free up credit granting capacity for the extension of a new loan or for the purchase of securities by the commercial institutions. The place of "investments" in the total "bank credit" means that banking institutions do not require that borrowers take the initiative in enlarging on the extension of credit and, in any event, the bank may want to keep its investment position fully extended. In the second case, the use of excess cash on the public's part to purchase an interest-bearing asset does not extinguish the cash but simply transfers it elsewhere. As to the facts in the case is the matter of whether accelerated growth in reserves leads to further growth in bank credit and deposit liabilities.

Overlooking the initiative that banks may take to increase bank credit and hence increase the money stock—in response to faster growth in bank reserves, as may come from open market operations by the central bank—Kaldor was thinking in terms of loan induced expansion of bank credit which gives rise to money balances (Kaldor 1982, 22-24). Writing about this as "credit money," he saw the amount of money in existence as being tied to bank credit, and he saw monetary policy as in an interest-rate/central banking orientation. Under it, as dealt with by Kaldor and Tobin before him, bank credit (incorrectly equated with money) simply expands at a given rate of interest.[12] Kaldor said (1982, 24), "the rate of interest of the Central Bank (the old bank rate, . . .) will be varied upwards or downwards as a means of restricting credit or making credit easier." (This old "bank rate," has variously been called the "discount rate," the "minimum lending rate" or the Bank of England's "dealing rate," without much difference of meaning.)

Referring to the Bank of England, Kaldor argued that the so-called "discount rate" is the main means of controlling reserves and that central banks cannot do this and maintain their function as a "lender of last resort" (Kaldor 1982, 25). Here he is both right and wrong. In the context of his own Keynesian control mode with fiscal policy in its primary place, he is right. On the other hand, as a matter of fact, the lender-of-last-resort function has never been limitless, and, as will arise much later, the central bank may not readily control the discount rate in Friedman's time frames because the discount/control mechanism concerns the difference between the discount and market rates (i), and another instrument for the creation of bank reserves exists in the U.S. case. The market rate, as I emphasize it, may depend on the expected inflation rate ($\dot{P}^e$), $i = i(\text{real}) + \dot{P}^e$. In addition, there is the further question of whether a lowering of rates (as in recession) actually coincides with faster growth in loans or whether there is some entire business cycle phenomenon to be contended with, as taken up much later in Section 6.4c.

Returning to the causation question ($\dot{M} \to \dot{Y}$, or vice versa), Kaldor puts the matter in terms of whether the quantity of money is "exogenously determined," to use the technical term meaning "outside" of the model.[13] There is the idea here of other variables being determined inside the model, whatever it may be.

In contrast, Friedman has the helicopter fly over the community and drop an additional load of bills from the sky or to accelerate a continuous dropping of bills (1969, 4-14). This would be for him a controlled event, or an exogenous event, to use Kaldor's terms. This helicopter activity is analogous to open market operations where bank credit is created and money balances arise. The steps in the money creating, Friedman "helicopter" process can be summarized thus:

Step 1: Open market purchase of securities increases reserves (check in payment received by investment bank or securities dealer)

Step 2: Check deposited at commercial bank (increase in M) and cleared to increase reserves

Step 3: Increment in bank reserves, R, supportive of credit expansion, $\Delta \dot{B}_c$, via investments in bank portfolio

Step 4: Credit expansion supports money stock growth, money stock greater than desired (helicopter money); causation $\Delta \dot{R} \to \Delta \dot{M} \to \Delta \dot{Y}$

The securities trading department at the central bank may do the following: purchase securities in the open market, pay with a check drawn on the central bank, watch the check clear via in increase in reserves (R), and expect the commercial banks to increase bank credit as investments. As this latter expansion comes about, the money supply increases. From the borrower's point of view, the money expansion is inadvertent, since the borrower is looking for a loan (a source of *funds* to the borrower) and not a stock of money balances to hold.

Further—and of special importance where I see discount rates as playing a special role—no single rate is announced to the press. The Fed's traders simply enter the market to buy or sell on the most favorable terms, and there are no limits to the ultimate growth of the Fed's portfolio of securities. If the Fed's chairman wishes an announcement effect, such as may accompany a discount rate change, he/she may make such an announcement of intentions, as Greenspan did on the occasion of the stock market crash of 1987 (Frazer 1988, 686). In any case, when the Fed's traders enter the market as heavy players, the New York dealers are able to determine the entry.

Via Friedman's route, an injection of reserves (R) becomes associated with an increase in deposits (the major part of the money stock), in addition to "helicopter money" causation—$\Delta \dot{R} \rightarrow \Delta \dot{M}$ (also $\Delta \dot{B}_c \rightarrow \Delta \dot{M}$). An excess of "actual" money balances over a "desired" amount on the part of agents (say, in relation to income) leads to the spending of excess balances, the stock of which is fixed by the central bank for the system as a whole. The spending then simply adjusts nominal income upward until "agents" hold the balances they "desire" in relation to income. Here the causation is from money creation (the "helicopter") to income. An expectations mechanism could enter, as it does in the analysis in Section 1.5b, where an expected "inflation rate" contributes to higher interest rates via $i = i(\text{real}) + \dot{P}^e$.

As incorrectly viewed by Kaldor (1982, 22-24), this foregoing excess of "actual" over "desired" balances would be extinguished and the activities of the "helicopter" would be for naught (Kaldor 1982, 22-24). For Kaldor, the money stock (M) depends on the demand side of the market for money and credit and not on the central bank or supply side. In particular, as developed shortly, Kaldor has the government's deficit spending (PSBR, and, I add, the Bank of England's funding policy) determining income (Y). There is financing of the deficit by having the central bank support it. The support of this financing of the deficit by the central bank increases reserves and the money supply, and the government's induced spending leads to the need for more money balances ($\dot{Y} \rightarrow M$). Since the money stock held is related to income, M $= k(...)$, Y, the income causes the money supply (i.e., $\dot{Y} \rightarrow \dot{M}$ not $\dot{M} \rightarrow \dot{Y}$). In Kaldor's terms, the money stock is endogenous, as noted in Figure 3-6.

This process in which money is endogenous can be summarized as follows:

Step 1:   Deficit spending on the part of the government enters (say, PSBR) as two things come about—as the government engages in the purchase of goods and services (via defense, welfare or entitlement programs, or whatever) with checks drawn on its account at the central bank, and as the central bank accommodates the governments spending via "funding policy."

Step 2:   The government checks are deposited by households and firms.

Step 3:   Deposits arise further but less directly as the non-central banks meet the demand for bank loans by households and firms.

Step 4:   The central bank accommodates the commercial (or non-central) banks via a sufficiently low "bank" or "pound sterling" money market rate (or in the United States, via the discount rate and by keeping the "discount window" open).

Keynesians and Kaldor have viewed income velocity (Y/M) as being affected by the interest rate—for example, in the context of bank-credit expansion à la Kaldor above, and in Tobin's earlier analysis. Friedman, on the other hand, has velocity dependent on the adjustment between desired and actual balances and the variable factor k(. . .) in Keynes's cash-balances approach to the quantity theory of money where the factor k(...) may vary in response to the expected inflation rate, among other expected rates.

Kaldor is joined in this foregoing view of the central bank as a means of accommodating the government's financing and loan expansion by those I identify in the subsequent text as post-Keynesians. Indeed, I include Kaldor among them.

3.3e Monetary and Fiscal Policy as Substitutes in Regard to Spending Effects

The central banking arrangements in the United States and the United Kingdom (as in the cases of the Federal Reserve and the Bank of England, respectively), differ somewhat, but the controlling principles do not differ all that much. In any case, to illustrate the point that monetary and fiscal policy are substitutes for one another as regards spending effects, I combine features of the two respective arrangements. First, recognize the central bank as the government's banker, such that the Treasury department maintains check transferable deposits at the central bank, and the central bank is fully funding the PSBR and serving as the direct purchaser of the financial instruments for the financing of the government's deficit.

This outlined arrangement applies to the Bank of England in connection with the United Kingdom's PSBR. In the United States, the Federal Reserve would be precluded from directly providing the funds for the financing of government deficits, but it can do so indirectly. Treating the accommodation as direct simplifies the exposition.

Taking reserves as a one-fifth fraction of deposit liabilities, and proceeding with an open market purchase valued at 20 million pounds sterling (of government or other securities), the following changes would occur: (1) the securities firms dealing with the central bank would receive checks totaling 20 million; (2) as the checks cleared through the central bank, bank reserves would be credited for 20 million; and (3) with no currency drain from the reserves on the part of the public, the commercial banks could increase deposit liabilities by a total of five times the initial open market purchase. Of these five parts, one part would be the initial deposits by the dealers, and four parts would be due to the expansion of bank credit. The credit multiplier would be the five minus one, for a multiplier of four. The books at the macro commercial bank would be in balance. The OMO causes the expansion of money balances, "helicopter money," and so on.

Next, let the government conduct a fiscal policy with a "fully funded" PSBR of 20 million pounds. The following comes about: (1) the government's spending occurs as a part of GNP (or Y); (2) the checks received by the public get deposited (a 20 million increase in deposits); (3) as the checks clear, the central bank has accommodated the government in effect by the full funding of the PSBR. The purchase of government securities appears as an asset of the Bank and the government's account receives credits against which checks are drawn. As the government draws against its account, the central bank substitutes a liability to the Treasury for a liability in the form of the reserves extended to the macro commercial bank. In sum, the money stock and bank credit expand just as in the OMO's case, only the causation is reversed; $\Delta Y \rightarrow \Delta M$ instead of $\Delta M \rightarrow \Delta Y$. (The whole illustration could proceed in terms of time rates of change, the government's and private sector's shares of GNP, and so on.)

But, why not a combination—a little fiscal policy with complementary monetary policy (say 50 percent fiscal and 50 percent monetary)? In reference to expansive policy, I could have the financing of the government's PSBR, which would account for say one percentage point of an acceleration in money growth of from 3 to 5 percent. The other percentage point could come from an expansion in money growth. The substantive point here is that the effect of the fiscal policy on income growth is dependent on monetary policy. If the latter is not accommodated by the money- and credit-creating process, then from the strictly domestic point of view, the financing of government debt by the sale of securities in the open financial markets crowds out private financing and hence the private sector.

The monetary policy and the fiscal policy with accommodation, as outlined, are not different in terms of the growth in the money stock and income (i.e., $\dot{M}$ and $\dot{Y}$). However, having the fiscal policy dependent on the monetary accommodation is one reason for *Milton Friedman's law* (Frazer 1988, 568, 650-651, 731), which states that inflation, as in the preceeding accelerated growth case, *is everywhere and every place a monetary phenomenon*. Said differently, the effects on total spending and inflation, in the cases just covered, would be the same, whether the policy was entirely monetary or entirely fiscal, in the Kaldor sense.

The separation of effects problem (Equation [1] in Section 2.5) reenters the picture. The policies are substitutes for getting the same effect on income. As arose earlier, if there is accelerated growth in money stock from 3 to 5 percent, and if this is entirely the result of the "full funding" of the PSBR, the combined effect on income of a two percentage point increase in money growth and the separate effect of the fiscal policy does not exist. There is only the two percentage point effect.

An equally bad-case scenario for the illusion of the separation of effects—such as I ascribe to Equation (2) under experiment 4 and the earlier discussion surrounding it (Section 1.4)—would be for an event to occur to alter the more ordinary spending behavior of the public in such a way as to increase the velocity of money ($\Delta Y/M$, of Figure 1-2a) and contribute to a rise in the price index (the P of PQ and Y/P) and the interest rate (i) in Equation (2) [via i = i(real) + $\dot{P}^e$]. Such a possibility may arise, for example, from a U.K. case of the late 1980s, when shares in government-owned companies were sold to sizable groups of private citizens at prices below market prices for the shares, as those prices materialized. The expected result from such enlarged holdings of liquid wealth would be greater spending and a rise in prices. The accompanying consequences would be, furthermore, very destructive of the possibility of controlling the money stock (M) by any possible control of a direct sort over the interest rate (i) and income (Y) in Equation (2) of Section 1.5a and experiment 4 with its given parameters (a_0, a_i, and a_2).[14]

3.3f The Government Budget Constraint and Expected Inflation

Closely related to the view of monetary and fiscal policy, as substitutes as regards spending effects (Section 3.3e) is the government budget constraint. It grew out of the context where deficit spending by government could be viewed in highly favorable terms considering Keynes's investment multiplier, namely, the factor 1/(1 − b) in Equation (4) in Section 1.4c.

In the presence of inadequate spending by the private sector, the favorable view is that deficit spending can be substituted to get a multiple impact on income thus:

$$\Delta \text{ deficit spending } \left[\frac{1}{1-b}\right] \text{ - } \Delta Y$$

However, an analytical/ideological problem arises in giving attention to the financing of the deficit. When that is allowed for, the nice effect of deficit spending is reversed,

$$-\Delta \text{ in deficit } \left[\frac{1}{1-b}\right] \text{ - } \Delta Y,$$

and divisible into monetary and "crowding out" effects, by way of the government budget constraint. Setting international financing of the deficit aside, the constraint is that the deficit must be financed by the sale of bonds to the public or by the central bank's accommodation of the financing. These limited alternatives in relation to the deficit may appear thus:

$$\underbrace{\frac{dR}{dt}}_{\text{monetary policy}} + \underbrace{\frac{dB}{dt}}_{\text{crowding out}} = \text{deficit}$$

the flows of international capital aside.

In the first term is monetary policy and not fiscal policy, and in the second term is the crowding out of the private sectors financing, and thus the crowding out of the private sector in relation to the public sector. There are no net nice gains that appear when the financing is excluded, except that some may regard the "crowding out" of the government sector as desirable on ideological lines.

The approach that excludes the importance of the financing as a part of the deficit process is very much on the political left of Hotelling's line. By the same token, the elevation of the importance of the financing places the budget-constraint concept on the right of the line.

In any case, the analysis does not end with the financing of the deficits, when the effects of deficits are seen as potentially inflationary (as in Greenspan's testimony, Section 1.2b)—monetary accommodation and all. At that point deficit reduction gains as the potentially stimulating effect from fiscal policy. It comes from the lower long-term bond rates and the strengthened perception that interest rates may have bottomed out. So, the analysis goes a full 180-degrees from deficit spending as fiscal stimulus to deficit reduction as fiscal stimulus.

3.3g The Naive View of the Transmission Mechanism

Much is often said and envisioned about how the central bank transmits its effects, via accommodation of deficits, inflation and wage rates, and otherwise. A common and rather naive view is fostered in part by focusing on the central bank's discount rate and related short-term market rates (say, i_s). In this view, a sort of cost accounting emerges. It overlooks the importance of open market operations à la "helicopter money" lines, the role of credit and money multipliers (FY 1966, Section 3.3), the role of liquidity shifts, and the place of psychological time with respect to the financing of planned expenditures.

The four steps in naive view are as follows:

Step 1.   Reduced cost of funds to credit granting and other depository institutions, that is, $- i_{discount\ rate}$.

Step 2.   The reduced cost of funds $(-\Delta i_{discount\ rate})$ means lower cost of funds to the credit granting institutions.

Step 3.   Step 2 in turn means a reduction of interest rates to borrowers because credit granting institutions face a lower cost of borrowing.

Step 4.   Step 3, in turn, means an expansion of loans and greater spending.

3.4 THE DEUTSCHE BUNDESBANK (A "STRONG" FED/FRIEDMAN/MONETARIST INSTITUTION)

With roots in the period of allied occupation (Kennedy 1991, 6, 11, 12; Klopstock 1949), the Deutsche Bundesbank was established with an essentially federalist structure under the Bundesbank Law of 1957. I refer to the Bank as a strong Federal Reserve, as well as a Friedman/monetarist bank for three overlapping reasons.

First, it has a federalist structure (regional or Länder central banks, LCBs, an enlarged number since German unification in 1991), with a Central Bank Council (CBC). It resembles the Federal Open Market Committee in the United States. Like the Board of Governors, which sits in Washington, the CBC's membership is regionally distributed with the final power over appointments given to elected officials.

Second, the Bundesbank is even more "independent" than the Federal Reserve within the framework of government. Indeed, it is independent of review by the Bundestag, although like the Federal Reserve there is no escape from the ultimate need of public support. This is thought to be very strong in Germany because of the dramatic inflationary episodes experienced in the early 1920s (German reparations and all [Schacht 1927, 1931]), in the early post-World War II years (Kennedy 1991, 6-10) and because of the Bundesbank's later success in establishing the deutsche mark (DM) as the preeminent currency in Europe and the "anchor currency" for the European Monetary System (EMS), which is discussed in Chapter 4.

Third, and in addition to structural similarities, the Bundesbank has a package of instruments for implementing monetary policy that is similar to that found at the Federal Reserve, since the U.S. banking acts of 1933 and 1935. In addition to setting minimum reserve requirements and conduction open market operations, it administers a discount rate and closely related lombard rate (Bundesbank 1989, Chapter 3). Although not intended as permanent sources of reserves, the discount rate applies to bank borrowing from the Bundesbank under fixed borrowing quotas, where as the lombard facility is unlimited except by the cost of borrowing. Under the arrangement, the borrowing banks turn over eligible, short-dated securities to the Bundesbank under agreement to repurchase them. In close relation to the discount rate, the lombard rate applies to loans from the Bundesbank "to bridge temporary liquidity needs on the part of credit institutions" and to repurchase agreements. Via the facility connected to the repurchase agreements, borrowing is unlimited, except for the interest-rate cost, which serves as a ceiling for the cost of money market funds.

More important than the discount and lombard rates, however, is the Bundesbank's overall use of its instruments and liquidity management as a means for attaining growth rates for a broad M3 measure for the money stock. This achievement comes about via a "complex transmission mechanism"

(Bundesbank 1989, 104), which I see as relating to Friedman's time frames since the mid 1970s. In addition, even statements in the original Bundesbank Act suggest congeniality with "quantity theory of money" based economics.

There is very minimal similarity to the Bank of England as a central bank, and very little hint of the i-regime orientation I see as Keynesian.[15] Apart from allied occupation and the noted influences, the other hints of Germany's central banking past still go back to rudiments of the quantity theory at a time when the economics was simpler. Such rudiments appear in a lecture Hjalmar Schacht (1877-1970) gave at the University of Wisconsin in 1964.[16]

In the Wisconsin lecture, the money stock, production, and prices are clearly interconnected, along with inflation rates and exchange rates (Schacht 1964). He saw the latter as a means of checking "the validity of one's judgment." Continuing, Schacht said, "Whereas the gold standard had provided certain automatic checks, a managed currency is completely dependant on the observation and study of economic development, especially of price level and foreign exchange rates."

Although the lecture offers no hints of Friedman's restatement of the quantity theory (the time frames, the inflationary/deflationary expectations), there is a lot of what I call in older terms "the real bills" doctrine (FY 1966, 116-117, Section 8.1; Frazer 1994a, Sections 5.4, Chapter 5 note 5, Chapter 7 note 3; Schacht 1967, 85; 113-118), and there is no mention by Schacht of interest rates in connection with central bank policy. Updating the "real bills" doctrine, as it were, gives the idea that the expansion of bank credit should accompany growth in production—that there should be something "real" to accompany the credit expansion if inflation were to be avoided.

Like some Bundesbank officials of a later time, Schacht deserves the title "financial wizard," which was given to him. Although there is no highly formal economics in his *The Magic of Money* (1967), insights abound. Schacht devised economic programs and helped implement them. There were emphases on production and containing inflation.

In Schacht's Reichsbank scheme for revising the German economy over the 1934 to 1939 period, elements along the following lines combine. First, some public works programs were set in motion. Second, a rearmament program was set in motion. It was viewed in part by Schacht as a burst of autonomous spending to get the economy moving in a world where private-sector savings had been virtually destroyed.[17] And, third, a combined means of raising capital for production and creating money balances came about. In this latter instance, suppliers who filled state orders for real goods got paid by drawing up bills of exchange that were accepted by a separately formed company. It had a paid-up capital, partly subscribed to by four large industrial firms, and the bills of exchange were guaranteed by the state. Viewed as "commodity [or real] bills," the bills paid a low 4 percent interest and were discountable at the Reichsbank in the same way that eligible paper would be discounted at the Federal Reserve in the United States. Since the commodity bills were highly liquid, and acceptable as payment, they took on the form of money balances, became widely held outside of the Reichsbank, and grew in amount with production (including for the secondary spending that came about in the private sector).

As production and wages grew, tax revenues to the state grew to provide the means of payment for the public works and the armaments. Overall, by such arrangements, the means of payment for products and services grew along with the growth in production. There was no "pushing on a string" as in the United States at the time of the 1937-38 recession and the great depression generally. Although rearmament entered as a part of the arrangement to employ the unemployed, armament itself was not necessary to the function of the monetary means for economic revival.

3.4a The Transmission Mechanism

In the Bundesbank's discussion of "the complex transmission mechanism," includes the following: the determination of the money aggregate of choice; the money stock as an "intermediate target" (say, between money market liquidity and the price level and sustainable growth in income); cyclical (or "transitory") and long-run behavior of "velocity of circulation"; the complexity present in hitting targets and maintaining the credibility of targeting; success in doing so; and the inflation "premium" (i.e., "expected inflation rate," present in the interest rates).

The Bundesbank summarizes its position thus:

(1) At the *instrumental level* the Bundesbank decides on suitable individual measures designed to create the desired conditions in the money market.

(2) At the *money market level* the Bundesbank establishes suitable short-term operational aims for bank liquidity and money market rates which will make achievement on the annual target for the money stock and the key economic goal variables appear attainable in the longer run.

(3) At the *intermediate target level*, which is represented by the annual monetary target—growth of the central bank money stock or (as from 1988) of the money stock M3—, the Bundesbank more or less continuously throughout the year examines whether, when and, if necessary, to what extent deviations in monetary expansions from the target path should be corrected through adjustment of the conditions in the money market and the other financial markets (1989, 109).

What I see is

| the management of liquidity by means of OMO, with use of the discount and lombard rates for facilitating liquidity adjustment | $\Bigg\}$ | the immediate targeting of DM M3 | $\Bigg\}$ | $\pm\Delta\dot{P}_{DM} = 0$ and growth (Figure 1-4) |

There is no public sector borrowing requirement here, no use of fiscal policy to control monetary policy, and no control over the demand for money via the long-term (or even the short-term) interest rate. Such an approach is an alternative to that relying on fiscal policy and interest rates.

In reference to the discount and lombard windows, the Bundesbank's text says:

[T]he discount and lombard windows can take on a sort of "buffer function" which offsets the monthly deficits or surpluses in central bank balances held by the credit institutions, in so far as these are not neutralized by discretionary market interventions on the part of the central bank. Since the money market has been managed more flexibly, this "buffer function" has lost significance because fluctuations in the banks' central bank money requirements are largely offset through fine-tuning measures by the Bundesbank—primarily by securities repurchase agreements. (1989, 106)

However, apart from the uses of the discount and lombard windows, the print media of London and New York have often focused on upward and downward movements in the bank's administered rates as signaling some condition about the actual acceleration/deceleration of the money and credit aggregates. They are often improperly supported in this by economics textbooks, although I have introduced the impriority of doing so.[18] Further, Bundesbank spokespeople have on occasion noted the peculiar effect of lowering discount and lombard rates, which is illustrated in Figure 1-1 and called a *Bundesbank effect*, namely, *a lowering of the administered short rates $(-\Delta i_S)$ can lead the bond market to actually set higher rates $(+\Delta i_L)$ when the lowering action is interpreted as an inflationary move.* Indeed, in discussing rates on long-term bonds, the Bundesbank says: "the long-term rate is predominantly determined by market factors which the Bundesbank . . . can influence only indirectly, such as interest rate movements abroad and inflationary expectations [say, i = i(real) + $\dot{P}^e$]" (1989, 73).

Summary statements by others to the Bundesbank's approach to "targeting" include several elements: "projected growth of productive potential" (say, Friedman's trend path, Figure 1-4); "desirable changes in capacity utilization"; and "expected changes in money velocity [Y/M]."[19] Continuing, essentially in a Friedman rule context, Kennedy notes allowances for changes in the money supply that do not rigorously reflect expected production and price variables because distortions may occur. Later Kennedy says (1991, 102) the position of the majority on the CBC conforms to established *Bundesbank theory.* Taking what may be a Friedman/long-run view, she notes real factors and forces are beyond the reach of monetary policy. Continuing, she says: "Money and money supply *represent* a reality; they affect production and the real economy, but cannot substitute for other factors."

3.4b The Bundesbank, the Economics, and the Polity

As to legislative intent, Ellen Kennedy points to its absence with respect to how the Bundesbank's price-stability/growth/protection-of-the-currency goals were to be achieved. Rather these were left to economic argument, somewhat along the line of the "rule of reason," so seen by Robert Bork in the case of the U.S. anti-trust laws (Frazer 1988, 319-319). On the one hand, Kennedy notes expectations aroused by the political left and the Stability and Growth Law of 1967, which came at a high point for Keynesian/interventionist argument. On various occasions, she sees this (1991, 26, 32-33) as a view in which economic success had been found via state intervention (Kennedy 1991, 21, 33, 42, 53). On the other hand, a breakup of the Social Democratic Party (SDP)/Free Democratic Party (FDP) coalition under Helmut Schmidt was followed by the FDP's gaining ground and by a so called conservative shift in the early 1980s. The FDP was pointed to as the proponent of so-called "neo-liberalism" ("social market economy," Friedman monetarism, I say). It also is said to run "perfectly parallel" to the Bundesbank's view, and the CBC's president Karl Otto Pöhl's tenure during the 1980s, plus it is also associated with Helmut Kohl's Christian Democratic Party (CDP).

So, in the early 1980s and afterward, the Bundesbank faced the conflicting claims of Keynesian interventionist policy, economic growth, and stability (Kennedy 1991, 42-54). Referring to the "neo-liberal positions that already formed the basis of both Mrs. Thatcher's policy and that of Ronald Reagan" (Kennedy 1991, 42-47), Kennedy notes Pöhl's 1981 positions:

"A deficit country cannot afford a policy of low interest rates." . . . High interest rates were the unavoidable consequence of deficits and currency devaluation. Low interest rates could only be expected if Germany's "stability advantage" was regained; monetary policy must not be used to pursue extraneous economic goals. (1991, 45)

Later—in reference to 1986 conditions in the Federal Republic of Germany and the United States/James Baker led moves to get Germany to lower interest rates and thereby obtain faster economic growth—the Pöhl/Bundesbank positions are stated thus:

1. [T]here was no such thing as growth with inflation; rather an inflation-free economy was the prerequisite for growth. (Kennedy 1991, 65)

2. "The level of monetary stability we have achieved at present is the most important foundation for continuous upturn. Every citizen, not least employees and pensioners, profits from stable prices." The "economic ecology" of recovery was right . . . . stable prices, a solid fiscal policy, moderate wage agreements. All this allowed a public policy in the Federal Republic which resulted in low interest rates, and the Bundesbank would continue to permit enough growth in the supply of money during 1986 to keep the recovery going. (Kennedy 1991, 66)

Viewing the economics and the polity overall results in an independently stated affinity with Hotelling's line (Figure 3-5). There the Keynesian economics appears centrist. The Friedman/monetarist economics appears on the political right.

3.5 ALTERNATIVE ANALYTICAL AND CENTRAL BANKING SYSTEMS: AN OVERVIEW

Kaldor and some other analysts who dealt with Friedman's so-called monetarism as it appeared in London in the early 1980s (Frazer 1988, Chapters 14, 15; Halcrow 1989, Chapter 10) continuously returned to Leon Walras's general equilibrium as set forth in his famous book (1954; FY 1966, Section 5.2; Friedman 1955; 1969, 2-14, 102; 1974, 145-146; Kaldor 1980, 86-140). Along such lines, Kaldor reviews Walras's account and some of its highly abstract technicalities, in relation to the monetary unit, in relation to what he calls "modern monetarists," and in relation to the quantity theory of money. In the critical evaluation, however, an interesting result appears. Most notably there are institutional and operating bases for distinguishing Friedman and Keynesian causation ($\dot{M} \rightarrow \dot{Y}$ and $\dot{Y} \rightarrow \dot{M}$, respectively).

The institutional and operations distinctions suggests that, aside from the study of the history that generated the data Friedman analyzed, the actual implementation of policy should be considered. There are the money and credit aggregates orientation and the institutional arrangements for implementing it (the accounting controls over bank reserves, as via the bank reserve equation, the means for accounting for the money and credit aggregates, and OMO as a means of controlling bank reserves, and hence bank credit and the money stock). Friedman's orientation in these matters is in terms of the growth rate for the money stock, adjusted for secular changes in the velocity of money [Y/M or its inverse, k(. . .)] and the Keynesian/Kaldor orientation is simply a nullification of that mode.

3.5a Monetary Accommodation and Discipline

To deal with these respective modes, consider a monetary policy indicator, and surrogates for it. Using the symbol $\tilde{M}$ for the indicator, $\Delta\tilde{M}$ is monetary accommodation and $-\Delta\tilde{M}$ is monetary discipline. As the indicator approaches the zero limit ($\pm\Delta\tilde{M} \to O$), monetary neutrality results.

The velocity ratio (Y/M) enters the indicator as a multiplier for the accelerated (decelerated) growth in the money stock. At the time of the changes in the money-stock growth rates, the changes times the current multiplier indicate the impact on total spending. Said differently, the velocity ratio indicates the extent of the work done by the accelerated (decelerated) part of the growth in the money stock.

In the context of the Friedman system, I expect inflation with monetary accommodation, we expect interest rates to vary with it too, and I expect a taming of inflation under monetary discipline, although Kaldor and the Keynesians would look to theories of market power for the explanation of inflation (Frazer 1994a, Chapter 3; Section 7.3). Further, I indicate the monetary policy, as just suggested, irrespective of whether the central banks attempt to announce monetary (or money and credit) policy in interest-rate or money aggregate terms.

Kaldor mistakenly related the Walrasian equations to Friedman, as have others, probably because of the New Classical School's (NCS's) connection with Robert Lucas at Chicago, with Frank Knight at an earlier time, and because of an emphasis on cyclical time frames in terms of Figure 1-4a and Wesley Mitchell.[20] The NCS's economics does in fact, however, end with market clearing conditions and a long-run position associated with the equations.[21]

As stated in *The Legacy* (Frazer 1994a, Chapter 9, note 1), I set aside the NCS's rational expectations (RE) on five grounds: (1) it has had no demonstrated impact on economic policy; (2) it is not primarily oriented toward the study of money, or monetary policy; (3) NCS notions that may bear on the present study are more readily visible in terms of the Friedman system; (4) the NCS's RE in effect separates the theory of money from the theory of production and hence offers no clear definition of money à la Keynes and Friedman (Chapter 1, note 4); and (5) it adopts the rather antiquated view of risk found in classical probability and in Frank Knight's work (Frazer 1994a, Section 3.2g; Knight 1921).

In this long-run, Walrasian equation context, all markets clear, there are supply and demand relations for each product market, and there are no unsatisfied buyers or sellers. Moreover, the prices in the various product markets in relation to one another are determined by a solution to a system of Walrasian equations, where as the absolute prices are determined in the quantity-theoretic expression $M = (T/V)P$. The symbol P here is a price index for all transactions (including the stock market), whereas in the Friedman system the prices are for the current output of goods and services only [M = k(. . .) PQ]. Proceeding from it, and the equilibrium time paths, as in the notion of time trend—and changing all stock and flow quantities in the economic system (say, e.g., mainly M and Q) at the same rate—the price level (P) remains unchanged. This statement says, in other terms, d(ln M)/d(ln Q) = 1. The statements are in fact what we see as M/P and Y/P, Y/P = Q, in Section 1.5a and Equation (1) of that section.

Main elements of the NCS's RE are (1) the definition of rationality,[22] (2) the definition of risk as actuarial probability, and (3) the definition of the transitory component of business conditions (Figure 1-4a) as a state where agents have incomplete information.[23] The rationality concept becomes that whereby agents have rationality in the long-run (i.e., when they have complete information).[24] The agents are seen as forming expectations according to the best economics available (i.e., as anticipating the future as economist would by way of fairly ordinary economics and the econometrics in fashion during the period of Friedman's work with Schwartz [FS 1982, 1991], and Friedman [1991]).

In this context, where rationality abounds, there is a stable state of business conditions. Monetary policy is taken into account by the agents when it is known, but then it is viewed in such a way that monetary policy can have no influence on the business-condition outcome unless the agents are tricked (i.e., given incomplete information). An interesting proposition follows.

Proposition. A stabilization policy on the part of the government is not required, because in the anticipation of stability agents will be rational and stability will come about from their acting rational without the government policy.

There is a corollary.

Corollary. The only way the government's control mechanism can have its effects is by tricking the agents—generating what amounts to information they do not have.

The difficulties with this view of the NCS's RE are several. (1) There is no room for agents to process new information of an episodic/exogenous sort, such as we encounter with personalistic probability in the Friedman system. (2) There is no room to assess the likely outcomes of central bank responses and the prospects for debt monetization such as discussed in the summary statement of the evolution of views on the effects of fiscal policy. (3) It makes no allowances for changes in the structure underlying the formation of expectations in the mid 1960s such as I point to (psychological time, New York's revenge, and so on. (4) The NCS's RE makes no allowances for destabilizing responses to possible episodes on the part of agents. In other words, the NCS's RE eliminates consideration of a good bit of what agent behavior in financial markets and central banking is about.

3.5b Lender of Last Resort, and Endogeneity and Exogeneity

Kaldor also makes something of the implication that "the superstructure of credit money varies in strict proportion to 'base money' whether the latter is thought of as gold in the vaults of the central bank or simply as the amount of bank notes printed by the central bank and brought into circulation through the discounting of 'eligible' bills [say the discount window] and/or through open market operations" (Kaldor 1982, 46). And he raises further questions about the control over the expansion of money in a "credit money" system—as introduced earlier under the bank credit and causation topics—about the "lender of last resort" function, and about the exogenity matter (also identical to the causation matter, in his account).

And again, Kaldor said, the money supply cannot be exogenously determined (Kaldor 1982, 46-47), although it appears to be so under monetary discipline in the United States and in the United Kingdom, too. A part of the analytical difficulty is that under the U.K.'s control arrangements, even with monetary discipline, the money stock is driven by fiscal (and "funding") policy, bank credit changes, and the activity via the discount window. And again, Kaldor's reason is that the discount windows must stay open. (However, he is thinking of extreme cases, such as the disastrous waves of bank failures in the United States in the early 1930s, at a time when the Federal Reserve did not use either the discount facilities or open market operations to save the banks). Continuing with his reasoning, Kaldor said: "Precisely because the monetary authorities cannot afford the disastrous consequence of a collapse of the banking system, while the banks in turn cannot allow themselves to get into a position of being 'fully stretched,' the 'money supply' in a credit-money economy is endogenous, not exogenous."

To support his case about endogenity, Kaldor referred to statements in a memorandum by the U.K. Treasury and the Bank of England to the effect that they used interest rates and fiscal policy (the financing of deficits by the central bank, called public sector borrowing requirement) in determining monetary policy. On the occasion cited by Kaldor, the governor of the Bank of England, Gordon Richardson (who was replaced in 1983), had said the following: "The main strategic instruments for influencing the growth of money supply are interest rates and fiscal policy—tax rates and public expenditures" (Commons 1980, 20). Rising to the occasion, after reading the British document of 1980, called the "Green Paper" on *Monetary Control*, Friedman commented:

I could hardly believe my eyes when I read, in the first paragraph of the summary chapter, "The principal means [of controlling the growth of the money supply] must be fiscal policy—both public expenditure and tax policy—and interest rates." Interpreted literally, this sentence is simply wrong. Only a Rip Van Winkle, who had not read any of the flood of literature during the past decade and more on the money supply process, could possibly have written that sentence. Direct control of the monetary base is an alternative to fiscal policy and interest rates as a means of controlling monetary growth.

Of course, direct control of the monetary base will affect interest rates (though not in the way that is implied in chapter 4 of the Green paper), but that is a very different thing from controlling monetary growth through interest rates. (Commons 1980, 57)

3.5c Problems of Control

To be sure, there were problems of control with respect to the control mechanism in the United Kingdom during the change from a Keynesian-era interest-rate regime to a Friedman-type monetary-aggregates regime (Frazer 1988 Chapter 15). Continuing, with these problems aside, Kaldor (1982, 48) said: "These instruments [fiscal policy and interest rates] operate, not on the supply, but on the public's *demand* for money." The instruments as Kaldor views them operate "*directly* by changing the public's desire to hold bank deposits in preference to other financial assets, or *indirectly* by influencing the level of expenditure on consumption and investment".

So what I see is that Kaldor actually adopted the bank-operations mode I associate with a Keynesian orientation, rather than a Friedman monetarist one. To be sure, Kaldor had in mind (1) a set of credit-policy actions and fiscal policy (measured as a deficit, or in British terms, the public sector borrowing requirement, PSBR) and (2) Keynesian "demand [spending] management." The first calls for (a) keeping the discount window open without restricting use by raising the discount rate and (b) having unlimited government expenditure (unlimited PSBR) up to the point of Keynesian full employment. Via this attention to instruments and the PSBR, government spending up to Keynesian full employment means that the government spending determines income. Monetary policy is subordinated to fiscal policy, and, were the matter of inflation arises, Kaldor would contain it via the use of direct controls over prices and incomes policy generally (1982, 61-62).

Kaldor's case is a priori, but it relies on operations of a particular sort. Under the institutional arrangements he deals with in the U.K., income growth causes money growth ($\dot{Y} \rightarrow \dot{M}$). As to the empirical question about causation, there was no predominate deficit policy with supportive monetary policy, such as that advocated by Kaldor, during most of history from 1867 through 1975, over which FS analyze data (FS 1982).

Although not exactly a part of convention during the 1867-1975 period as a whole, Kaldor's position is quite explicit—the government engages in deficit spending up to "Keynesian full employment," and the central bank finances the deficit (the extent depending on "funding policy"). Quite clearly the government determines income and the financing of the deficits, and the means of entry into the sterling money market determines the money stock. Kaldor thus offers the explanation of reverse causation ($\dot{Y} \rightarrow \dot{M}$). However, as the matter turns out much later, the Bank of England has operated in the sterling money market, and it has lacked accounting control arrangements comparable to those in the United States (the bank reserve equation etc.). The Bank's orientation (the money market operations, the funding policy, the absent of the accounting arrangements) is latent in the approaches of Keynes, the Keynesians, and the post-Keynesians. Even as the Bank attempted monetarist policy along Friedman's line in the early 1980s, they were limited in fact from doing so by control and accounting arrangements quite different from those found in the United States. What is found under two governors of the bank of England is an approach quite foreign to Friedman's. It is that of controlling money demand (and the stock supplied too) by controlling interest rates and giving a direct role to fiscal policy (PSBR, and the Bank's "funding policy"). (This approach is symbolized by Equation [2] of Section 1.4a.)

Kaldor also said the money stock cannot be determined exogenously, whether $\dot{M} \rightarrow \dot{Y}$ with feedback or $\dot{Y} \rightarrow \dot{M}$ with feedback. However, there is no absolute determination of either exogeneity in the first instance or endogeneity in the second. Rather from an econometric model point of view, I come to find references to degrees of exogeneity or endogeneity. Argument along institutional lines are more decisive, notably, where the government gives a primary emphasis to monetary policy, the money variable is exogenous on the adage "the buck stops here"; and where deficit spending and central bank financing of the deficit receive primary attention, the money variable is endogenous in the sense that a monetary expansion is drawn into being by the government's requirement that the central bank accommodate the deficit.

Following exercises along the lines of Friedman's "helicopter money," and Kaldor's endogenous money, I find only one effect on income from accelerated growth in the money stock. The Kaldor fiscal-policy effect is a substitute for the Friedman helicopter effect. The respective policies and their effects are substitutes. The distinct policies are not additive. Instead, the government enters differently in the respective cases. Given that role, I can recall the place for the different ideological positions on Hotelling's line (Figure 3-5). The result—via the political orientation and experiments 4 and 5—is that the policies themselves are the result of i and M orientations. I say they are politically driven (or exogenous under the experiences we encountered).

3.5d Traversing Fiscal Policy

As these remarks should indicate—when juxtaposed to earlier comments on the Keynes/Keynesian, income-expenditure block, and the Greenspan comments on fiscal policy—the views of a fiscal policy role since Keynes and the beginning of Keynesian/macro economics have traversed some diverse routes. In the order of their appearance on the scene they are the following: First comes the idea of a direct stimulus effect from deficit spending. Operating via a multiplier without regard to financing the deficit the effects were viewed on a priori grounds as considerable. (This was later to be countered from the political right, as viewed on Hotellings line, by the government budget constraint). Second is the operating mode of the Bank of England, where the control of the money aggregate depended on fiscal policy and interest rates, as

$$\ln M = a_0 + a_2 \ln i + a_3 \ln Y$$

(This goes undisputed as an operations approach to controlling the stock and demand for money balances, but it is seen at odds with the Friedman-system's control prospects, which are an alternative to control via interest rates and fiscal policy. Also, by this route, and in connection with the government budget constraint, note the monetary and fiscal policy as substitutes.) Third is the Greenspan account of the effects of fiscal policy referred to as deficit reduction (Frazer 1994a, Section 4.5). At this point, the twist on the interpretation of fiscal policy comes with a new emphasis on long-term bond rates where I see the role of expectations in the private sector, bond market by way of

$$i = i(\text{real}) + Pb[\dot{P}^e] \, \dot{P}^e$$

It is absent of any direct influence on the Federal Reserve's part, except to the point that the Greenspan Fed showed some firmness on the deficit problem and the containment of inflation. There was no Arthur Burns/William Miller approach here.

Indeed, the stimulating effect of fiscal policy by this third route is a 180-degree change from the stimulating effect found in the Keynesian/macro convention as depicted by the first route above. The 180-degree change supports the psychological/probabilistic emphasis we have given to interest rates and what I called elsewhere (Frazer 1994a) an open ended analytical system.

3.5e Hypothesis H_{TW}

Finally, as presently introduced, views of the banking system are latent in the teaching and theoretic counterparts of the alternative analytical systems (hypothesis H_{TW}). After all, Keynes was most familiar with the institution and practices in the City of London, when he wrote the *General Theory*; Lord Kaldor was practically stating the predominating fiscal policy approach of his day, when he dealt with the causation matters; and M. Friedman was aware of the accounting arrangements for bank reserves, the system of money and credit multiplies, and open market operations of the sort found in the United States. Along with the view that the teaching of economics in U.S. colleges and universities had drawn quite heavily on British writers, such as Marshall and Keynes, is the added view that the distinct alternative analytical systems and banking views stated in this chapter cannot be readily meshed together by simple means. The adoption of a strenuous ceteris paribus, separation-of-effects approach may appear to enhance the prospect of combining the diverse approaches pointed out, but the approach does not enhance an understanding of how the world works.

NOTES

1. The interest rate is regressed on velocity and then the simple regression is reversed as a means of obtaining the bounds on the true regression coefficient. In doing this, I proceed as FS do (1982, 224-225, note 18) and encounter the extension of Edward Leamer's idea to more than two variables. Friedman said "that applying an upper and lower limit is really the most effective way to have some idea of knowing what I do know and what I don't know."

The Leamer problem can be stated thus: As variables are added to the regression equation it is extremely difficult to set limits on the separate regression coefficients, and beyond some point it may not be possible to set the bounds at all.

2. The method employed in this study of U.S. data was in several parts. First, time-to-maturity profiles for the government securities holdings of eight institutional groups were constructed. Then, maturities in dollar amounts for the various holdings for the respective group were treated as percentages of the respective totals to obtain profiles analogous to probability distributions. This was so that mean distributions, mean values (M), standard deviations (σ), and other measures of central tendency could be constructed to obtain graphs and information such as shown in Figure 3-7.

Next, the maturity profiles and the measures of central tendency so obtained were used as time series for the 1960s to study the stability of the profiles over time for the respective groups. Although, the yield curve (e.g., Figure 3-2) itself varied considerably, during the decade of the 1960s, the time series showed that the profiles were stable and coincided with the future needs of the groups. The groups included nonfinancial corporations where the results were later related to the planned financing of industrial corporations (Frazer 1994a, Section 5.4, Chapter 6, note 6).

3. Friedman advanced the idea of stable statistical phenomena over time, while focusing on his time frames (Figure 1-4), allowance for episodic change (and not simply a "flat out" stable velocity ratio), and the function shown earlier (Equation [1] in Section 1.5a).

Along this line and in the case of the change in the structure (i.e., the change from Figure 3-1 to Figure 3-3) we may proceed to reestablish the old relation (Figure 3-1) by adjusting the U.S. series for the episodic changes of the 1970s and 1980s. For that purpose, the interest rate appears to be guided more by the level for the expected inflation rate, whereas velocity depends more on the change in the rate from one level to another. As a result, the interest rates are driven up faster and to a higher level than velocity.

The analytical problem with the velocity ratio is that disproportionate changes are occurring in both the denominator and the numerator of the ratio when inflation starts to move persistently in one direction. As the liquidity preference analysis in Section 1.5b would indicate, there is a penalty for holding money balances (the denominator) and spending shifts upward from path C, to B, to A as this penalty occurs and places a premium on holding real goods.

Figure 3-7
Examples of Time-to-Maturity Profiles for Selected Institutional Groups, U.S. Data

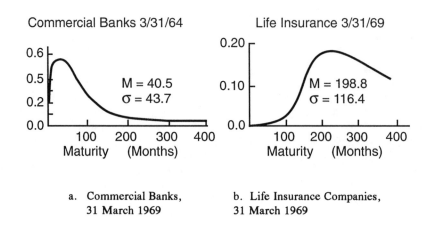

a. Commercial Banks,   b. Life Insurance Companies,
    31 March 1969   31 March 1969

This change in the permanent components as it affects spending on real capital is illustrated in Figure 3-8. The accelerated growth in money balances changes the path in nominal terms from C to B. The additional shift from path B to A is due to the premium on holding more real capital as the inflation rate moves from 0 to 2 percent. There is, parallel to this, a penalty on holding money balances and hence the move from path B to A in Figure 1-7a.

This search for a stable relation, has been discussed in terms of allowing for the expected inflation rate and for changes in the payments mechanism in the United States in the early 1980s. In the United States in the early 1980s, allowances for episodic change also called for adjusting the money stock measure M1 for the presence of NOW and super-NOW accounts at a time of deregulation in the banking system (Frazer 1988, 654-659).

Figure 3-8
Accelerated Growth (3 to 5 percent) in Capital

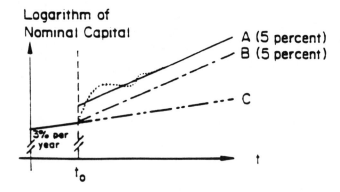

4. This was more formally called the Congressional Budget and Impoundment Act of 1974. It altered the budget timetable and gave focus to the notion of an overriding budget or fiscal policy. It did so by establishing budget committees in each house of Congress with the responsibility for setting income and expenditure targets and hence a budget surplus (or deficit) target. To help carry out its objectives and to assess the economic impact of various legislative actions, it established the separate Congressional Budget Office. The new budget office paralleled the Office of Management and Budget (OMB) in the Executive Office of the President.

5. The account of Paul Volcker, the Federal Reserve's chairman from 1979 to 1987, is consistent with the dating of the U-Turn in the Federal Reserve policy of controlling inflation by money and credit aggregates means. As also found in Frazer (1988, 555, 642, 648-649, 669-670), Volcker's account is to the effect that the Fed's announcement of October 6, 1979 reflected a change in operating procedure and not in the monetary policy to control inflation by means of monetary and credit aggregates, absent of the "quick fix" and record inflation rates in early 1980 and early 1981. (Volcker in Volcker and Gyohten 1992, 170-172)

6. Kaldor's most formal paper on the controversy is reprinted in Wood and Woods (1990, vol. II, 1-28) along with a comment by Friedman and Tobin's rejoinder.

7. Christopher Sims pursued the issue of causation by further introducing a statistical test for the existence of "unidirectional casualty." It is a variant on a criterion provided by Granger. Where applied, the rather restrictive Sims/Granger test supported the prospect of causation from money to income. Even so, we encounter Friedman thus:

I think that the Sims and Granger methods only deal with those variables that are involved in the correlation. They don't deal with third variables that may influence both. It may be that this time-relationship is deceptive because, for example, take a very simple case. If I have a pure curve and I enter into another series which is a derivative of that sine curve, if I go through the Sims technique, I'm going to get one of those causing the other either way. I'll get a mutual causation both ways, and of course that's nonsense. (Frazer and Sawyer 1984)

The graph for a sine curve (Y = sine X) is shown in Figure 3-9.

Figure 3-9
The Graph for a Sine Curve (Y = sine X)

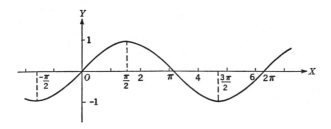

8. The term "exogenous variable" is close in meaning to what the early American Keynesian Alvin Hansen called an "autonomous variable" in reference to Keynes's discussion of highly volatile capital expenditures. Controversy over the term "exogenous" raised the defining standard (Frazer 1973, 102-105); namely, an exogenous variable in a stochastic model (say, a regression equation) is a variable whose value in each period is statistically independent of the values of the random disturbances in the model in all periods.

The concept of an autonomous variable is close to the ordinary notion of independence. Moreover, the term "exogenous" can refer to a variable in a system of structural equations or can imply the idea of an outside variable in relation to the economic system under consideration, such as the U.S. economy. The term, even so, has its origin in formal usage, where controversy did not abate (FS 1991, 41-44). Most likely, within the realm of econometric usage, degrees of exogeneity and endogeneity exist, at best.

By contrast, I view monetary accommodation as meaning causation from income to money and hence view the money stock as endogenous. Monetary discipline takes on the reverse meaning.

Friedman himself did not like the use of the term causation. In connect with it, however, he warned about infinite regress (Frazer and Sawyer 1984). For example, we start saying money growth was a cause, and then we say: Why money growth? Why not Friedman who offered the idea? Why not those who taught Friedman? The issue is more constrained. It is the choice between one of two series (M and Y), where feedback is present, and where the responsibilities of monetary and political authorities are recognizable. I say "The buck stops at the policy making authority."

9. As discussion and references attest, I consider central bank operations in connection with economic theory and turn to policy officials on occasions where they have taken positions. As I proceed with this, among those drawn upon are Paul Volcker the Federal Reserve chairman from 1979 to 1987, where special problems arise in doing so (Volcker and Toyoo Gyohten, hereafter VG 1992). Most notably, I draw on Volcker's authoritative reflections on international monetary affairs but encounter conflicts with the distinct Friedman system. This comes about mainly to the extent that Volcker, like Bank of England governors, rather consistently views monetary policy as working through interest rates (in VG 1992, 233, 236, 243) whereas the Friedman system offers an alternative.

Although Volcker gives prominence to international and exchange rate matters and attributes prominence to expectations, speculation, and open markets, as we do (Chapter 4), he also treats rather conventionally the workings of interest rates, even in relation to international capital flows. Moreover, he refers to fiscal policy as something to be coordinated with monetary policy (Volcker in VG 1992, 236 and 292) as if the two were offsetting and not interdependent (as in Sections 3.2e, 3.2f below). In particular, Volcker's leanings come out when he discusses "monetarists" in the U.S. presidency of Ronald Reagan (in VG 1992, 173-184).

I expect the basis of Volcker's orientation on fiscal, monetary, and interest-rate matters consists partly of the prospects in hypotheses H_{CB} and H_{TW} of Section 1.1 and partly of what I allude to in introducing the separation-of-effects matter (Section 2.5).

10. The early stages of open market operations are taken up by Lester Chandler (1958), and Frazer and Yohe (FY) review these changes plus take up the banking acts of 1933 and 1935 (FY 1966, 146-153, Section 8.1).

11. Gold is initially economized by the operation of a fractional reserve banking system, and then it is further economized where holdings of a key currency, such as the pound at one time, can be used to provide additional reserves. A key currency, is one that is widely accepted in the world. It is accepted especially by the central banks of the less visible countries as a reserve for the broader money and credit aggregates.

12. Recall that the interest rate is the price received for extending credit and paid for obtaining credit (as distinct from money balances and thus not to be confused with M1, M2, and so on).

13. Compare note 8, above.

14. Referring back to Paul Volcker (note 9 above) and the views he expresses on domestic policy in the United States there are conflicts with his reporting which arise in the perspective of the monetary/fiscal policy links we offer. These extend to the dating of the U-Turn as it relates to monetary policy in the United States (Section 3.2e) and to matters concerning Volcker's view of the independence of the Federal Reserve. The matters of independence takes on added importance when we later return to the U-turn hypothesis (Section 1.1), to the Bundesbank (Section 3.4), and to the European Monetary System (Chapters 5, 6).

In the analyses I offer, there are in Volcker's accounts (1) an inappropriate sharp distinction and (2) a conveniently blurred distinction. The first is that between an interest-rate oriented view of monetary policy and a distinct view of fiscal policy (Volcker in VG 1992, 120, 292). This distinction leads to a separation of the effects of the monetary and fiscal policy on inflationary prospects and so on.

The blurred distinction is that between interest rates and the money stock (including after allowances for velocity) in addressing matters of monetary ease and tightness. In this instance there are elements of what we see as Equation (2) in Section 1.4 (Volcker in VG 1992, 164-166), where a short-term interest rate may be used to put a money aggregate on target, and there is the rather clear and distinct view of proceeding rather directly to control reserves and a money aggregate without intervention via interest rates (Volcker in VG 1992, 166-167).

Further, in the Friedman system, as opposed to the Keynesian one, there is control of money and credit aggregates as an alternative to fiscal policy and the interest-rate orientation (as summary remarks indicate, Section 3.5). In addition, there are numerous ancillary matters   I invoke about fiscal policy, debt, the potential for debt monetization (Section 2.2) but especially the money-aggregates orientation alters the perception of the Federal Reserve's independence within the framework of government (Frazer 1988, 259-261). Along the lines we take up, it does this by revealing the power of the Federal Reserve to nullify the fiscal-policy intentions of the U.S. Congress (Frazer 1988, 259-261)' and by becoming a substitute for fiscal policy (Section 3.3e). In turn, this independence matter is present in Paul Volcker's account, although Arthur Burns took a different track and cited the same authority. Volcker says: "The Federal Reserve, which is deliberately designed to be independent from the executive branch, reports directly to Congress, which was given the power by the Constitution to 'coin Money, regulate the Value thereof, and of foreign Coin.' The Federal Reserve is responsible for *monetary policy* pure and simple, no adjectives." (Volcker in VG 1992, 232)

15. When Schacht does lapse into a reference to interest rates (1967, 152-152) it is to the rate of discount set by the Bundesbank and the use to "combat domestic inflation [of the mid 1960s] with a high rate of discount and by granting credit charily at a high

rate of interest." Except for the rub that this may attract "even more foreign money" the discount-rate matter could simply be in reference to the management of liquidity by the Bundesbank.

I find no hint of open market operations of the special sort I refer to (Section 3.3) nor of a bank reserve equation in which the impact of an inflow of foreign currency could be exchanged for deutchemarks without any excess going into the creation of bank reserves. Quite simply the effect of this inflow of liquid balances, as it were, could be offset in the bank reserve context by open market sales of securities.

Schacht refers to the effects of the inflow of foreign currency beginning in 1957 and extending into the mid 1960s as "imported inflation" (1967, 145-146) which suggests even further that he was unaware of the use of open market operations to nullify the inflationary effects of an inflow of foreign balances on bank reserves. On the other hand, Schacht was correct in seeing the open economy world with fixed exchange rates as one in which strictly domestic matters on the policy front could not be conducted independently of international matters. Nevertheless he argued (1967, 145) that the inflow of foreign currency (say a balance of payments surplus) beginning as early as 1957 should have been channeled into purchases of foreign securities and property rather than be monetized.

16. Dr. Schacht, who was president of Germany's central bank from December 1923 until March 1930, resigned over disagreement with the German government. Reappointed Reichsbank president in March 1933—following Adolf Hitler's election as Chancellor—Schacht became powerful in the realm of economic policy during the early years of the Third Reich. In January of 1939 Schacht was dismissed from his various posts and from the Reichsbank presidency over economic/political conflicts (Classen 1987, 254-255) arising from his defense of the Reichsbank's monetary policy (Schacht 1967, 117). An authority in his time, he never regained economic/political prominence, beyond the lecture circuit and as advisor to developing countries. Indeed, the early post-World War II German Chancellor Adenauer had urged him not to return to public life (Schacht 12967, 187).

17. This economic program is viewable in terms of the Kahn/Keynes, public works multiplier (Frazer 1994a, Sections 5.2b and 9.2), except for one big difference. That difference is that a partly private-sector plan for the financing of the primary and secondary streams of spending was added. This added feature connected to well-known banking concepts, which in turn tied the growth of money and credit to the growth of production.

18. Also in Frazer (1994a, Section 5.4c) is "psychological time" as it bears on the effects of interest rates on expenditure plans by industrial corporations.

19. See, for example, Kennedy citing an unpublished manuscript by Scharrere (Kennedy 1991, 84, 102).

20. In more detail concerning origins, and exclusive of the connections to Knight and Friedman's "Wesley Mitchell connected" work, the NCS can be associated with the following: an early paper by Lucas and Rapping (1969), early and related papers by Robert Barro and by Barro and Hershell Grossman (including Barro and Grossman 1971; Barro 1977, 1981, 1984). If there is any common connection these people appear to have, it is centered around Carnegie-Mellon University. John Muth was there when he wrote his 1961 paper and until 1964; Lucas's 1969 paper with Rapping was written at Carnegie-Mellon; Sargeant was there in 1968-69 after receiving a Ph.D. from Harvard, and before moving to the University of Minnesota where he encountered Neil

Wallace; and Rapping, a Chicago Ph.D., spent the 1960s there as a full professor before making a break with his past at Chicago and with the NCS.

Barro's textbook (1984) reflects some of the characteristics of the NCS. First, however, it presents only a view with no meaningful attention to alternative theories and hypotheses. This is contrary to Friedman's approach where there are always competing theories. To get its overall result, there is a good bit of distortion and one-sided referencing of statistical results. The overall result is the neoclassical dichotomy,

$$M = \underbrace{(Q/V)}_{\text{const.}} P$$

Although there is incongruity in holding output constant and treating growth paths for the money stock (M) and the price index (P) in the long run, this is what occurs. In other words, the text deals with growth in money balances as found in Friedman's work, but without the dynamics found there. The dynamics found in Friedman include the monetary theory as a statement of motion, the cycle/trend distinction, the parallel growth in money and output that yields greater price-level stability, the interaction between the real goods and monetary sectors, and the treatment of the volatile Cambridge k (the reciprocal of the velocity ratio).

The inharmonious past of Chicago, which the NCS drew on, was that of Knight and Friedman. In viewing economics, Knight backed away from the prospect of its becoming an empirical science. He simply saw it in terms of ethical behavior, a proper code of behavior, and the risk part extended to insurance (i.e., to actuarial risk). On the other hand, Friedman moved in an empirical direction. Uncertainty was something in the mind of the agent, and the analysis of uncertainty was linked with the demand for money, as it was for Keynes.

21. To state the Walrasian equation system, let S be the supply function, and D the demand function, and then take account of the supply-demand equality for each item and the general equilibrium of the economy as follows:

$$S_1 (p_1, p_2, \ldots, p_n, A, M) = D_1 (p_1, p_2, \ldots, p_n, A, M)$$

$$S_2 (p_1, p_2, \ldots, p_n, A, M) = D_2 (p_1, p_2, \ldots, p_n, A, M)$$

$$\vdots$$

$$S_n (p_1, p_2, \ldots, p_n, A, M) = D_n (p_1, p_2 \ldots, p_n, A, M),$$

where p_1, p_2, . . . , p_n are the respective prices of the n items, including money as one item, and where A, in combination with the average stock of money (M), is an index of the nonhuman wealth of the economy.

The system could be expanded by including other variables and parameters (for taste, expectations, and so on). Given the values for the parameters A and M and the prices in the present instance, the system contains as many unknowns (the quantities) as equations, and presumably a solution exists.

However, there is one major complication. One of the n items is money, and the price of a single unit of money is one dollar. Thus one of the prices in the system must be the number 1. In such a case, one would have a redundant equation, and although this need not prohibit a solution, earlier economists were concerned that it might. Consequently, they excluded the equation for the demand for money in their statement of general equilibrium and spoke of simply a numeraire or unit of account, but to account for the demand for money, an identity (albeit one that can be extracted from the Walrasian system of nonidentical equations) was used. The identity was named Walras's law. It can be denoted as follows:

$$\sum_{i=1}^{n} p_i \, q_i^{(S)} = \sum_{i=1}^{n} p_i \, q_i^{(D)}$$

where the left-hand member is the sum of all of the products for the respective prices (p_i [i = 1, 2, . . . , n]) and the corresponding quantities supplied ($q_i^{(S)}$ [i = 1, 2, . . . , n]), and the right-hand member is the sum of all the products for the prices (p_i [i = 1, 2, . . . , n]) and the corresponding quantities demanded ($q_i^{(D)}$ [i = 1, 2, . . . , n]).

The use of the law to refute the notion that money is simply a numeraire to be excluded from the determinant system of equations is straightforward. Those demanding commodities are prepared to exchange an amount of money (e.g., currency and transferable balances) or some other commodities of equal value, and those supplying goods are prepared to accept in exchange their equivalent value in money (e.g., currency and transferable deposits) or other commodities. Note, in particular, that the exchange does not necessarily require the use of money in the specific sense of currency and transferable deposits. The exchange may involve units of items other than currency and transferable deposits, and the item chosen is independent of the item called money, although all values are expressed in terms of the unit of account (say $ or £, or DM as defined in Chapter 1, note 4). In fact, Walras's law says that the supply of and demand for any single item omitted from the n items must be equal and not just the supply of and demand for units of currency and transferable deposits. That is, if the value of the goods supplied is equal to the value demanded for all but the first item as can be assumed from a system of n − 1 items and n − 1 equations, then for the first item

$$p_1 q_1^{(S)} = p_1 q_1^{(D)}$$

or

$$p_1 q_1^{(S)} - p_1 q_1^{(D)} = 0$$

$$p_1 \left(q_1^{(S)} - q_1^{(D)} \right) = 0$$

and

$$q_1^{(S)} = q_1^{(D)}$$

It makes no difference which equation I choose to drop from the initial system of n equations and n unknowns. The first was simply a convenient one to pick.

It follows from the requirement imposed by Walras's Law, and the solution to the $n - 1$ system of equations, that the quantity and price of the first item are also determined by supply and demand conditions. Since $q_1^{(S)} = q_1^{(D)}$, the n prices and n quantities are determined. The redundant equation, therefore, is harmless and causes no difficulty in the initial statement of general economic equilibrium.

As implied by the initial equilibrium equations, the solution is n specific prices on n specific quantities, given the quantity of money M. Since the n prices relating to each other and their absolute values make up the price level, the equations must also determine the price level, and presumably this is determined whether prices are high or low (inflated or deflated), given M. There must be one price level at equilibrium, and others will produce disequilibrium. But this is also implied by the equation of exchange where the concern is with the respective prices on all transactions or it is implied by the cash balance approach to the quantity theory where the concern is primarily with current output alone. In the former case, for example,

$$M = (T/V)\ P_T \tag{1}$$

where T (= const.) is the constant dollar value of all transactions, V (= const.) is the velocity of money balances with respect to the total of transactions, and P is the average of prices on all transactions. In the case of current output,

$$M = (Q/V_y)\ P_y \tag{2}$$

where Q (= const.) is current output, V_y (= const.) is the income velocity of money, and P is the average of prices on current output. In both instances, the higher the price level, the greater the amount of money balances needed for effecting expenditures, although differences in the two expressions take on importance when growth trends and the stock market prices are introduced (included in Equation [1] but not [2]). This is because stock market prices are tied to economic growth and grow with it over the long run, whereas bond prices (as in inflation to the interest rate) and the index of prices (P_y) for the current output of goods and services are constant when the money stock (M) and real output (Q) grow at the same rate.

If the price level (P_y) is high for a given money stock, the demand for money will exceed the supply, since people will hold money in lieu of spending it (i.e., velocity will decline). The effective demand for other items will then decline, and presumably the prices and current output of those items will decline to some equilibrium path. The converse in the case of lower prices would also hold. The general equilibrium system would work the same way; if prices are above the equilibrium level, prices and/or output will be forced down, and vice versa.

Thus far, at a moment in time (or in terms of averages for a period), the price level is determined. This is true for the quantity theory approach and statement of general equilibrium, given underlying conditions. However, if there are changes in the underlying conditions (say, a change toward the prospect of a decline in prices), a rise in the demand for money occurs in connection with its store of value function (defined in Chapter 1, note 4). In the product-market (quantity-price) terms of the figure below this means less demand for output. The conclusion is that a positive (negative) shift in the community's demand to hold money gives rise to a decline (rise) in velocity and output as illustrated in Figure 3-10 (the move from point A to B). If output adjust faster than prices, as when recession occurs, the result is an unemployment level of output (q_u). On the other hand, if and when supply conditions (and wages as a special price) adjust to the demand shift condition, the end result is at point C and full employment output (q_f).

22. Following John Muth, the NCS offered a quite stringent definition of rationality, which I may call "super rationality." Muth's paper, titled "Rational Expectations and the Theory of Price Movements," appeared in 1961, over a decade before interest in it picked up. He dwelt on prices, as his title might indicate, and a rather general view of rationality, notably, "Rationality" is the formation of expectations in such a way as to be "essentially the same as the predictions of the relevant economic theory." However, Muth did not claim complete rationality in every respect. He said (1961, 330) that the assumptions can be modified and "systematic biases, incomplete and incorrect information, poor memory, etc., can be examined with analytical methods based on rationality."

As to super rationality, I see agents forming expectations on the basis of the best economics available, including profit and utility maximization, now extended over time, Walrasian equations and the conditions they imply, the classical dichotomy, and knowledge of the actuarial probability distributions for the outcomes. This concept of rationality was wholly extended by the NCS to mean rationality in terms of the economic models and the mechanical structure, including that of actuarial probability.

23. I may call what I offer as the NCS' RE a caricature, because I abstract from the details found in the NCS books. I did this because—in contrast to Keynes and Friedman, where somewhat unified bodies of work can be closely identified with the principal figures—so many were involved along the way, and because the principal

Figure 3-10
A Strengthened Preference for Money Balances with and without
Wage (Cost) Adjustments

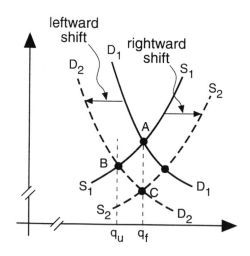

figures have written so much of a highly technical nature from which I abstract (Lucas 1981; Lucas and Sargeant 1981; Sargeant 1987).

Argo Klamer's *Conversations with Economists* (1984) contains views of other economists on the NCS.

24. Amazingly against this background, the U.S. President Bill Clinton called for a lowering of German interest rates on June 30. The media reporting was then accompanied by the announcement that the Bundesbank lowered its discount and lombard rates (from 7 1/4 to 6 3/4 and from 8 1/2 to 8 1/4 respectively), which is not to say the long-bond rate.

Of course other conditions than the President's public request were about to influence the Bundesbank decision. Even so, I encounter in the media/White-House matter on the references to the long-term rate, in the background case, and the administered rates, in the July 1 case, extreme instances of drawing upon the significance of "the" long rate when convenient and detaching the announcement of symbolic administered rates from the former when it is convenient rhetorically to do so for public consumption.

Chapter 4

The Exchange-Rate and Reserve- and Capital-Flows Mechanisms

4.1 INTRODUCTION

The exchange-rate and reserve- and capital-flows mechanisms have varied somewhat from the concept of the classical gold standard with fixed ties between gold and countries' units of account, and the wide acceptance of gold as a monetary reserve. However, the principles of an anchor for the monetary unit (such as gold at a fixed price or, more recently, the anchoring of selected currencies to the deutsche mark) and the fractional reserve banking system (as illustrated in Figure 3-6) have not varied much since David Hume (1711-1776) tied such a system to the simplest of the quantity theories of money and the idea that a country's price level was governed in some way by the stock of money.

Starting with gold as the reserve asset of choice, and fixed ties between gold and currency units, results in fixed exchange rates, the gold-flows mechanism, and a set of classical conditions. The fixed rates at which the currencies exchange for one another are the means for extending abroad the prices of goods found in the various countries. Then, allowing for competition in the export of goods and services, the country with the lowest prices is favored, and gold flows in as foreign currencies are exchanged for gold. The inflow of gold increases reserves, and the system of money and credit multipliers comes into play, the money stock expands and, domestic prices rise. As this happens, the conditions are set for a reverse set of changes to occur.

Adding the prospect of substitutes for gold reserves (such as currencies that are as good as gold), the functioning of the gold-flows mechanism does not change much. In the post-World War II years, the U.S. dollar was such a currency for a time, as I will indicate, and then with a history as a "hard currency" the deutsche mark became widely accepted and came to serve as the preferred monetary asset within the European Monetary System.

Introducing the concept of floating exchange rates (Friedman 1953), and adding other prospects, the exchange-rate and reserve-flow mechanisms become more complicated as the experiments with government policies occur. However, the newer prospects for Europe still reflect fixed-rate and reserve-flow mechanisms without much departure from the past.

Adding the managed, floating rates, and recognizing other prospects, I see two "pricing means" at a national policy level for a country to improve the export of its competitive goods. One is that of lowering the domestic price level, and the other is that of lowering the price of the currency in the foreign exchange market, where such may be feasible. Completely managed rates and the use of administered controls over market prices aside, however, these two means are inseparable—lower prices for goods improve the value of a country's currency, and vice versa. What I come to see is that in the presence of free markets, the policy connected variables of Equation (1), Section 2.5, are inseparable for the purpose of controlling GNP (or GDP). The ideology (Hotelling's line, Figure 3-5) reenters the picture. The economics with the market-economy orientation appears on the right of the line. The economics with the forced compliance appears more to the left. It is not absent, even in plans bearing on the European Monetary System. There is a Keynesian/Kaldor prospect.

Other complicating prospects presently appear only in the background. They are that the money stock governs the price levels, after allowances for economic efficiency, technological changes, and the turnover of money balances, and that a country's export of competitive goods are most favored by lower prices relative to those of trading partners.

Within the accounting arrangements where all these foreign transactions are recorded, the central bank enters from the point of view of the i-orientation, as well as from the alternative M-orientation. In the interest-rate view, the central bank can be seen as being able to raise and lower interest rates as a control variable with the view to influencing the international flows of short- and long-term capital (viewed as financial instruments). In general, the i-orientation's control prospects rely on the separation of effects by a combination of force and analytical means. With respect to Equation (1) in Section 2.5, and a new variation of it, there is the twofold set of prospects—that of controlling the price index, exchange rates, interest rates, and fiscal and other matters separately from one another and that of arriving at a separation of effects by artificial analytical means. In the realm of practical affairs, the two require one another. Hence, the move to the left on Hotelling's line where I classify the economics as to its ideological content.

4.1a   The Managed System

The managed financial system entered on the international side in the 1920s, at the same time it entered with respect to the domestic side, and again the Federal Reserve Bank of New York was involved. Its involvement came about when the decision was made for Britain to return to the gold standard in 1925 at the old parity of $4.87. With respect to that standard, Hjalmar Schacht reported thus:

Internationally the gold standard was maintained by the fact that the Bank of England was prepared not only to buy gold at a fixed price, but also to sell. . . . Even if . . . other central banks . . . undertook similar obligations, it was still the . . . trust in the Bank of England which gave paper money . . . status as gold.

Referring to the period in which neoclassical economics could take money for granted, Schacht continued:

This trust was so great . . . that no-one . . . gave . . . thought . . . that the gold standard, which the whole world adopted in . . . the last quarter of the 19th century, was not a currency standard which carried any international obligations [but was a fractional reserves, gold standard with the Bank of England]. (Schacht 1967, 63)

Then turning to Montagu Norman, Schacht recalled as follows:

Germany was not only the country . . . Norman gave financial and banking assistance. In the 'twenties the Bank of England helped many foreign central banks. While the French . . . had eyes for none but their own interests, Norman recognized the need to revitalize . . . world trade. This was certainly also in the interest of England. The Sterling currency was the world's main trading currency and served all. . . . It was Norman's aim to make London the centre of the international payments system . . . as it had been before the First World War with benefit to the entire world. Not until after the Second World War did London lose this position. (Schacht 1967, 82)

However, Keynes's perception was a bit different. It was that the pound was over priced, plus there was the conflict over prices and wage adjustments. And, as reported in various places (e.g., Frazer 1988, 424-425; FY 1966, 146-151), the New York Fed's Benjamin Strong moved to contain some downward movements in U.S. prices to ease the difficulty confronted by the British, with the consequence that bank credit gave added support to the U.S. stock market boom from which terrible consequences followed.

As the crash ensued, there were waves of bank failures, and a failure of leadership at the Fed's Board in Washington as the money and credit aggregates contracted (FS 1963, 407-419). And then, in connection with all this and other European matters, American willingness to grant loans to Germany to help pay World War I reparations came to an end. German debt payments stopped and its economy collapsed in July 1931.[1] The United Kingdom departed from gold in September 1931, and the United States in March of 1933.

Approaching the end of World War II, however, the post-World War II world was expected with much determination to make international financial arrangements work. The first step, again as widely told (FY 1966, Chapter 22), was the U.S. sponsored, international meeting in Bretton Woods, New Hampshire, in 1944, which gave rise to the International Monetary Fund (IMF) among other things, and new roles for gold, the United States, and the workings of what is known as the goldflows mechanism. Numerous developments follow. Crucial phases of the post-World War II experience are listed and annotated.

Phase I (IMF, 1944-1973). The IMF was charged with making the old gold-flows mechanism work and with implementing an exchange rate mechanism (ERM) to facilitate the workings of gold within the context of balances of international payments. The ERM was one of fixed exchange rates, such as accompanied the pre- and post-World War I gold standards, but with two differences. They were that the limits within which the rates were fixed—as illustrated in Figure 4-1 with a hypothetical dollar/pound exchange rate—could be more readily adjusted by way of agreements with the Fund, under certain conditions, and that the IMF had some elementary features of a bank.

As the figure indicates, there were upper and lower limits ($2.37 and $2.33) about a par rate that constituted the fixed rate (actually a rate with limits).

Figure 4-1
A Hypothetical Rate on Foreign Exchange between the United States and the United Kingdom from the U.S. Point of View

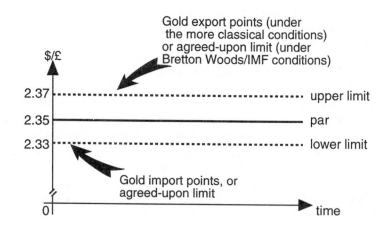

These were originally set by adding and subtracting the cost of shipping gold at the par rate, but under IMF arrangements, until the 1971-73 period cited later, they were agreed on limits within which the rate could fluctuate. It would be pegged within these limits by purchases and/or sales of one country's currency through a fund, with the country ultimately being ready to exchange its currency for gold, as where the price of the country's currency could fall (say, $/£ price falls to the $2.33 limit). As implied by the "adjustable peg" reference, the ban concerning the par value and the par value itself could be adjusted through agreement with the IMF.

There were, and still are, member countries to the IMF, there is voting on the part of members, and there are in effect balances held and contributed by member countries, and lines of credit available to them. Like a bank, these can be drawn on to facilitate adjustments in the accounting balances for the respective member countries. The voting and member contributions to the IMF depend on the extent of participation of the member countries in the total amount of trade conducted internationally.

Early on there were contributions of gold to the Fund, but these were reduced and in part replaced in 1970 by bookkeeping units of "paper gold" called standard drawing rights (SDRs). The SDR units were valued as a basket of major currencies. Volcker and Gyohten point out that the SDRs were "meant to serve as a supplementary reserve asset and source of international liquidity." However, VG say (1992, 334), "It [the SDR] has not functioned as a major substitute for the dollar in countries' foreign reserves, although it is used to provide needed liquidity from time to time, especially by developing countries."

Early on the U.S. dollar's tie to gold at $35.00 per fine ounce for official purposes was a crucial one, and gold still flowed from one country's account to another as it did under the old classical gold standard.

In general, the gist of what the IMF did was to provide liquidity to member countries in the short term to ease the burden of making adjustments in balances of international payments. If a member country persisted in having payments difficulties, two main things could happen. For one, additional liquidity could be provided by tying the extension of further credit to agreements concerning corrective fiscal and monetary policies, which were seen as the sources of difficulty to begin with. For another, the country could be allowed to devalue its currency (i.e., to adjust the entire pegged-rate mechanism, illustrated in Figure 4-1). In the case of the British, for example, where post-World War II adjustments seemed common, the entire set of rates in Figure 4-1 would be adjusted downward (i.e., the $2,37, $2.35, and $2.33 numbers).

The act of devaluation was thought to give a country some advantage to export goods and possibly reduce unemployment by effectively reducing all its prices to foreign buyers. However, as the world has become more integrated as to production, a common fear has come about, namely: a depreciated currency may bring more inflation domestically by raising import prices. Also, with the move toward floating rates which we turn to in phase 4, the short-run effects of even relative extreme exchange rate changes comes into question. Volcker says (in VG 1992, 152):

Supporters of floating rates had strongly expected that rate changes would produce a better balance of international payments. But we found that the mechanism did not work quickly enough to shift trade flows and help bring equilibrium, and therefore a certain disillusionment arose about this function of the regime. As a result, attention shifted, or rather expanded, to demand management policy and especially its multilateral coordination at summits.

Phase 2 (A Super Central Bank). Even as U.S. deficits were becoming crucial in the early 1960s, the international system's tie to gold and the possible limits on its supply and liquidity generally were questioned (FY 1966, 550-555). Out of the questioning grew an interest in converting the IMF into a super, international central bank, complete with money-creating powers and the like. The prospect was advanced by Robert Triffin for a world money supply (1961), with all it potentially might entail in terms of a loss of sovereignty and a managed, global financial system.[2]

Phase 3 (Open Market Operations in Foreign Exchange). Confronting a need to support the dollar by means other than its tie to gold in the early 1960s, the Federal Reserve Bank of New York came to conduct open market operations in currencies with the view to maintaining pegged exchange rates in February of 1962, as the dollar showed its early sign of vulnerability. The arrangements have since varied, but through "swap agreements" the major central banks agreed to exchange currencies and maintain a "swap network" for attempts at limiting the more extreme, speculative swings in the foreign exchange markets.

Described by Paul Volcker (in VG 1992, 31), the initial "swap network" consisted of "prearranged" short-term lines of credit among the major central banks and treasuries, enabling them to borrow each other's currency almost instantaneously in time of need." Volcker mentions that "so-called Roosa Bonds were invented, enabling the United States to borrow foreign currencies from other monetary authorities, currencies that could be used instead of gold when a country wanted to convert unwanted dollars."

As seen with hindsight by Volcker the plain implication of the swap arrangements was that the dollar needed defending. He saw it as a step toward America's "changing fortunes" with respect to its competitive position in the post-WW II world.

The central bank arrangements did not end with the early 1960s. Volcker and Gyohten define an official "swap agreement" thus:

[A] central bank agrees to provide a supply of its own currency to another central bank for an identical amount of its currency. Typically, the stronger currency will be drawn to intervene in support of the weaker. When the pressure comes off the weak currency and its reserves are rebuilt, the money is repaid, and the sway is thus unwound. The agreement usually includes guarantees to offset any change in currency values. (VG 1992, 334)

Phase 4 (Closing the Gold Window). The phase 2 prospects did not materialize for the IMF, but the dependence of the IMF arrangements on the role of the dollar foretold the doom to the arrangements it fostered (phase 3). In summary, the difficulty was threefold: the IMF's dependence on the dollars as a stable (or gold-standard) currency, the United States's commitment to exchange gold for foreign held dollars when they were presented to the United States by foreign central banks; and the United States's domestic conditions. The United States's monetary authority had started to accommodate government spending and price increases, and Keynes's "labor standard" was breaking down. This was occurring at a time when Germany and Japan were coming on line as economic competitors and the United States was running deficits in the balance of international payments.

Faced with domestic policies at odds with foreign policies, the Nixon White House chose to close the "gold window," to support the demonetization of gold, to devalue the dollar in two steps, and to lead the United States's trading partners toward a floating of currencies in the foreign exchange markets.[3] Dramatic changes followed: the dollar's exchange value varied inversely with the U.S. inflation rate (Figure 4-2a); and the dollar declined in terms of its exchange value as measured against the trade-weighted index of ten foreign currencies (including the deutsche mark [DM], and the Japanese yen [¥]). The decline was later reversed in the early Reagan years, as inflation was brought under control, as also shown in secular trend terms (Figure 4-2b). The trends shown are readily comparable to the trends in Figures 2-1a and 2-2b. Juxtaposing the respective trends, the United States's domestic monetary policies of the 1970s and the 1980s are reflected in the exchange rate data. The policy effects are in the direction expected.

Phase 5 (the Freedom Issue). The principal proponent for the move toward floating exchange rates on the academic front was Milton Friedman. In the fall of 1950, while a consultant to "the then Marshall Plan agency," he offered an analysis of common market prospects that became the basis for "The Case for Flexible Exchange Rates" (Friedman 1953).

The idea, combined with the problems confronting the dollar, in the late 1960s and early 1970s, was to bring about the move toward the float and support from unlikely quarters. On one hand, there was Friedman, and the "freedom" issue present in his economics viewed as a the whole (Frazer 1988, Chapter 12, 1994a, Section 3.4). He had set freedom (extending to voluntary association in markets, and payment according to the value of the marginal product) as the highest goal. When he extended his advocacy of freedom

Figure 4-2a

The Correlation between the U.S. Inflation Rate (Consumer Price Index, 1982 = 100) and the Exchange Value of the Dollar (Trade-Weighted Index, 1982 = 100), 1970:I to 1990:III

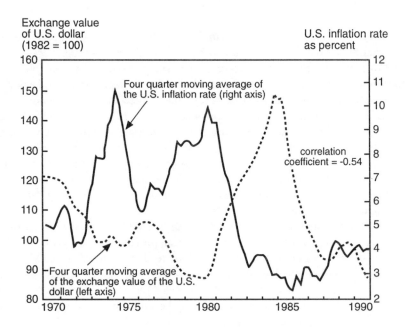

Note: The data are smoothed using a four-quarter moving average.

Source: Board of Governors of the Federal Reserve Systems

internationally, it meant that countries should be free to follow whatever domestic economic policies they choose to follow. These policies could be closed economy policies, to which the floating exchange rate would adjust.

In a second instance, Friedman was joined in his advocacy by the Keynesians in the Nixon White House and possibly others so inclined (Frazer 1988, Chapter 8). They were to be given the freedom to follow the domestic policy they selected, which included deemphasizing the U.S. responsibility for the dollar.[4]

Abandoning all this seemed proper on the part of the U.S. politicians and officials of that day. A part of the economic problem that began to emerge afterward is that only real cost and goods adjustments ultimately matter.

Figure 4-2b
Trends in the Exchange Value of the Dollar

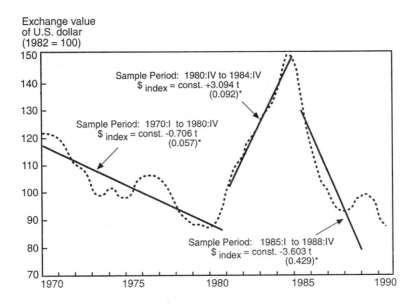

*Significantly different from zero at the 1 percent level of significance.

Including such internationally known proponents as Paul Volcker (in VG 1992), there were of course those who wanted to see the dollar as a sound currency for conducting transactions around the world. In the end, it all comes back to sound monetary policy of a disciplined, noninflationary sort which Friedman and gold-standard enthusiasts had advocated. Volcker said (in VG 1992, 233), "I think all authorities would agree that, at the end of the day, monetary policy will be a more powerful influence on exchange rates than intervention [in the foreign exchange market] which tells you where the final balance of power lies."

Phase 6 (Negotiated Policy). In the move toward floating rates, the United States and its leading trade partners appeared never to want full floating as a response to complete freedom in the pursuit of domestic policies. Rather negotiations and discussions at economic summits appears to move toward a way of managing world affairs concerning money and exchange rates.[5] The gist of the meetings has been toward a freeing up of trade policies and the pursuit of a zero-inflation goal, as in the Federal Republic of Germany and European Monetary System case.

In such negotiations concerning trade policy, price competition reenters the picture. There are questions about eliminating government subsidies to industry, and even the view that sustained devaluations of a currency are a means of subsidizing domestic industries. In these cases, the weight of the argument favors price adjustments and competition rather than trading off high inflation for a weakened currency.

Both the idea of price adjustments and that of the tradeoff can be seen in terms of the ratio of the purchasing power parity exchange rate [e.g., (P_{US}/P_{UK}) $\approx$ \$/£] to the market exchange rate (e.g., \$/£),

$$\frac{P_{US}/P_{UK}}{\$/£}$$

The empirical prospect is that this ratio will come to approximate the number 1—that if the exchange rate is fixed, the relative price levels will adjust, such that the ratio approximates the number 1; that if inflation occurs in the United States (ΔP_{US}), the dollar price of the pound will rise to adjust for it and keep the ratio in line.

Furthermore, in this context, we see why speculation in relatively free, "floating rate" exchange markets comes to center on speculation about what the monetary policy of the respective governments will be, that is,

$$\text{over } \pm\Delta\dot{M}^e{}_{US} \rightarrow \pm\Delta\dot{P}^e{}_{US}$$

$$\text{and } \pm\Delta\dot{M}^e{}_{UK} \rightarrow \pm\Delta\dot{P}^e{}_{UK}$$

Confronting the empirical prospect, Friedman reported that the ratio of the price relative (P_{US}/P_{UK}) to the exchange rate (\$/£) was approximately 1.12 in the secular trend context of the years 1868-1978. The analysis of data he offered is illustrated in Figure 4-3. Where the ratio hovered about the 100 year average, for the most part, until the disruptions of the 1930s and the U.K. experience with attempts at controlling policy variables by direct means (e.g., price controls, and devaluations of the pound through the IMF arrangements). When the currencies were allowed to float (phase 4), the ratio of (P_{US}/P_{UK}) to (\$/£) came back to the historical position it held much earlier.

The empirical result gives some historical perspective and support for "*the law of one price.*"[6] Namely, allowing for transportation and location costs, a market basket of goods will come to sell for approximately the same price at similar locations within the respective currency areas.

Phase 7 (The Private Sector). The accumulation of dollars abroad, the move toward floating exchange rates, and that of freeing up of trade contributed to the rise of foreign exchange dealers and markets and a greater mobility of privately owned capital. This has been such that the effects of central bank

Figure 4-3
**The Ratio of Purchasing Power Parity Exchange Rate (P_{US}/P_{UK}) to the
Market Exchange Rate ($\$/£$), 1868-1978**

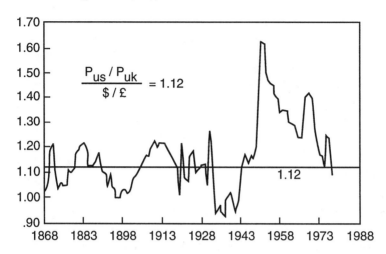

interventions in the foreign exchange markets are greatly reduced relative to the
private sector sources. Along such a line are statements by Bundesbank
officials, namely, "foreign exchange interventions only have a lasting effect
when supplemented by monetary policy" of a disciplined sort on the domestic
front. And, quoting Ellen Kennedy (1991, 93), it is "seldom helpful to shore
up a currency [through intervention in the foreign exchange market when that
currency is] under severe market pressure."

Viewing speculation in exchange markets as essentially speculation favoring
or disfavoring one set of monetary policies or another, and taking note that
private capital can flow toward the "strong currency," "low-inflation,"
productive country, central banks and their governments are pressed to avoid
spurious monetary policies. This is an example on the international side of
what I labeled "New York's revenge" and cited later as a special Bundesbank
effect.

Phase 8 (Tariffs). Following reaction to a stronger U.S. dollar in the 1981-
1985 period, Ronald Reagan's strong free-trade advocacy, and record U.S.
imports from abroad as a response to the strong dollar, tariff sentiments gained
strength in the Democrat-controlled congress as a means of protecting selected
U.S. industries from foreign competition. So it was in part as a counteraction
to the isolationist thrust, that we got the Baker-led move to bring down the
foreign exchange value of the dollar (Section 3.2e, Figure 4-2).[7] This was
with the view of making imports more costly to U.S. citizens and exports more
desirable to foreign nationals. However, there was no prior basis for expecting
that as large decline in the value of the dollar as occurred (Figure 4-2), would

have such a small and possibly unmeasurable effect on the U.S.'s trade balance. A complication was that some exported U.S. products and services may have included imported parts and components that become more costly in such a way as to impede decline in U.S. prices.

In addition, at a negotiating level, Secretary Baker sought to reinforce the declining dollar by pressuring the Bundesbank on its interest rate and money supply policies (Kennedy 1991, 56-74). What he sought was higher inflation for the Germans (or, in code words, "lower interest rates" and "faster economic growth"). In contrast, the Bundesbank's position (Kennedy 1991, 65) was that "there was no such thing as growth with inflation" and that "an inflation-free economy was the prerequisite for growth."

Further, as the U.S. tariff debate occurred, a focus came to bear on anticipations about the effects of the isolationist move, and in fact it was averted. However, in forming the anticipations, the argument shifted back to the 1930 Smoot-Hawley tariff act, passed by the isolationist Republicans of the day. The act came with the worldwide isolationist moves following the 1929 crash of the U.S. stock markets, related failures at reestablishing the gold standard, and the default on the German reparation payments for World War I. In the climate of the time, Britain, France, Italy, and Canada also enacted tariffs that depicted what was called a trade war.

The idea in referring back to the early 1930s events during the mid-1980s debate was that in the mid 1980s, success at imposing tariffs might bring about similar conditions to those of the 1930s. The debate provides an example of *psychological time*, which I introduced in Section 1.5. *It is, in the present case, that in the formulation of expectations in response to an important episode (such as that of the tariff matter in the U.S. Congress) the agents look back at some prior, comparable episode (such as the Smoot-Hawley tariff act) and not simply at the current episode with fixed lags in calendar time.*

Phase 9 (Avoiding Renewed Inflation). In trading a fall in the dollar's value for a reduction in monetary discipline at the close of the 1980s, very little room was left to the Federal Reserve to confront the reduced spending in the U.S. in the fall of 1990, as uncertainty came about in response to United States budget settlements and the Iraqi invasion of Kuwait. Further, as the U.S. economy moved into the 1990-91 recession and the sluggish recovery that followed, the Federal Reserve gave the impression of avoiding efforts that would renew the inflation and further weaken the dollar (e.g., Figure 3-4).

The U.K. economy also confronted some renewal of inflation at the close of the 1980s (Figure 2-1b), recession, and the need to avoid inflation. Their need was compounded by the U.K.'s entry into the European Monetary System (EMS) in October of 1990 at the DM/£ par rate of 2.95 (or £/DM rate of approximately 0.34). Looking back at the IMF, exchange-rate mechanism (Figure 4-1), we have by comparison Figure 4-4. The pound was initially permitted to move within a range of 6 percent in either direction (i.e., from a low of 2.77 DM per pound [or 0.36 pounds per mark] to a high of 3.12 DM

Figure 4-4
Exchange Rate between the Pound and the DM on U.K. Entry into EMS

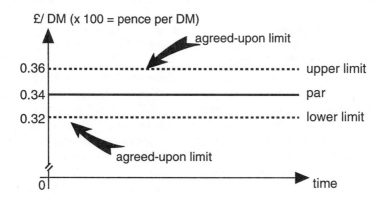

per pound [or 0.32 pounds per mark]). As seen in phase 11, however, the U.K. Prime Minister John Major suspended Britain's link to the exchange rate mechanism, and, by the time of phase 12, the ERM had undergone even further stresses in what appears in part III of the text as EC efforts to force the compliance of the domestic economies to suit the presumed requirements for European integration.

Phase 10 (The EMS). As indicated at greater length in Section 4.4, the EMS's existence came about in 1979, as a core of European Economic Community (EEC) countries joined together with a view to creating a European monetary system. Its prospects took on added significance in 1989, when an EEC committee's Delors Report appeared (Report 1989, and Tygesen 1989). The Report offered the prospect of a new central bank for Europe and even the prospect of attaining a "common currency" for EMS member countries with a zero-inflation rate goal.

The Report and the prospects it contained harked back to the post-World War II IMF arrangements and the super-central bank prospects it had (phase 2). There was a mechanism consisting of fixed exchange rates, a hard currency (the DM in the EMS case) to which other currencies could be tied, and an official currency unit called the European Currency Unit (ECU) with which trade imbalances could be settled. In addition, there was the prospect of a monetary authority that would have powers extending to control over the fiscal policies of the EMS member states. In short, the EMS came on line with a very strong IMF orientation, as to exchange rates and central bank power, and a very strong fiscal-policy oriented view of the central bank such as we encounter at the Bank of England (Section 3.3d).

Thatcher—the U.K.'s monetarist-oriented, prime minister from May 1979 until November 1990—initially reacted negatively to the Report's proposals, the loss of sovereignty prospect (the freedom issue, phase 5), and then hesitantly announced the U.K.'s entry into the EMS in October 1990. One argument for her doing so was that the British government might have more influence on the future outcome of a European monetary system. Even so, Thatcher had been opposed by some of her own ministers for her hard line toward the U.K.'s entry into EMS, and in the end, her hesitance led to her loss of the party leadership (Young 1991, Chapter 24).

In any case, what direction a European monetary system would ultimately take became an issue. Would a central bank emerge with operations along M-orientation lines (voluntary association and all)? Would it emerge along Keynesian lines (the fiscal policy, i-orientation line)? Would European integration move the world toward major currency blocks consisting of the DM-anchored ECU, the dollar ($), and the yen (¥)? At the simplest level, the notion of a "common currency" had great appeal.

To many in Britain and on the continent, the vision of a common currency was that of a single system of currency notes and coins to replace the jumbled numbers on the display boards at banks and corner exchanges in London and at the larger European entry ports. There was the prospect of crossing borders and entering the shops of one or another of the states and using a currency free of the exchange rate costs, hassles, and uncertainties over prices that had accompanied the exchange of currencies in EMS member countries.

Below this appealing surface, however, was Thatcher's voice, which had been a part of the leadership in the late 1970s and early 1980s, with respect to the freedom issue and the taming of inflation by monetarist means. Consequently, she saw the greater complexity.

Phase 11 (Ten Days in September). Fifteen months after entering the EMS, at a meeting of European Community (EC) member heads of state in the Dutch town of Maastricht, the British were able to insert an "opt out" clause to a new EC treaty. Taken up later, the Maastricht treaty provided for steps toward monetary and political union, except that in early June, Denmark's voters narrowly opposed ratification of the treaty. Their doing so left open a number of questions and prospects for other referenda.

Shortly after the Denmark vote, the French scheduled one to reaffirm support for currency union. However, as the time for the French referendum approached, the outcome of the voting in France, too, appeared narrow and uncertain and strains with respect to currency alignments began to appear, first in some non-EC member Nordic countries, which had attempted to tie their currencies to the Mark, and then in Germany's effort to support Italy's currency in accordance with its commitment to the EMS's exchange rate grid.

The week of guarded uncertainty started when Finland floated its currency. But, more dramatically, the Bank of Sweden (the Riksbank) moved to defend the krona. First, they did so by raising the bank rate from 16 to 24, and then to 75 percent. The finance minister Anne Wibble said, "The Sky's the limit." So, it was soon to be. As the matter turned out, Sweden raised its bank rate further to 500 percent. Although less dramatic in the extent of its actions, the Bank of England soon followed suit to defend the pound by first raising its bank rate from 10 to 12 percent then to 15 percent.

Ten days of crisis and realignments started on Friday. A chronology follows:

Friday, 11 September. The Bundesbank and the Bank of Italy were unable to stop the lira from falling below the floor imposed by the EMS's exchange rate mechanism.

Sunday, 13 September. There were two events. First, after an unprecedented Sunday meeting of its Council, the Bundesbank announced a 1/4 percentage point cut to 9 1/2 percent in the lombard rate and a 1/2 percentage point cut in the discount rate. Bundesbank president Helmut Schlesinger explained that the Bank had been caught in a "foreign exchange trap." It arose from Germany's obligation to support the lira on currency markets under ERM rules though German inflation was still too high and money supply targets were not being met. (*Financial Times*, 15 September, 1992, 1)

Second, Brussels officials announced that the pound—along with the DM, the French franc, and some other EMS countries—would be revalued by 3.5 percent while the lira was devalued by the same percent for an effective devaluation of 7.0 percent. Also, at a meeting near London, EC foreign ministers warned about a financial and political crisis if the Maastricht treaty on European union was rejected by the French referendum on September 20th.

Monday, 14 September. European share and bond prices rose temporarily on the news of the cut in German discount and lombard rates, even as some observers expressed disappointment over the small cut in the short-term rates. Also, on Monday, Bundesbank president Schlesinger said "there is no room for more." (Later inactions confirmed his position.)

Tuesday, 15 September. The pound hit a new low against the DM within the EMS's exchange rate mechanism. Also, the German news agency, DPA, reported that Bundesbank president Helmut Schlesinger had suggested that weekend realignments in Europe's exchange rate mechanism had not gone far enough to reduce tensions in the currency markets.

Wednesday, 16 September. Sterling's membership in the European exchange rate mechanism was suspended after the largest assault by currency speculators on the European ERM since the EMS's formation in 1979.

Thursday, 17 September. As the week approached its end, the markets settled down to await the outcome of voting in France on Sunday. The following occurred: the European Commission mounted a defense of the single currency idea, in anticipation of voting in France on Sunday; the lira underwent a "temporary withdrawal" from the ERM; the Bundesbank declined to deliver further cuts in interest rates; Spain's peseta was devalued by 5 percent; and the Bank of England pared its bank rate to 10 percent. Referring to the week's activities, the *Wall Street Journal* (18 September, p. 1) noted that "Currency Traders Play High Stakes Against Central Banks."

Sunday, 20 September.   French voters gave a reprieve to the Maastricht treaty by a narrow 50.95 percent-to-49.05 percent margin.   It offered further uncertain prospects for restoring movement toward the EC goals of economic and monetary union.

Reflecting on the days of crisis, some recalled the time the gold window was closed.   In doing so, the British chancellor deplored the exchange-rate chaos. Others noted that routine trading of currencies for commercial transactions, as opposed to speculation, counted for only a small 5 or 10 percent of currency transactions.   France and Germany were still seen as trying to save the EMS's plans.   Mr. John Major, the British prime minister, on the other hand, was calling for the reform of the ERM.   In his hesitancies about Britain's return, there was the suggestion that Major was becoming a Thatcherite (*Financial Times*, 22 September, 1992).   At the same time, the Bundesbank's Helmut Schlesinger was serving notice that the reentry of the lira and sterling to the ERM would call for negotiation.

Meanwhile, Milton Friedman (*Wall Street Journal*, 22 September 1992) once again chose an opportunity to point out the frailty of fixed exchange rate systems for countries with disparate political and economic systems.   For him, it was the freedom and sovereignty issues all over again.   As the last days of September passed, the lira and the pound were still declining.

These days of September 1992 passed, Sweden had apparently averted the run from its currency, although the actual yields on short- and long-dated market instruments did not approach the heights of 500 percent to which the Riksbank raised the bank rate.   On the other hand, the lira and the pound were still declining.   Against the dollar, the pound was down over 14 percent from a recent high of almost $2.00.   Looking backward at the incredible support operation, which spanned a fortnight in September, the *Wall Street Journal* (1 October 1992) cited estimates that the German, British, Italian, Spanish, and Swedish central banks had on balance lost between $4 and $6 billion to the currency trading operations.

Phase 12 (Nine Months Later in 1993).   Nine months after the September 1992 episode, the British Parliament faced its vote on the Maastricht Treaty, and thus the move to a super-central bank and a single currency, and the French franc became the focus of the struggle with the ERM.   Even as the Parliament gave John Major a narrow vote of confidence and approved the Treaty on July 23, the speculation built against the franc.   The French, who had been a main player with the Germans, were containing inflation at 2 percent but running a record 11.6 percent unemployment rate.   Doubting that the French and a few others had the willpower to stay with the deutsche mark, speculators continued to dump French, Danish, Spanish, Portuguese and Belgian currencies in exchange for the EMS's anchor currency.

In this atmosphere, the central banks again appeared unable to maintain the prior ERM arrangement.   So EC finance ministers, meeting in Brussels over the August 1 weekend emerged with another of the dramatic EC announcements. Most notably, the ministers and central bankers agreed that seven of the nine currencies in the ERM could rise and fall as much as 15 percent above and 15 below the agreed-upon-par rates.

This was in contrast to the plus and minus 2.25 percent bank which had been maintained for the French franc and most of the other currencies. Confronting its own problems of a 4.3 percent inflation rate, east and west integration, and a fast-growing money stock, the Bundesbank steadfastly concentrated on its main task.

To be sure, the stresses of 1992 and 1993 on the ERM casts some doubts on the outcomes and targets set by the Maastricht Treaty and on the progress toward European unification. More fundamentally, however, I pursue the differences in the Friedman-monetarist orientation and the Keynesian one and ask a few questions; namely, will a two-tier monetary system emerge from the Maastricht arrangements, which were fractured by the events of September 1992? Will those countries most able to maintain a tie to the DM hold together while others remain on the side? What, if any, difference does the central banks hypothesis H_{CB} (Sections 1.1 and 3.1b) and the alternative approaches (Section 3.3) make in the establishment, organization, and function of a central bank?

4.1b Balances of International Payments

Like many other data sets, balances of international payments were more a concept than carefully recorded sets of data before World War II. Since then, some have come to be stated in detail and to be carefully annotated (Kemp 1975). However, even allowing for that reality, I still simplify and simply point to basic, balance-of-payments accounting notions, preliminary to illustrating matters at hand.

Quite briefly, a country's balance of payment is a statement of changes in accounts over a period of time, such as a year or quarter, for one country in relation to the rest of the world. As just suggested, the principle accounts, and the ones I focused upon above a certain line, are the "trade" account (or the slightly broader measure known as the "current account") and the capital account. Below them is the "official settlements balance." This includes some purchases and sales of securities between central banks for official purposes, but mostly the flows reported under official settlements are flows of monetary reserves. Historically, there were movements of gold and titles to gold. For much of the history since the U.S. Federal Reserve came about, and particularly following congressional actions in 1933 prohibiting U.S. citizens from owning gold, changes have been made in titles to gold, which was held several floors below street level at the Federal Reserve Bank of New York. Overall, in reference to the balance of payments, for anything given up (say, exported), a country gets credits (denoted as +'s) and for anything acquired a country gets debits (denoted as −'s).

As implied, a line can be drawn across a balance of payments statement, usually below the capital account, and any imbalance in the recordings above the line (say a net deficit, −'s > +'s) must be offset below the line. Hence, there must be balance overall, except for errors and omissions. The plus amounts balance the minus amounts, expressed in a country's own currency.

A simplified balance of payments statements, such as just described, may be as shown in Figure 4-5. As shown there, a line can be drawn on the balance of payments statement and the net imbalance above the line must be met by an offsetting balance below the line. We speak of a surplus (net +'s) or a deficit (net −'s) above the line. The surplus then must be offset by exports below or the deficit above by imports below.

The desirable picture from a world community point of view is for countries to have balances in the balance of payments, at least in the long run. However, from either a gold standard or business tradition, a "favorable" balance of payments meant exports on the trade account and imports on the monetary reserve account. Under the old gold-standard conditions, a country sought to sell goods and acquire gold as a desirable asset. The competition between countries then was to sell goods and services and to acquire gold. These matters appear in the history to have been set aside for a time in the Keynesian era, when the financial trappings were set aside from the real goods side. In some measure, the sentiments reflected Keynes's hint in the *General Theory* (1936, 159) that capital development should not be "a by-product of the activities of a casino." But, returning to the financial matters, weak currencies mean a failure to export goods and services at competitive prices and weak currencies usually mean unemployment and a loss of status among nations.

Figure 4-5
Simplified Balance of Payments Statement

	Credit (+)	Debit (−)
1. Trade		
2. Capital Short-term Long-term		above the line balance (net)
3. Monetary reserves (gold, paper gold, international reserves generally, as case may be)		below the line balance (net)

As stated, official balances-of-payments statements overall, such as described, were slow to come about. Even so, their presence is implied in analyses of trade, central banking, and in international banking. In the broad historical context, deficits on the trade accounts were met by the export of monetary reserves (principally gold at times and even paper gold, where the IMF has added standard drawing rights as a means of official settlements). The use of the label "a payments deficit" has meant a deficit met by the official settlements (say, e.g., an export of gold). As flows of capital, viewed as financial instruments, have grown, particularly in the United States in the 1980s, attention was given to the trade account and the U.S. trade deficit. Meeting such deficits by private-sector capital movements grew in proportion to the official settlements role after the United States closed its gold window and moved the world toward the managed and somewhat dirty float.

4.2 PRICE LEVELS AND THE FLOWS OF INTERNATIONAL RESERVES AND CAPITAL

The acceptance of assets to serve as international monetary reserves and a fixed exchange rate arrangement by several major countries provided a mechanism both for regulating price averages and for facilitating adjustments in the countries balances of payments. This mechanism—which so characterized the years from Waterloo to World War I, a time in the interwar period, and the Bretton Woods period until 1971—remained somewhat intact at the close of the twentieth century. Exchange rates were not exactly adjusted, as under the initial IMF arrangements, but the managed float and voluntary cooperation between countries led to very much the same results as the old exchange rate arrangements; namely, trade imbalances call forth price-level adjustments.

The old gold-flows mechanism (whether with "adjustable peg" or "managed float" rates) can be outlined for two trading partners or one country and the rest of the world (say, P_{US}/P_{UK} or $P_{US}/P_{rest\ of\ world}$). Beginning with two price levels and a constant at some base time,

$$P_{US} - P_{UK} + \text{const.} = 0$$

Following this base time, monetary reserves are attracted toward the United States when

$$P_{US} - P_{UK} + \text{const.} < 0 \qquad \text{(flow toward United States)} \qquad (1)$$

and toward the U.K. when

$$P_{US} - P_{UK} + \text{const.} > 0 \qquad \text{(flow toward U.K.)} \qquad (2)$$

In effect, the more favorable prices in the United States such as implied by inequality (1), would attract reserves to the United States because of an increase in the U.S. exports to the United Kingdom and a decrease in U.S. imports from the United Kingdom. The relatively more favorable prices in the United Kingdom, as implied by inequality (2), would induce an outflow of reserves from the United States because of a decrease in U.S. exports to the United Kingdom and an increase in U.S. imports from the United Kingdom. I proceed from that position even though I know full well that: (1) there are people at the Federal Reserve, the Bank of England, and so on that manage the reserves; (2) these people react to their governments, and possibly to what is acceptable to the financial markets; (3) participants in the private sector's foreign exchange, money, capital, and real goods markets are second guessing the policy actions and inactions, plus their results; and (4) ultimately governments are responsible for guiding monetary policies in a world I depict in terms of reserves and capital flows.

In addition to the respective price levels (P_{US}/P_{UK}, etc), there are the other variables for the respective countries domestic reserves (R_{US}, R_{UK}, etc., denoted R_o, as the case may be), the corresponding money stocks (M_{US}, M_{UK}, etc., or simply M, where M_{US} and so on should be clear from the context), the respective reserve ratios (effectively $r = R_o/M$, for country A, country B, etc.), and the corresponding money multipliers ($1/r$, etc., and say, $1/r = 5$ for $r = 0.20$). In brief, there is the money demand side (e.g., Figures 1-2 and 1-6 and the quantity theory expression $M = k(. . .)PQ$) and the money supply side (helicopter money).[8]

It is important to look again at the theoretic expression, $M = k(. . .)PQ$ and the bank reserve equation introduced in Section 3.3b. In that equation, gold flows were a main determinant of monetary reserves, but the final arbiter was the central bank with its open market operations in the government securities or commercial securities markets. In a simple form,

$$R_o = G + \text{residual}$$

Here R_o is reserves available to the public's banks, and G is gold (or "paper gold" and international monetary reserves generally). In the regulatory mechanism, the gold- or reserve-flow (ΔG) shows up as an inflow of reserves (ΔR_o). Under fractional reserve banking, such as has characterized the historical periods dealt with here, there is a multiplier ($1/r$) effect on the money stock; that is $\Delta R_o (1/r) = \Delta M$, and so on.

The regulatory mechanism is as shown in Figure 4-6. Note, at the start of period 1, a condition where $-\Delta P_{US}/P_{UK}$. It leads to a more favorable U.S. export position on the trade account of the balance of payments. The capital account in the balance of payments aside, for the time being, there is an inflow of monetary reserves to the United States. If the U.S. central bank takes no

Figure 4-6
A Regulatory Mechanism with Respect to Relative-Price Levels

Period 1. Fixed Exchange Rate System,
$-\Delta \ P_{US}/P_{UK}$ (or rest of world)

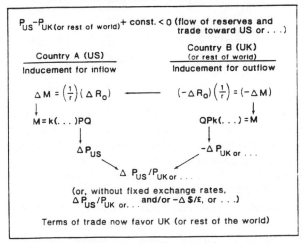

Period 2. Fixed Exchange Rate System,
$\Delta \ P_{US}/P_{UK}$ (or rest of world)

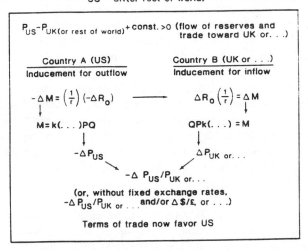

Figure 4-6 (continued)

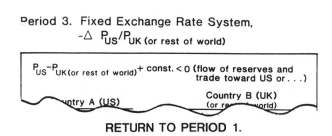

Period 3. Fixed Exchange Rate System,
$-\Delta \ P_{US}/P_{UK}$ (or rest of world)

$P_{US}-P_{UK \text{(or rest of world)}}+ \text{const.} < 0$ (flow of reserves and trade toward US or . . .)

Country A (US)

Country B (UK) (or rest of world)

RETURN TO PERIOD 1.

action to neutralize these by the use of offsetting open market operations, there is upward pressure on the U.S. price level. The reverse is going on in the United Kingdom. Reserves are declining and so on, provided it wishes to maintain a competitive trade position.

By the start of period 2, matters have reversed, $\Delta P_{US}/P_{UK}$. The terms of trade favor the United Kingdom. Provided the Bank of England does not neutralize the inflow of reserves, their condition, too, is soon reversed, $-\Delta P_{US}/P_{UK}$. We are back to the start of period 1.

Competitive forces in the real goods and product markets are present. However, as we have reported earlier, exchange-rate changes can be substituted for inflation-rate changes, and at times countries may be reluctant to deflate. They may, instead, attempt to get trading partners to inflate their currencies. When this was actually tried by the United States in the 1970s, 1980s, and early 1990s with the Federal Republic of Germany and the Japanese government it did not work so well. The prospects, since Keynes wrote about "sticky prices," point back to the old prospect of price adjustments.

With the decline in the importance of a primary reserve asset—such as gold (or even the gold backing of reserves on deposit at the central bank, as in the U.S. case before the closing of the gold window)—the pursuit of reserves declines in importance and the maintenance of a "hard currency" status gains in importance, as in the case of Germany (phase 9). It implies monetary discipline (Figure 4-2), a favorable-trade position, and a capital-inflow position. Notably, in the terms used in Figure 4-4, it is as shown in Figure 4-7.

In ranging over the phases of the managed financial system since World War II, the moves from "pegged" (Figure 4-1) to managed exchange rates (phases 3, 4, 5, 6, and 7), and the further freeing up of world trade under Margaret Thatcher and Ronald Reagan, the apparent growth in the abundance of private-sector capital has given it an upper hand in terms of capital movements from one country to another and in terms of the determination of exchange rates. Governments can no longer both pursue accommodative/inflationary domestic

Figure 4-7
The Balance of Payments and Capital Flows

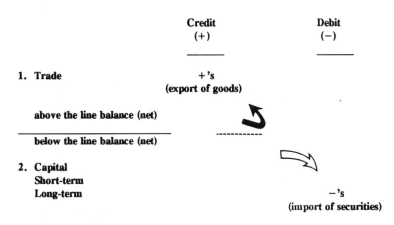

	Credit (+)	Debit (−)
1. Trade	+'s (export of goods)	
above the line balance (net)		
below the line balance (net)		
2. Capital Short-term Long-term		−'s (import of securities)

policies and use resources on a adequate scale to peg exchange rates without regard to the abundance of private capital funds and economic realities of production and efficiency in the respective domestic economies (Melamed 1988, 344, 399, 407). When the private sector becomes suspicious of the sincerity and soundness of a government's position, there is little the government can do, short of using military force, to stop an outflow of capital funds and a decline in the exchange value of its currency.

4.3 FOREIGN EXCHANGE MARKETS AND POLICY-CONNECTED VARIABLES

A portion of the money balances of each country engaged in foreign trade is exchanged for those of other countries, also engaged in foreign trade. The portions depend on the extent of the trade of each country in relation to its domestic economy. Both the trade and the economies are thought of as growing, in the presence of technological change (Frazer 1994a, Sections 1.4b, 3.2e). As trade and capital flows balance out, there is no surplus or deficit of a country's currency in the exchange of goods, services, and capital.

The exchanges of currency are variously made through banks and other facilities in financial centers. The larger banks operate special departments, which employ traders who are devoted full time to the purchase and sale of currencies with speculative gains from trading in mind. As a consequence, these departments serve the useful function of making and maintaining both spot markets, where currencies are more immediately exchanged, and forward markets, where currencies are purchased or sold at a current rate for future delivery.

The forward markets help exporters cover themselves (or hedge, or make a counterbalancing transaction) against losses due to potential changes in exchange rates between the time of entering into a commitment and discharging it. However, the purpose in elucidating these arrangements is not the arrangements themselves but rather that of taking further note of legends, myths, and reality with respect to how the central banks and governments enter in relationship to the foreign exchange and money markets. This purpose revives the prospect of government control of exchange rates, the price-level/exchange-rate "trade-off," and the virtual impossibility of separating by artificial means the policy-connected variables in Equation (1) of Section 2.5.

4.3a Covered Interest Arbitrage, Capital Flows, and Exchange Rate Volatility

A portfolio manager confronted with the opportunity to purchase ninety-one-day Treasury bills in London or New York provides an illustration. If the rate on these bills is higher in London than in New York, then the manager may get a greater return without additional risk by buying the bills in London, provided there is assurance of eliminating risk by converting pounds into dollars at a given rate at the maturity date of the bills. This particular covering of risk is called covered interest arbitrage. It comes about when the possibility of a loss from exchange rates changes over the time to maturity of the investment is covered by a purchase of forward exchange to coincide with the time to maturity.

The profitability of moving funds from one financial center to another depends on (1) the yield spread between investments of relatively comparable risk and maturity in the respective centers and (2) the relation of the two currencies in the spot and forward exchange markets. The American investor wishing to switch from U.S. Treasury bills to U.K. Treasury bills, because of the yield spread, then may first purchase sterling in the spot market in order to buy British Treasury bills in London. At the same time, the portfolio manager must execute a forward sale of sterling to coincide with the maturity of the investment in order to ensure some extra return from the yield differential and to avoid the effect of any possible depreciation of sterling that might offset the gain. There is zero interest arbitrage incentive when the gain (loss) from the interest differential is just offset by the discount (premium) on forward exchange.

The incentive and the tendency toward parity between the yield differential and the discount (or premium) can be simply illustrated, as in Figure 4-8. There the interest differential in percent per annum between the yield on a particular type of security in the domestic market and the yield on a comparable type of security of the foreign country is shown on the vertical axis. In addition, a positive differential indicates a higher interest rate in the

Figure 4-8
Interest Arbitrage Incentive: Foreign Yields Less Domestic Yields, Plus the
Discount (−) or Premium (+) on Forward Exchange

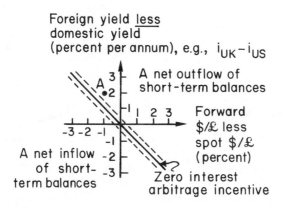

foreign country and a negative differential indicates a lower interest rate in the foreign country.

On the horizontal, the discount (minus) or premium (plus) on the forward exchange of the foreign country is shown as a percentage per annum. The interest parity line is the diagonal that intersects the lines representing zero interest differential and the zero discount or premium. Any point on the interest parity line represents an equilibrium for the yield spread between rates in the respective countries and the discount or premium on forward exchange. For instance, a point on the interest parity line corresponding to a 2 percent interest differential also corresponds to a 2 percent discount on the forward exchange axis. Now, when the discount or premium on forward exchange gets out of line with the zero interest arbitrage incentive (or so-called interest parity), a positive (or negative) incentive emerges and the switching of funds from one financial center to the other becomes profitable, without the need to incur additional risk. This can be illustrated by reference to point A in Figure 4-8.

At point A in Figure 4-8, the yield in the foreign country is two percentage points higher than the yield on a similar type security in the domestic economy, and the forward discount is only one percentage point. The net outflow of funds (the reverse of the movement of the short-term capital as securities) could appear on the balance of payments accounts of Figure 4-4, illustrated in figure 4-9.

The lesson concerns the way short-term funds (and hence the reverse movement of capital viewed as financial markets instruments) can be moved around by changes in the relation between interest rates in the financial centers "under some circumstances" and in the short run. These qualifications are

Figure 4-9
Capital Flows and Monetary Reserves

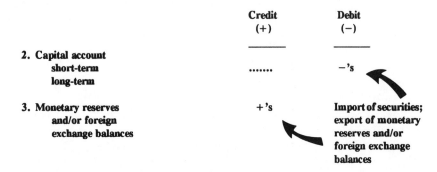

	Credit (+)	Debit (−)
2. Capital account short-term long-term	....	−'s
3. Monetary reserves and/or foreign exchange balances	+'s	Import of securities; export of monetary reserves and/or foreign exchange balances

needed because contracts may be denominal in various currencies for various lengths of time, because the covering of all risk is not possible, and because sizable capital flows may come about exclusive of the interest rate incentive as a result of such changes as were perceived in the U.S. economy by foreign investors in the 1984-85 period and in Germany in the 1991-92 period. In the United States case (Frazer 1988, 684-685), the inflow of capital funds accrued even as the short- and long-term rates were declining in the U.S., as the spreads/between the U.S. and foreign rates narrowed, and as the U.S. inflation rate declined (Figure 2-2a).[9] In the German case, Germany moved from being an exposter of capital funds toward being a more intense user of capital funds following the unification of the eastern and western parts of Germany. At the time, the Federal Republic of Germany not only contained inflation and maintained a strong currency at the same time, but, after the frantic weeks of crisis depicted in phase 11, Germany had both the lowest money market and ten-year bond rates in Europe.

As the U.S. and FRG examples indicate, attracting capital funds may be more a matter of extending the markets perception of a stable economy, with a potential for profitable production, than high nominal interest rates. It should also be noted that, as indicated by the broken lines in Figure 4-8, on strictly yield-differential and spot-forward differential grounds the incentive must be in excess of a transaction cost of one-half percent per annum before it becomes worthwhile to move funds from one market to another because of transaction costs.

In the preceding illustration, the movement of short-term funds abroad on a sufficiently large scale would tend to restore the parity between the yield spread and the discount (or premium) on forward exchange. Although I doubt the power of such a movement in relation to other market forces in the short-run time frame of Figure 4-8, the movement of funds in the illustration could work to restore parity in two ways: (1) it could increase the forward discount by way of a price-raising force in the market for spot exchange and a price-depressing force in the forward market and (2) it could lower the interest rate differential as funds were transferred from one market to another. In other words, the tendency in effect would be for any arbitrarily selected point, such as A, to be propelled into the locus of points corresponding to zero incentive by setting in motion adjustments in interest rates in the respective countries and in the spot and forward exchange markets.

The example of covered interest arbitrage focuses on Treasury bills. However, as Kubarych pointed out in 1978, "There are . . . many short-term financial instruments in the U.S. and in other major countries available to international investors and arbitragers" (Kubarych 1978, 44). A decade later, Arthur Burns (the Federal Reserve chairman from 1970 to 1978) pointed to the numerous variants of covered interest arbitrage (Burns 1988, 30-32). Among them were "currency and interest rate swaps" involving firms and internationally linked financial institutions.

Continuing on the broader aspects of covering against risk from exchange-rate volatility, Volcker (the Fed chairman, 1979-87) points out, "There is no sure or costless way of hedging against all uncertainties." He says (in VG 1992, 293), "the only sure beneficiaries [of exchange rate volatility] are those manning the trading desks and inventing the myriad of new devices to reduce the risks--or to facilitate speculation." Along similar lines, Toyoo Gyohten says (in VG 1992, 307): "In the market itself, traders strongly prefer volatility, because they make more money out of it than from stability. Businessmen, by contrast, prefer stability because it allows them to plan ahead."

Turning more toward the stable economic order, Volcker recalls the traditional case for an open economic order. He points out that it rests on the idea of "comparative advantage," namely: "that countries and regions concentrate on producing what they can do relatively efficiently, taking account of their different resources, the supply and skills of their labor, and the availability of capital." Continuing Volcker says, "But it is hard to see how business can effectively calculate where lasting comparative advantage lies when relative costs and prices among countries are subject to exchange rate swings of 25 to 50 percent or more." (Volcker in VG 1992, 293)

4.3b Exchange Rates, Interest Rates, and Central Bank Matters

The discussion of zero interest arbitrage incentive and incentives for net outflows and inflows of short-term financial claims provides the framework for examining the effect of interest rate and exchange rate changes on the movement of short-term balances, and it points out possible interrelationships between yields in the financial markets of one country and those in the financial markets of other countries. In addition, Figure 4-8 and the accompanying balance of payments exercise harks back to the earlier time of central bank operations when interest rate movements were thought to be quite powerful in their effects and readily attainable on the part of central bankers. Little was said about the mysteries of the business and Keynes's himself thought the "bank rate" to be potentially quite powerful.

In such an orientation, there are two possibilities for indirect monetary control over the movement of short-term balances and possibly even long-term balances. One is quite old and traditional. It involves an increase in the rate on short-term funds on the domestic side. In reference to Figure 4-8, this would narrow the yield differential between the domestic and foreign financial centers. In doing so, it would also reduce the incentive for an outflow of short term balances. If the differential were narrow enough (or negative), depending on the discount (or premium) on forward exchange, a rise in the domestic rate may even provide the incentive for a net inflow of currency reserves and other short-term balances (or even gold, in its day).

Although Montagu Norman, the closed-mouth governor of the Bank of England from 1920-1944, doubted the interest rate he controlled had this power, the central banking legend has lived on in many quarters. Indeed, it was about in the crises days of September 1992 and even before. As reported earlier, Sweden raised its bank rate from 16 to 24 to 75, and then to the unheard-of level of 500 percent to stop a run against its currency and an accompanying outflow of capital funds. For its part, the Bank of England raised its bank rate from 10 to 12 to 15 percent with the hope of raising market rates and averting the run from the pound, all without noticeable effects. In the terms of Figure 4-5, the hoped-for effect would appear in Figure 4-10:

The prospects for even greater effects from interest-rate changes also abounded in the months approaching phase 11. During them, the U.S. and the U.K. governments bashed the Bundesbank, ostensibly for not lowering interest rates to achieve "faster economic growth."[10] All this was, of course, in the face of "the Bundesbank effect." As lamented in the *Wall Street Journal* (25 September 1992, A8): "Oh, sure, Nicholas Brady is still at the Treasury helm,

Figure 4-10
Monetary Reserves and Capital Flows: An Old English Lesson

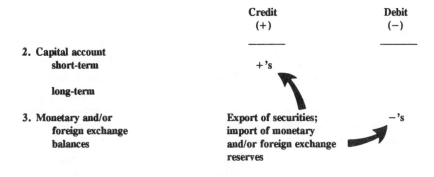

an Ahab chasing 'lower interest rates' around the globe. But his credibility with financial markets is somewhere south of the Italian government's."

Still another possibility for monetary intervention comes from open market transactions in foreign currencies, as discussed earlier. Under the February 1962 authorization of phase 3, the New York Federal Reserve Bank could purchase and sell foreign currencies through spot or forward transactions in the open market at home and abroad with a view to influencing market conditions. The power here too may be greatly exaggerated, but other central banks haveit and the prospects for using this power remain and appear in the print media on occasion, as they did in phase 11.

Of course, the difficulty with respect to the legend, the exaggerated power, and the print-media reporting is the interdependence of the monetary and other economic variables and the tendency to view some key variables as if they were separate from others for control purposes. As noted, (1) interest rates are intimately linked to inflation rates and inflationary prospects, although more at some times than at others (FS 1982, 572); (2) the inflation rates and prospects are linked to the exchange rates (Figure 4-2); and (3) all are linked to the money and credit aggregates and their prospects.

Indeed, the actual exchange rates depend very much on the currency traders and speculators, since phase 4, and speculations about what particular currencies are going to do in the markets depend very much on the anticipated monetary policies and the success of the respective countries as reflected in their balances of payment. The speculators, in such a context, process a lot of information bearing on the credibility of central bankers and their governments and the future results of their actions as they may be reflected in currency values.[11]

Central bankers especially may like the markets to be orderly in order to better serve currency exchanges and not simple speculators. With this in mind, they may justify intervention to correct disorderly conditions and they may attempt to mitigate speculative swings in some currencies that have been thought to go beyond the parity price.

With the added uncertainty that came to surround monetary policy after the United States' 1971 closing of the gold window, the speculative trading in foreign exchange was broadened by the creation of futures markets in currencies and some highly liquid money markets instruments such as U.S. Treasury bills and the IMF's SDRs (a reserve asset for selected, official purposes). These markets, like those for commodities such as corn and wheat, gave small speculators a chance to enter the markets in currencies under conditions where the forward markets operated by banks are confined to large, asset-sized participants. The first such futures markets was in fact created in 1971 at the Chicago Mercantile Exchange. And such have been created elsewhere since.

Pieces on the foreign exchange markets contain all the elements of other financial markets, such as those for stocks and bonds and shorter dated instruments where interest rates are determined. First, the marketable debt instruments are highly homogeneous (or can be placed in groups of homogeneous instruments) and characterized by their liquidity (ease of conversion to cash, possibly without loss of principal or purchasing power), where, by contrast, real capital is very illiquid and may have highly specialized uses. Second, financial markets clear rapidly, whereas real goods markets adjust less rapidly to changes. Said differently, the traders in the financial markets process information quite rapidly, particularly in the presence of the widespread use of electronic equipment, display screens, and the like, and this is reflected immediately in the exchange rates, whereas changes in the trade accounts for countries may respond much slower to changes.

To be sure, there is much more than simply direct changes in price levels and exchange rates that are at hand, as anticipations enter the picture. As I indicate, exchange rates are connected to speculation with respect to anticipated monetary policies and inflation rates, and the rapid processing of information. Toyoo Gyohten, a career economist in the Japanese Ministry of Finance until retirement in 1989, offers a summary statement along such lines:

Factors that market practitioners take into consideration certainly have changed over time, and on the whole they have multiplied almost beyond our calculation. In the early days of the floating regime, we thought that medium- and long-term elements such purchasing power parities and balance of payments adjustments would still have a major influence. But then short-term capital flows and interest rate differentials [also connected to inflation rates] became very important. But aside from that, there was the explosion of information technology, which promoted quick shifts of focus. One moment the market will be focusing on interest rates, the next on balance of payments data, and then on political developments. So it is difficult to pinpoint the decisive factors in short-term movements [once anticipator prospects later]. (Gyohten in VG 1992, 161)

Where Gyohten waxes somewhat metaphysically about short-term exchange rate movements, we may also recall his reporting on fine tuning and standard econometric models (note 10).

4.3c Supply and Demand

There are ordinary notions of supply and demand, and there are less ordinary notions, as shown for a currency in Figure 4-11. All other things being equal, a rise in the dollar price of pounds can be expected to result in the offer of a larger quantity of pounds supplied, and similarly a rise in the dollar price of pounds may be expected to result in a reduced quantity of pounds demanded. These quantities of course are being viewed quite unreasonably as being measured in the unit of exchange with exchange-rate changes themselves having no influence on the purchasing power of pounds. In other words, the pound

Figure 4-11
The Dollar Exchange Rate and the Supply of and Demand for Pounds

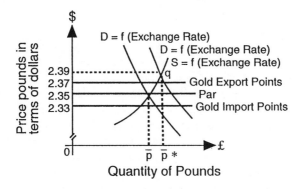

Quantity of Pounds

is going down in value, but its purchasing power in the United Kingdom is rendered unchanged by extremely artificial means (or, said differently, the exchange rate is increasing, but it is doing so without any decline in the United Kingdom's price index).

Schedules thus obtained by the artificial means would appear against the backdrop of a vertical axis, as in Figure 4-11, and with a horizontal axis depicting the quantity of pounds, as in Figure 4-11. This leads to the case of fixed exchange rates, limits set by gold points, and the initial schedules intersecting at a point where the price is $2.35. In the historical context, the gold standard originally set these limits, and over the post-World War II years until 1971 they were an integral part of the exchange rate agreements with the IMF. The responsibility for confining rate fluctuations to these limits was that of the central bank or a government stabilization fund.

In the post-war years prior to 1961, the U.S. Treasury maintained a relationship between gold and the dollar by setting the price of gold at $35 per fine ounce (or $1 per 1/35 ounce). Dollar-rate changes were effectively limited by this and by the interventions of other members of the IMF in the market to establish the limits on their own currency in terms of dollars. In February 1962, however, the Federal Reserve System announced its decision to enter the exchange market for its own account (phase 3), and later of course, the system of fixed exchange rates was abandoned to what turned out to be the managed float system.

In the early post-World War II context, the introduction of an increase in the dollar demand for pounds, as in Figure 4-11, results in a tendency for the dollar rate on pounds to increase, as from the $2.35 price, as the value of the dollar depreciates in accordance with the equilibrium price of $2.39. To limit the exchange rate at the upper limit agreed on, the Bank of England would enter the foreign exchange market to sell pounds for dollars. They would in effect shift the supply schedule to the right until the equilibrium point fell within the gold points, and, in the process, there would be other possible adjustments. For example, as the Bank of England acquired dollars in exchange for pounds, it might elect to exchange the dollars for U.S. gold, say, at the price of $35 per ounce. At least, this could have been the case before the closing of the gold window in 1971.

Now, these supply and demand schedules might change for some fundamental reasons concerning the prices of merchandise imports and exports, capital inflows and outflows, and central bank intervention, and the changes in one schedule can involve a movement along the other schedule as the quantity of the currency in question flows onto or off the market. Moreover, the schedules in question may shift, and do so simultaneously, in response to speculative shifts resulting from changes in expectations concerning monetary and other prospects. The shifts may occur in the short-run time frames with or without supply/demand/quantity flows taking place and they may give rise to changes in exchange rates that are not too differently from those described in phase 11.

After 1973, of course, the fixed-rate system, as depicted by the gold points in Figures 4-1 and 4-8, no longer abounds, and some exchange rates come to fluctuate more widely than under the fixed-rate regimes. Moreover, the financial resources of the private sector have grown to such an extent that they may at times dominate (e.g., phases 11 and 12). Even so, the exchange rate systems are still subject to some intervention by central banks.

With respect to the growth in foreign exchange markets and the managed float, the arms of the cross in Figure 4-11 are likely to be floating around as traders adjust from both the supply and demand sides of the market to the same information. The information being processed concerning the future of the currencies, and the monetary policies behind them, are likely to swamp the effects of small changes in the actual quantities of a currency coming on or being taken off of the market in the short-run time frames.

Whatever the case with these markets, two means of bringing about trade account adjustments in countries' balances of payments and the movements of short- and long-term capital are (1) the relative price levels (say, P_{US}/P_{UK}, for the U.S. and U.K. price levels, or $P_{US}/P_{rest\ of\ the\ world}$ for the larger balance of payments picture) and (2) the exchange rates. The exchange rates will reflect anticipated central bank and related government policy bearing on price-level competition with trading partners, the general stability and profitability of the economic systems, and the like. To be sure, the earlier outline of the exchange rates under the managed float suggests that balance of payments adjustments will rely fundamentally on the relative price levels and related policies in the same way they did under the Britton Woods arrangements with the IMF at the center. Under those arrangements, the IMF could provide temporary relief to a country from having to immediately adjust its trade position, while extending its relief on the expectation of fundamental reforms (monetary discipline and all).

Under the managed float arrangement, countries start to cooperate in a less formal way than when they relied more heavily on the IMF's drawing facilities, but they nevertheless are still in the position of receiving cooperation for temporary relief on the prospect that some domestic policy reforms, not unlike those imposed by the IMF, will come about. This is much like the old gold-flows mechanism, which was central to the working of the old gold standard, and to the later Britton Woods arrangements, but with some added questions.

One question is whether exchange rate changes (devaluations and revaluations) are really as significant in correcting balance-of-payments disequilibria as once thought by J.M. Keynes of the 1920s, economists generally, and the post-WW II central bank officials and ministers of finance. The answer appears that they are not, possibly because they simply mirror the inverse of central bank prospects for inflating and/or deflating the purchasing power of the currencies. As to the fact of the exchange rate changes, and not entirely irrespective of inflationary/deflationary prospects, Paul Volcker offers a summary of some events in his book, *Changing Fortunes* (with Toyoo Gyohten, 1992, 294):

One of the ironies of the story of this book is that, after repeated depreciation of the dollar since 1971 to the point where it is 60 percent lower against the yen and 53 percent lower against the deutsche mark, the American trade and current account deficits are nevertheless much higher than anything imagined in the 1960s. Conversely, among the major industrialized countries, those with the most strongly appreciating currencies enjoy higher savings rates, stronger productivity, more competitive industries, and finally, the strongest trade balances. (Volcker in VG 1992, 294)

Another question that arises is not just about the old mechanism's existence, but rather about the prospect of currency blocks consisting of the DM-anchored ECU, the dollar ($), and the yen (¥). Concern in various quarters is not so much that such regional blocks may come about. It is rather that, should they come about, they will not turn protectionist and inward, all to the disadvantage of global open markets and the efforts of former command economies to put market-economy systems in place (VG 1992, 297-298, 305-306).

Reflecting along idealistic lines on possible deutschemark, dollar, and yen blocks, Toyoo Gyohten concludes thus:

I would like to dream of something that would work perfectly in an ideal world. I would envision a situation in which the three countries agree to remove all restrictions on the use of their currencies, pledge they will have no exchange controls and no capital controls--and then agree to make all three currencies common legal tender in each others' countries. They would not have to surrender their monetary automony, nor intervene to support their currencies, not commit to any fixed rate at all. (Gyohten in VG 1992, 309-310)

4.4 EUROPEAN INTEGRATION: THE MOVE TOWARD THE ECU/DM BLOCK

Key steps in the effort to move toward European integration were first with respect to markets and then money and political union. They include the Treaty of Rome, 1957, which established the European Economic Community; the founding of the European Monetary System, 1979; the Single European Act of 1987; the *Report on Economic and Monetary Union in the European Community* (in short, the Delors Report, 1989); and the Treaty on European Union (also called the Maastricht treaty, 1991). The first step was taken when six European states moved to advance the idea of a common market. In time, membership grew until in the early 1990s the twelve-nation group confronted even greater prospect for growth in membership as non-member countries Austria, Sweden, and Finland saw trade positions with the EC threatened by the absence of membership.

In the period following the founding of the EEC, fortunes did not wax and wane so much as other realities sat in; most notably, the achievement of the sought-after single market for real goods on the part of some large countries with independent political systems appeared to also require monetary and political union. To be sure, in theoretic/economics terms, the areas of money and polity were elevated within the economics of how the world works.

The EMS emergence can be traced to the British Labor Party politician Mr. Roy Jenkins. He had advocated a single market for Europe (Ludlow 1982, 37; Young 1991, 410), served in Harold Wilson's cabinet, and moved to bring the EMS about while serving as president of the European Commission in 1977. It entailed the cooperation of the German Chancellor Helmut Schmidt and the French President Valéry Giscard d'Esting in an era when a body of economics reigned that was quite different from that of the later British Prime Minister Margaret Thatcher.

The motive behind the German interest was seen as threefold: a need to identify more strongly with Europe in order to mitigate Germany's legacy from the Social Democrat era of the 1930s and World War II (i.e., in order to "buy goodwill," Kennedy 1991, 75), a means of stabilizing exchange rates among European trading partners, and as a means of forming a currency block for confronting the unstable dollar. The French interest can be seen as the desire to improve the role of a larger governmental unit and to contain politically the future role of Germany as an economic power. Collectively, the EMS came to be seen as a means of both taking advantage of the strong DM by tying to it and of confronting the United States on more equal terms at international summits.

The economic arguments supporting a common market to begin with included the ordinary ones of comparative advantage; free trade (specialization, the division of labor); and economies of scale, as where larger economic units may find lower minimum cost points on the U-shaped average cost curve. The single currency arguments included the removal of the transactions costs of moving from one currency to another and the removal of the need for up-dated information about trends in different currencies and the legal status of entering into contracts in one currency versus another. To be sure, however, the one-market and one-money arguments were extended to encompass the greater mobility of labor and capital. And, in juxtaposition to all of the one-market/one-money arguments, there was the loss of sovereignty that Margaret Thatcher lamented. Her biographer Hugo Young said:

This came to seem all that really animated her. It was the subject of the most significant intervention she made in the House of Commons before declining to leave elective politics. A federal Europe and a single currency, she counselled, would amount to "the greatest abdiction of national and parliamentary sovereignty in our history". It was fitting, and not at all surprising, that this should be her cause, for it was over this that her conduct of the prime ministership had finally broken the tolerance of her party. (Young 1991, 598)

Matters evolved considerably after the 1957 and 1979 dates. Despite supranational institutions called the Commission of the European Communities (in brief, the Commission), the Court, and the Parliament, power within the EEC still resided in the hands of member governments (Ludlow 1982, 12). So in December of 1974, the European Council of the Member Heads of State or Government (in brief, the European Council) was formed. An important feature was its voting with respect to EEC matters; notably, a unanimous vote was required on all matters before the European Council. Connected to it have been numerous committees, such as the Committee of Central Bank Governors, the Monetary Committee, and the Economic Policy Committee. The first of these links with the 1973-established European Monetary Cooperation Fund (EMCF), which appeared as the arrangement for supplying and accounting for the ECUs.

The ECU was the new currency unit. Starting merely as a unit for settling accounts between European central banks, it has become a currency in its own right. Even though made up from a weighted average of EMS member country currencies, the ECU has traded at a value of its own.

The Single European Act of 1986 modified the original Treaty of Rome (also called the EEC treaty) by inserting a chapter making it clear that "the EMS and the ECU are the instruments for the progressive liberalization of economic and monetary union." Continuing, Sunt (1989, 5) said that the 1986 act is the first clear reference to the ECU in an EC constitutional document. *The Economist* (July 11-17 1992) said the act "demolished any lingering British pretense that the creation of a European common market could somehow be kept separate from ideas of political union." In doing so, it points to European states as "agreeing to accept each other's commercial rules as adequate," and as agreeing to frame more common commercial rules by majority vote.

Later, in December of 1991, in the ancient Dutch town of Maastricht, came the Treaty on European Union (also called the Maastricht treaty), which added amendments to former EEC treates, most significantly the Treaty of Rome. As summarized by *The Economist* in a special edition (July 11-17 1992, 10, 13, and 14) four points stand out. (1) It formally dubbed the former EEC the European Community (or just EC), in recognition of a broader scope of activities. (2) Specific steps toward a monetary union and a single currency were set down. Most notably a deadline of January 1, 1999, and conditions for moving toward a single currency and a EuroFed bank were set down. (3) In effect, the European Council and its secretariat were promoted as the power center of the union, and thereby a government by states was promoted. (4) The treaty makes "a first proper attempt," the *Economist* said, "to limit the ambitions of European central government" by retaining at the state level those things that cannot be better achieved by emerging European central government.

Also at the Maastricht meeting, strict economic criteria were set for EC member nations to meet before belonging to the European central bank and circulating a common currency, and an "opt out" clause was inserted by the British. Most notably, the British parliament would have to approve later whether to scrap the pound for the new European currency.

Moreover, the latter clause was seen as applying to other EMS member countries. By April 1992, the Deutsche Bundesbank was issuing warnings about the economic risk of a single currency, although in France progress toward union remained popular, and by early June 1992, voters in Denmark threw uncertainty into the plans by narrowly opposing ratification of the Maastricht treaty. And then, in response, the French president scheduled a referendum with the close outcome reported for phase 11, and in close alliance, Britain and Italy suspended membership in the EMS's exchange rate mechanism. So it would seem that all was not certain about developments with respect to the twelve-member EC and the somewhat smaller EMS.

However—following the voting in Denmark and in the wake of currency turmoil in September 1992 (phase 11)—European Community leaders appeared to get back on track. Although divided over the goals, the means of achieving them, and the events of September, two days of negotiations in Edinburgh, Scotland, in December 1992 resulted in agreement on overcoming Denmark's rejection and on other EC matters. Within a suitably ambiguous text, the EC leaders allowed for another referendum by Danish voters, altered language to leave as much legislation as possible to individual member states, gave official status to the existing seat of Parliament in Strausbourg, France, and left open prospects for the location of new EC institutions (*Wall Street Journal*, 14 December 1992).

In a second referendum in May 1993, following the earlier rejection, Danish voters approved a subtly modified Maastricht treaty by a comfortable margin of 56.8 to 43.2 percent. A few days later on May 20, following assurance from Britain's John Major that ratification did not force Britain to rejoin the Exchange Rate Mechanism, the House of Commons voted 292 to 112 to ratify the treaty.

As matters started out, influence in the EEC and the later EMS arrangement was seen as being symmetrical in so far as burdens to adjustments were seen. In contrast to this vision, however, the EMS has became more of an "hegemonic" system by virtue of the dominant economic role of Germany and the high regard given to the Bundesbank, as discussed later. In any case, membership in the EMS gained relevance by virtue of its members being able to tie their currencies to the highly regarded deutsche mark. When previously high inflation countries such as Italy tied to the DM, they were immediately able to issue bonds at lower interest rates (with reduced inflation premia), and lower interest cost loans could be obtained in the countries by using contracted amounts expressed as ECUs. The politicians themselves were seen as being more able to sell austere, deflationary policies to their constitutants by citing the need to achieve a stable exchange for the DM.

A Bank of England official confided that the United Kingdom would not be in the EMS were it not for the advantages of tying to the deutsche mark. He further noted that if the Federal Republic of Germany (FRG) faltered in the progress that was set on track at Maastricht, then that progress would be dramatically set back. To be sure, the prospects for movement toward one market and one money for a core of EC countries did not seem inevitable in the Maastricht time frames.

On the relative success if the EMS's "hegemonic" system, even irrespective of outcomes within the Maastricht time frames, Paul Volcker concludes thus:

That success has been possible because within the area there has, in fact, been a dominant economic power and a predominant currency . . . With only limited exceptions, the nations of the Community have, in fact, been willing to nail their currencies to the strong mast of the DM. They have done so in the conviction that fixed intra-European currency values are a critical complement to an economically unified common market, dependent for its operation on large flows of trade among the members. As long as the German economy has remained strong and its currency a bastion of stability, the constraints implied for domestic monetary policy for the other members of the European exchange rate mechanism have seemed worth the protection against inflation and instability. (Volcker in VG 1992, 295)

4.5 THE POLICY-CONNECTED VARIABLES, THE SEPARATION OF EFFECTS, AND IDEOLOGY

The classical, gold-standard arrangement was rather impersonal in its operation. It worked according to certain rules, and dispersed the power that might otherwise reside in a government-managed economic system. As J. M. Keynes indicated, its function was surrounded by mystery, respect, and certain amounts of awe and reverence. However, as Keynes reviewed the matters of the 1920s, he saw that the managed financial system had crept in. To be sure, some phases of it that bear on the present analyses, its conclusions, and extensions of national policies to an open-economy setting have been reviewed here.

At the domestic level, there are the i-orientation and its fiscal policy accoutrements, which I associated with $\ln M = a_0 + a_1 \ln i + a_2 \ln Y$ (Equation [2] in Section 1.4a), monetary accommodation, the causation issue, Lord Kaldor, and all. Moreover, these topics were extended to others; namely, to notions about controlling prices directly enter via theories of imperfect and oligopolistic market structures, where inflation may arise (Frazer 1994a, Section 3.2e); to the uses of force that arise that may extend to making the world fit the models (Frazer 1994a, Sections 1.1, 3.5); and to income redistribution via income policies and the uses of the tax and transfer powers of the state.

Juxtaposed to this, on the domestic level, was the M-orientation, which limited the government's function in fiscal, price-control, and market matters. It does several things, it suggests different utility and consumption functions (Frazer 1994a, Sections 3.2g, 3.3b); introduces the prospects of freedom and voluntary association in markets as an economic goal (Frazer 1994a, Sections 3.2c, 3.4); and pictures monetary neutrality ($\tilde{M} \approx 0$) as the attainment of the zero inflation goal.

Now, in the open economy context, the conflicts, issues, and choices take on international extensions. What appears domestically as the "freedom issue" becomes the sovereignty issue. The interest-rate orientation and its fiscal policy accoutrement still exist, and notions about a super-national central bank and different exchange rate mechanisms enter the picture.

Quite basically of course, countries' prices (as in a price index) are extended internationally by means of exchange rates. They are stated in terms of the unit of account (Chapter 1, note 4) for one currency in relation to another (e.g., the dollar price of the pound, $/£, the deutsche mark, $/DM, the yen, $/¥), and so on.

Exchange rates appear at times as fixed and at other times as variable, along the lines set forth in dealing with control arrangements and their ideological extensions. To the extent that domestic central banks bear crucial responsibility for price levels, and to the extent that currencies are freely traded in the foreign exchange markets, speculation in currencies reduces mainly to speculation over the prospects for monetary policy in the respective national states. So anticipations about the future enter with respect to central bank policies, domestic price levels, and exchange rates. As illustrated, these last two sets of prices bear on a country's prospects for importing and exporting goods and services as well as capital.

Not only does the classification of the economic positions—as to the political left or right on Hotelling's line—extend internationally, it is not independent of the analytical and statistical problem I call the separation-of-effects problem.[12] Indeed, the international extension of the domestic analyses indicates even more dramatically the economist's and policy maker's inability to separate the effects of policy-connected variables by other than forceful and direct control means. To be sure, Equation (1) (initially stated in Section 2.5 to symbolize the separation-of-effects problems) can be more elaborately stated. For example, for the United States,

$$\text{GNP and/or GDP} = \begin{aligned} &a_0 + a_1 i + a_2 \text{ \$/DM} + a_3 \text{ \$/Yen} + a_4 P_{US}/P_{\text{rest of world}} \\ &+ a_5 \text{ fiscal policy (with accommodation)} \\ &+ a_6 \tilde{M}_{US}/\tilde{M}_{UK} + \dots \end{aligned} \quad (1)$$

As taken up in connection with liquidity preference and overshooting (FS 1982, 572), $i = i(\text{real}) + \dot{P}^e$. So, in variants of this Equation (1)—the income velocity (Y/M) and liquidity shifts aside—the acceleration of M_{US} in the ratio of the currencies (M_{US}/M_{UK}) drives up U.S. prices (P_{US} in the ratio, P_{US}/P_{UK}), increases the dollar price of the foreign currency ($\Delta\$/£$), and raises the interest rate (Δi).

In somewhat parallel terms, monetary accommodation contributes to inflation and we have $\dot{P}^e$. And, finally, the accommodation ($\Delta\tilde{M}_{US}$), as will be shown, varies inversely with the exchange value of the dollar and likely such major currencies as the deutsche mark and the yen.

If direct force enters (say, exchange rate and price controls), by implication or otherwise, to make the variables in Equation (1) conform to government wishes, the location on Hotellings line moves from right to left. On the other hand, if monetary policy is neutral for a sustained period time ($\pm\Delta\tilde{M}_{US} \approx 0$), then $\Delta P_{US} \approx 0$, $i = i(\text{real})$, and the price relatives at the domestic level (p_1/p_2, p_2/p_3, . . .) work their own effects. The position is on the right of Hotelling's line.

Turning to analyses of data, note the following: a Keynesian-policy orientation that prevails in the United States and the United Kingdom; conditions and ideas that combine to bring a turn in the policy orientation, and policies that move more along M-orientation lines. Selecting approximately equal-length sample periods, which can be identified with the alternative analyses and approaches to policy, I choose roughly the decades of the 1970s and 1980s, respectively, for an examination of data series bearing on policy-connected variables. To be sure, this involves the monetary policy indicator that I previously linked to price levels, wages, and fiscal policy, even in the 1970s, and establishes a connection with the trade-weighted indexes for the dollar and the pound.

Taking into account prior analysis and findings bearing on inflation rates and interest rates, data analyses, reveal interdependent, policy-connected variables. The monetary indicator (whether accommodation linked to fiscal policy or discipline), the exchange rates, the inflation rates, and the wage rates come as an inseparable package. Even the 1970s efforts at experimentation and the forced compliance with the prospect of separating effects by artificial means does not alter the appearance of an interdependent set of policy-connected variables. In fact, they all appear to be linked to monetary growth and income velocity as the main determinants, whether under the conditions of the 1970s or the highly different one of the 1980s. Quite possibly the efforts at forced compliance—as where prices were controlled by direct means when monetary policy was accommodative—were simply a reflection of an inadequate use of force. Nevertheless, this concession does not alter the essentially ideological links with the respective analytical approaches.

What is revealed is that a host of economic variables can be controlled by direct means rather than by voluntary association in markets. Indeed, discussion of forced compliance appears with respect to EMS member countries as movement toward EMS goals comes about (Emerson et al. 1992, 100-101, 178, 189, 236-237; Kennedy 1991, 14, 31, 110). It is encountered, especially with reference to fiscal policy, probably because some states link fiscal policy to monetary policy (as in the case of the United Kingdom, and the Bank of England), and it appears in general where countries must meet the conversion criteria imposed by the system of fixed exchange rates. Even so, should the transition to one market and one money for a core of European states come about, it is not beyond the realm of possibility that a properly functioning monetary umbrella may fall into place, along with a commitment to voluntary association in markets and a breakup of the analytical state policy association between monetary and fiscal policy. Indeed, such a breakup in the linkage would be fostered should the fiercely independent Bundesbank impose its self-image of independence (Kennedy 1991, 19, 21, 31, 37, 54) on a EuroFed central bank.

NOTES

1. J. M. Keynes was the first with wide visibility to bring attention to the non-sense of German reparations as agreed upon at the Paris peace conference following World War I (Keynes 1920). Schacht also wrote on the matter (1931; and 1967, 16, 83, 87, 90-93).

2. As Volcker and Gyohten also point out, the Triffin plan was not the first for an international money. They point to the Keynes plan of 1942-43, and mention the "bancor" as the monetary unit (VG 1992, 9 and 324). The term "bancor" combined the word for bank with the French word for gold.

3. For Paul Volcker's personal account of the decision to suspend the convertibility of the dollar and its aftermath, see Volcker (in VG 1992, 74-90 and 101-128).

4. Referring first to the radical outside-the-main-stream nature source of the floating-rates idea (Volcker in VG 1992, 38), Volcker also points out "The ideas of free-market economist Milton Friedman . . . began to be taken more seriously."

Referring first to the Nixon White House, Volcker later describes a different setting:

The combination of accelerating inflation and the oil shock late in 1973 went a long way toward establishing floating currencies as the operational international monetary system. By mid-decade, they were sanctified by amendment of the Articles of Agreement of the International Monetary Fund. By the end of the decade they were so imbedded in academic thought, in government policy, and in banking practice, that those still longing for fixed rates on more than a regional or highly selective basis were relegated to the fringes of debate. (Volcker in VG 1992, 136)

Taking up an amendment to the Articles, Volcker says:

The rest of the new amendment was short on specifics, but the philosophical base was unmistakable. Stability in exchange rates, while devoutly to be desired, would have to emerge from "orderly underlying economic and financial conditions" rather than from any specific government decision to determine an appropriate rate. Nations were to avoid "manipulating" exchange rates, and the IMF itself was to exercise firm surveillance efforts so that efforts to distort the market through intervention or otherwise would be discouraged. (Volcker in VG 1992, 141)

Referring to a November 1975 meeting, "well removed from Paris," Volcker notes its purpose was to pronounce a "blessing on the Fund amendments."

5. Volcker recalls in VG 1992, 126-127) the early framework for the meetings of the groups of five and seven (the G-5 and G-7). He says of the spring-1973 meeting in Washington, following the demise of the Bretton Woods system, "there was a common understanding that it would be worthwhile to maintain the informal contact." Noting continued dissatisfaction in some quarters with the success of floating by the mid 1970s, Volcker reemphasizes the summits (in VG 1992, 137-139). On the G-5, see also Gyohten (in VG 1992, 134 and 152).

6. Lawrence Klein uses different methods and reports similar results to Friedman's which also appear in FS's *Monetary Trends* (1982, 412-417; and Frazer 1988, 549-552). A comparison of Friedman's approach and Klein's appears in Frazer (1984).

7. Volcker also gives an account of this Baker led move in some detail (in VG 1992, 229 and 241-247). He reports that Baker and Richard Darman readily joined efforts (begun at the initiative of the other G-5 countries to restrain appreciation of the dollar." He says:

A substantial slide down the exchange rate roller coaster began. When the dollar rallied for a while during the late summer, the new Treasury team triggered a joint, aggressive, and open effort to push it lower in what came to be known as the Plaza agreement because it was sealed at the Plaza Hotel in New York in September of 1985. (Volcker in VG 1992, 229) See also Gyohten (in VG 1992, 252-258).

The Plasa meeting was followed in February 1987 by another meeting of the G-5 referred to as "The Louvre" since it took place at the Louvre Palace in Paris. VG's chapter on it carries the interesting title "More Experiments in Economic Management."

8. This attention to the equation of exchange $[M = k(. . .)PQ]$ was around at the outset of the gold-standard/gold-flows/mechanism era, except the factor $k(. . .)$ was taken as fixed in the economics before J. M. Keynes and before M. Friedman. With Keynes and Friedman the factor $k(. . .)$ becomes a variable factor, plus with Friedman and the managed float system (Melamed 988, xix, 390, 392, 398-399) the variable

factor k(. . .) took on international significance. Perhaps surprisingly the focus on domestic monetary policy—purchasing power speculation and so on—comes more to the forefront in the foreign exchange markets.

9. Paul Volcker also saw fit to comment on the large and dramatic inflow of foreign capital funds to the United States which peaked in 1985 (Volcker in VG 1992, 178-179, and 228). He attributes it mainly to high interest rates in the United States (Volcker in VG 1992, 179) which, as I illustrate elsewhere, were in fact declining from the inflation-premium high, including in relation to foreign rates (Frazer 1988, 685). The dollar at the time was also becoming more expensive.

Continuing, Volcker said the inflow seemed "an obvious problem except to some dedicated members of the [Reagan] administration team who interpreted it all as a vote of confidence in U.S. policy." However, to be sure, the vote-of-confidence tack is the one most consistent with the facts.

10. It had come about at the time of the U.S.'s Carter presidency, and the later James Baker episode (Section 3.4b and phase 8 of Section 4.1a), as a means of relieving pressure on the U.S.'s domestic-policy and payments-deficits problems. At the time of the Carter presidency, the dollar was declining (Figure 4.2a) and payments deficits were soaring. Further, at that time the policy was Keynesian based and identified with the econometrician/big-model builder Lawrence Klein and what I allude to in the text (Section 2.5) and elsewhere with "the separation-of-effect problem" (Frazer 1988, 68-87 and Chapter 18; Frazer 1994a, Section 7.4).

Referring to early 1977 when Lawrence Klein made argument to a U.S. Congress and Secretary of the Treasury Michael Blumenthol traveled to an international conference in Japan (VG 1992, 146-147, 154, and 161), Toyoo Gyohten also refers to the failure as "an obsession with a fine-tuning approach" to foreign exchange markets. Gyohten went on to note the folly of the precise targeting of a 6.7 percent growth rate which was being recommended for Japan as a way of narrowing the U.S. trade deficit and lifting the world economy. Gyohten says:

The mentality of those days was totally wrong in trying to gear the performance of national economies to that kind of quantitative target . . . . This is really amazing in a world of market-oriented, capitalist economies, to talk as if national economic performance can be fine-tuned to that extent. (VG 1992, 162)

11. The developments on the domestic side are in turn the same developments which the foreign holders of the currency react to as they also speculate about the central bank's actions (or more to the point, what market participants will expect policy to be one quarter or a year hence). J.M. Keynes, we may recall (1936, 156), analogized the task of the speculator to that of a competitor in a competition to pick the winner in a beauty contest. In an effort to pick the winner, "each competitor has to pick, not those faces which he himself finds prettiest, but those which he thinks likeliest to catch the fancy of the other competitors, all of whom are looking at the problem from the same point of view." The solution to stabilizing the speculative activity, even so, comes back to the government's policy, namely: stabilize the policy to which the speculators react.

An added dimension in the foreign exchange markets is that the holders of the currency on the international, nondomestic side are assessing developments in several major countries. The international holders are dealing with one country's policies vis-à-vis another country's (and the market participants' expectations for those policies). I have relative central bank policies, and relative price levels (e.g., P_{US}/P_{UK}) similar to the system of relative prices, p_1/p_2 etc., which appears in Frazer (1994a, Section 3.2b).

12. This separation-of-effects problem with respect to analysis and the direct use of statistical methods could be stated as "the man-in-the-backroom illusion." The illusion is that the static constructs in economics (even call them partial analysis) can be found in the real world "directly" by known econometric methods (or means known to those in the backroom); that point elasticities can be computed from "directly" identified constructions; that predictions associated with the *ceteris paribus* method of impounding other things are tantamount to unconditional predictions (as in the case of some hard sciences); that a variable on the left-hand-side of an equation can be accounted for in terms of a "direct" and adequately detailed treatment of additional right-hand-side variables; and that uncertainty on the part of agents about economic outcomes can be separated from the main analytical systems adopted and taught in economics without damaging the relevance and fruitfulness of the systems.

Part III

Central Banking

Part III is an extension of the main subjects of the text in terms of some more or less hypothetical questions. The subjects include economic analysis broadly viewed, money, and ideology. In the broad view, alternative approaches emerge and react against the separation of the theory of money from that of production, the omission of money from the analysis of aggregate demand, and the prospect that prices are determined in markets exclusive of monetary analysis (Frazer 1994a, Sections 3.2e, 7.2b).

Even recognizing alternatives, the text offers a total analytical system in which the demand for money in income velocity (or liquidity-shift) terms and variations in the growth of the money stock impact numerous other key variables in the economic/analytical system so as to render virtually impossible the separation of effects of the distinct variables in any detailed sense by known direct means. Rather, special time frames enter along the lines of Milton Friedman's early moves to advance the monetary dimension of the business cycle research, which was set on a course by Wesley Mitchell. In the analytical part of this work, Friedman adopts the policy orientation, the definition of money, and other features of the analysis that were set on a course by J. M. Keynes.

A partially hypothetical question is how one would go about structuring and provisioning a new central bank on the basis of the analysis, the comparisons of central banks, the facts, the experiments, and the phases of post-World War II developments. Without ignoring the polity matters I associate with the economic analysis, I turn in Part III to summary statements of interest rate/fiscal-policy and money-stock regimes and reconsider some hypotheses and institutional concerns introduced in Section 1.1 and Chapter 3. Matters bearing on money, and central banks that provide it, are summarized and the European Monetary System, its goals, and the hypothetical question about a EuroFed bank are considered.

The main central banks introduced in the evolution of central banking are the Bank of England, the Federal Reserve, and the Bundesbank. The first is the oldest and is seen as characterized by traditions and rather old practices. The 1913-founded Federal Reserve initially reflected the bank-rate orientation of the Bank of England. However, open market operations of a special sort came about at the Federal Reserve Bank of New York and were later written into the Federal Reserve Act.

Among the prominent central banks, the Bundesbank is the newest. As such, it has benefitted from inflationary experiences following World Wars I and II as well as from the rise of interest in the money stock, the targeting of a money aggregate, and the velocity of money. To be sure, its success in containing inflation and providing a hard currency for the Federal Republic of Germany (FRG) make it a possibly prototype for a new European central bank.

Early in the move toward a central bank for the EMS member countries, British Labor Party politician Mr. Roy Jenkins, German Chancellor Helmut Schmidt, and French President Valéry d'Esting were main players. However, as an early Friedman monetarist, Britain's Margaret Thatcher later reacted negatively to the EMS developments. In doing so, she raised issues over sovereignty and the exchange rate mechanism, which brings the discussion back to Thatcher, Britain, and the sovereignty issue, which link to the matters of central bank involvement with fiscal policy.

As an early leader in the redirection of the 1970s policies bearing on inflation and efforts at controlling prices by direct means, Thatcher appears as a major political figure in what I have called the "Big U-Turn" and illustrated in reference to price indexes, interest rates, and exchange rates. Essentially, I see the U-Turn in connection with new ideas contained in the Friedman system of analysis and economic problems such as Thatcher confronted. Focusing on the Bundesbank's non-inflationary demeanor, its orientation as a central bank, and the notion of ideas impacting policy, draws consideration to Germany, the pervasiveness of changes in the 1980s, and the ideas concerning economic analysis, policy implementation, traditions, and practices.

The hypotheses from Section 1.1, which are reconsidered pertain to whether the numerous countries were simply following German leadership (H_{FTL}), pursuing policy in an autonomous way (H_{PA}), or reacting to crises and new ideas ($H_{U\text{-}Turn}$). The prospect that the data series in Section 2.2 were responding to policy regimes and the U-Turn changes suggests earlier notions about the pervasiveness of monetary influences and the exogeneity of forces impacting key time series.

These and other matters of importance to economic analysis and the European Communities parallel the separation-of-effects problem. Juxtaposing what I encounter in economic analysis for the most part, leads to conflicts with what I encounter in the EC experience with economic integration, most notably,

Economic Analysis	EC experience since the Delors Report
The separation of the theory of money from that of production	The need for monetary integration as a step toward the furtherance of economic integration
The separation of the theory of money from the polity	The need for moves toward political union to achieve monetary union (Staff 1992, 178-183)
The mix of fiscal and monetary policy	The money and financial matters emerge as primary with respect to the achievement of zero-inflation rates and economic stability (Staff 1992, 101-102, 106-107, 235, 236, and 243), whether viewed, in Kaldor, Friedman, or deficit reduction terms

In extending the exercise concerning the preceding partially hypothetical question I ask further why so much attention is given to "one money" or a German/France led, currency block to begin with. The answer centers on transaction costs and the exchange-rate uncertainties first introduced in Section 4.4. Most notably, the substitution of a single currency with a zero inflation rate for multiple currencies with diverse inflation rates and disparate central banking arrangements offers the following prospects on the positive side. First, the substitution reduces the direct cost of exchanging one money for another in order to make across-the-border purchases. Second, the one money with the attained zero inflation goal reduces the uncertainty associated with holding a given stock of money balances and undertaking long- and short-term contracts concerning the repayment of debt and future deliveries of goods and payments denominated in a currency of uncertain future value. Third, closely allied with reduced uncertainty are reduced costs of getting information about future prospects and legal statuses of entering into contracts in one versus another unit of account.

Tying a block of currencies to a single "hard" currency, via an exchange rate mechanism, is a step toward reducing uncertainties and information costs of the sort mentioned, but this action does not go quite all the way to reducing uncertainty through the acceptance of one monetary medium. Reduced uncertainty over transactions costs and future purchasing power are thought to encourage trade and the indirect exchange of goods through the acceptance of money. The choice reduces to one of the direct exchange of goods for goods, the indirect satisfaction of wants with a monetary medium, or some compromise. Hjalmar Schacht expressed the choices this way:

Regression to a moneyless condition, or the modern . . . exchange by . . . money
. . . are the alternatives. Money plays the role of the sorcerer's apprentice—created
to serve a master . . . who cannot now rid himself of his indispensible sprite.
(Schacht 1967, 65)

However, and most important, the market mechanism with a satisfactory
money umbrella disburses power and enhances voluntary association (Frazer
1988, 415, 434, 477, 491). The acceptance of the monetary arrangement
itself goes back to the definition of money, the speculative shifts in the
demand for money, business conditions generally, and the interplay of
money as a liquid asset and the real goods markets for less liquid assets.

Although Part III has a special focus (the central banks, the EMS, and so
on), awareness about money and central banks should be raised by the
experiences in the EC. Indeed, the need for that arises even as I confront
the prospect of transition from the multi-currencies arrangements of the EC
to "one money" and one common market. Moreover, although I dwell on
developments in the EC, the money and central banking lessons should not
be lost on countries seeking to undertake transformations from socialist and
disorganized states to market economies that require viable monetary
systems.

Chapter 5

Selected Central Banks and Alternative Analytical Systems

5.1 INTRODUCTION

In the perspective of a London School of Economics (LSE) professor, most economists tend to ground themselves in something. I review some cases, recall alternatives, reconsider the hypotheses from Section 3.1b, and consider the matter of a super-central bank and a super-national money for the member states of the European Monetary System. Although I am not indifferent about the outcomes for the EMS, the super-central bank and super-national money matters provide the opportunity for a rather practical exercise. It is namely, given the background in the alternatives analyses, their historical roots, and links to political positions, along what lines might I proceed in structuring and provisioning a new central bank (as to power, policy instruments, and accounting control arrangements). Further, in considering the matters of economic, political, and monetary union for such a diversity of European states, other facets of economics arise, notably, the efforts through the early 1990s at economic union suggest that economic union falls short without monetary union and that monetary union calls for political union. Parallel to these suggestions are others for economics as empirical science: *whether the economics of the real goods sector can be readily separated from that of the monetary sector and whether theoretic economics in fact has political dimensions of the sort introduced here.*

5.1a The Alternatives

The alternatives—with links to actual-policy orientations—are the Keynesian one (also with a post-Keynesian flair) and the Friedman system I offer. In the first, there is skepticism about money (the i-orientation, the liquidity trap, "pushing on a string," the attention to "bank loans," and the like and 3.2d) and, instead, there is the rise of fiscal policy. These positions are grounded in views about the separation of effects (by ceteris paribus or multiple regression means) and in views about fiscal policy and the state as instruments for stabilizing business conditions and possibly otherwise controlling prices and income distribution. To be sure, monetary policy is accommodative.

The Keynesian grounding in the separation-of-effects models has connections to the econometric fashion with respect to the multiple regressions, endogeneity, and many equations and unknowns (FS 1991, 40; Frazer 1994a, Section 7.4). This can be shown to be consistent with any position to the political left of the Friedman system's "monetary umbrella" (the Hotelling line, Figure 3-5). Moving in that direction, increasing amounts of governmental authority may be called for to bring the economic-policy-control prospects into compliance with the latent and hidden parts of the economics.

In the Friedman system, the grounding is quite explicitly twofold: (1) Friedman's view of economics as an empirical science (and not simply "positive economics," Frazer [1994a, Section 9.1]); and, consistent with it, (2) the "monetary-umbrella" view with freedom and voluntary association as goals (phase 5 in Section 4.1a and the "social market economy" ethic [Frazer 1994a, Section 3.2e]). The "empirical science" view, as distinct from just positive economics, is the search for repetitive phenomena (prediction beyond the sample period), and the extension of the study of U.S. data to that of the U.K. data, as in the shared experience hypothesis H_{SE}.

5.1b Institutional Concerns and the Hypotheses

From the LSE professor's perspective, whereby most economists ground themselves in something, the professor suggested that his colleague's feet were firmly planted in the air. Referring to himself, the professor said that he grounded himself in knowledge of the institutions. There had at least to be a consistency between the economics and the Bank of England, for example, such as encountered in two of the earlier hypotheses. In brief:

H_{CB}. *The Central banks.* Central bank traditions, operating procedures, and accounting controls influence the choice of economic theory on which government bases its central banking and financial markets policies.

H_{TW}. *The Theoretical works.* Underlying the theoretical works of the Keynesians and the later post Keynesians, on the one hand, and Friedman's monetarist work, on the other, are particular views of central banking arrangements, policy approaches, and means of intervening in the money markets.

For the present, H_{CB} is recalled with two objectives in mind. One is to explain the Bank of England's failure to put a Thatcher/monetarist regime in place, even as the U.K. government attempted to move policy along monetarist lines (Frazer 1988, 554-565). The second objective is to use H_{CB}, and the comparisons of the U.K. and U.S. cases that support it, to broaden the choice of central banking arrangements as I contemplate the implications of the alternative analytical systems for the establishment of new banking arrangements. And, finally H_{TW} serves as an explanation for the failure of the theoretic/academic economists to relate the highly important policy and operations matters to the alternative approaches taken up.

As to the Bank of England, it never made the operational, accounting control, and institutional changes needed for the implementation of policy along M-orientation lines. No doubt in part as a consequence, the policy maker at the U.K. Treasury (with its authority over the Bank of England) was doomed by a reversion to rather flawed ideas about policies and effects from an earlier past. Missing the announced targets for sterling M3, and using the faulty means for obtaining them, the officials saw themselves as losing credibility with the general public, the press, and the markets. As this occurred, the Bank reverted to the old traditional, bank, i-oriented way of viewing things (the haven of the static method, ceteris paribus and all), in the second half of the 1980s.

As to the revolutionaries themselves, J. M. Keynes's economics was very much rooted in his London experiences and his closeness to the Bank of England and the views fostered there, on the one hand. Friedman himself was very much influenced by the means of accounting for bank reserves in the United States, the place of open market operations in that accounting arrangement, and the money and credit aggregates arrangements that emerged there, on the other hand. I can even point to Phillip Cagan's work (1965) in this regard, since it was a part of the series of studies Friedman undertook with Anna Schwartz. Moreover, I have extended the prospects here by noting similarities in structure and means of policy implementation between the U.S. Federal Reserve, as it emerged from the 1930s, and the FRG's Bundesbank as it emerged in the post-World War II years.

5.1c The i- and M-Orientations Again

Now taking into account the alternatives, the divergent institutional concerns I relate to them, Margaret Thatcher's early monetarist leadings, and the emergence of the Bundesbank, I turn to the divergent prospects for the European Monetary Systems. On the one hand, there is the Delors Report itself, which appeared in April of 1989, with very much of a Keynesian/"phase 1"/IMF orientation, but with some apparent ambiguities of language. And, on the other, there was Margaret Thatcher who confronted it very much as a political leader with Friedman/monetarist connections, in what I dubbed the "Big U-Turn" (Frazer 1988, Chapters 14, 15), and there was Otto Pöhl and the

Bundesbank, which "combined with Germany's size, wealth and the asymmetric results of monetary *Realpolitik* . . . seem to secure the Bundesbank's . . . position as monetary hegemon of the European Community for the foreseeable future" (Kennedy 1991, 103). Furthermore, Kennedy saw the Bundesbank as being able to take advantage of "ambiguities of the text [i.e., the Delors Report] to secure its own position [with respect to domestic price stability]."

Referring to the phase of monetary integration, which immediately followed the Delors Report, Ellen Kennedy (1991, 108) continued thus:

[T]he Bundesbank won an important point in having Karl Otto Pöhl appointed to chair the committee considering what to do next. This part of the Delors Committee's remit is so vaguely drawn and offers so many possible interpretations that the German central bank will be able to find sufficient grounds to keep the matter under discussion for a very long time. Given its skill in reading European doctrine—especially when it comes to the fine points of monetary integration—the Bundesbank is poised to interpret (and reinterpret) the final Eurofed document until the contents suit its own norm of monetary stability.

Referring to Pöhl and his misgivings about the speed of monetary union in Europe, Kennedy (1991, 108) found him "declaring that he still had 'serious doubts that European governments, not just the British government, are really prepared to accept the consequences of a transfer of far-reaching powers over monetary policy to a supranational institution.'" Continuing with reference to Pöhl, she has him implying that "nothing would be as sound or secure as the Deutschemark had been." Describing Pöhl at a meeting of ministers in December 1990, "to discuss phase two of monetary integration in Europe," Kennedy (1991, 108) says: "Pöhl indicated, they would have only two choices—a real central bank (a Eurofed that acts like the Bundesbank) or a compromise that would negate everything the Germans stood for in monetary policy."

As stated earlier, the Delors Report placed on the table the possibility of a new central bank for Europe and "a common money supply for Europe." In the initial proposals for new currency arrangements, the federalist structure of the U.S. Federal Reserve and Germany's Bundesbank appeared as a part of discussions, as did the deutsche mark as Europe's soundest currency. The economic goal of a zero inflation rate was present, as were the Keynesian fiscal policy ideas of an earlier time. In the context of the Delors Report, these Keynesian ideas extended to an international dimension. It appeared early, where central-authority influence could be extended to some control over a sovereign state's fiscal policy.

Thatcher's monetarist leanings and the sequence of happenings with respect to her odyssey can be sketched as follows:

1. Margaret Thatcher embraced monetarist ideas as she led her party to political victory in May of 1979.

2. The prospects for taming inflation by monetarist means were held in place at the U.K. Treasury and at the Bank of England until the mid-1980s.

3. Missing targets for the monetary aggregate, sterling M3, and experiencing a loss of credibility in the media and with the public for doing so, the Bank of England reverted to the old traditional means of focusing on interest rates as the policy variable, although it did not go so far as to dismiss the money and credit aggregates from its deliberations.

4. Missing targets, accepting the frailty of accounting controls over the aggregates, and given the enormity of the privatization episode, which is discussed in Chapter 6, the U.K. Treasury and the Bank of England did a highly creditable job of imposing monetary discipline in the United Kingdom throughout the decade of the 1980s until near its close (Figure 2-1).

5. Facing the Delors Report's proposals in the fall of 1989, Margaret Thatcher split with her treasury minister Nigel Lawson and more or less sided with advisor Sir Alan Walters. (Walters had adopted a Friedman/monetarist approach early [Frazer 1988, 597-602], and in the fall of 1989 he strongly opposed the exchange rate mechanism called for by the Delors Report.)

6. By October 1990, following the swift unification of the Federal Republic of Germany and German Democratic Republic, facing political opposition for not joining the European Monetary System, and facing the prospect of some abatement of inflation, Margaret Thatcher announced the U.K. move to join the EMS. (The pound was set at a par of 2.95 DM.)

7. The possible argument favoring Thatcher's October 1990 action was that her government gained the leverage of being more influential in the final outcomes for a "EuroFed" bank, a possible common currency, and the like.

8. In November 1990, Thatcher was placed in the position of resigning as leader of her party. In part, the situation related to the matter of "sovereignty" with respect to the United Kingdom and the EMS. (The Thatcher mantle passed to John Major.)

9. Germany loomed large as the key player in the EC and the deutsche mark appeared as the anchor for monetary discipline in Europe.

10. Saying "there is more to setting up a monetary union than agreeing [to] the *constitution of a central bank* and the *tools of monetary management*," Governor Leigh-Pemberton of the Bank of England discussed the United Kingdom's support of a three-stage plan for moving toward the "hard Ecu" (European Currency Unit) as a substitute for national currencies (Staff 1991).

11. As reviewed in phase 11 (Section 4.1a), the United Kingdom, as well as Italy, had to withdraw from the EMS's exchange rate mechanism. The withdrawal was in part a vindication of Thatcher's position, although as indicated earlier, the British Parliament voted on May 20, 1993, to ratify the Maastricht treaty.

The United Kingdom's three-stage plan was not too different from that found in the Delors Report, apart from the later time table and optimistic prospects. First, the plan called for an exchange rate mechanism (ERM) that linked currencies to the DM. Second, the U.K. plan called for intensification of cooperation between European central banks. Third, the United Kingdom's approach in the plan was to set up a European Monetary Fund (EMF) with real operating functions. It was to become a *European System for Central Banks* with the function of helping familiarize people with the concept of a "supernational money" and ultimately issuing and managing a new common currency.

As Leigh-Pemberton saw the matter in 1991, "The Hard Ecu system would operate in roughly the same way as the *gold standard* during the years of its success." He said, "it is also similar to the way the ERM has worked with the *DM as the anchor*" (Staff 1991). The IMF had once been viewed along such lines in reference to the prospect for a world currency (Triffin 1961). Indeed, the IMF's SDR evolved as one means of settling accounts at the IMF, and the IMF played a key role in the fixed exchange rate arrangements before the United States closed the gold window in 1971.

Taking what I may call a Thatcher/monetarist/sovereignty route, I suggest a set of European central banking arrangements different from those found in the Delors Report and from those supported by the United Kingdom in 1991. In doing so, I return to the hypotheses H_{CB} and H_{TW} first presented in Section 1.1, and take up the operational, accounting control matters that are latent in the alternative analyses I discuss. Note, however, that the ERM Thatcher opposed may have had the political advantage of offering some EMS member government an excuse for disinflation and austerity in the short run. To be sure, the United Kingdom continued to follow an austere policy through the 1990-92 recession, as it sought to meet the criteria for phase 2 of the movement toward unification.

5.1d Pertinent Conclusions

The pertinent conclusions with respect to H_{CB} and H_{TW} are as follows:

1. The Bank of England of the 1980s was characterized by traditions and practices that are rooted in the late nineteenth century, the confrontation with the Baring liquidity crises, and the post-World War II age of fiscal policy.

2. The Federal Reserve was founded in 1913, with the "discount rate(s)" as the principal means of confronting liquidity crises (as in Bank of England tradition).[1]

3. The discovery of open market operations (OMO) at the Fed of New York, and the banking acts of 1933 and 1935 giving formal recognition to them, combine with accounting control arrangements to provide the operations-control arrangements underlying the Friedman system and the "helicopter money" concepts.

4. This link to the Friedman system is what I see with respect to the Bundesbank, its federalist structure, and related matters.

5. The United States and the Federal Reserve share the post-World War II age of fiscal policy with the United Kingdom and the Bank of England.

6. In the light of items 2, 3, and 5, the Bank of England is primarily an i-regime central bank and the U.S. Federal Reserve shares this arrangement in part.

7. In the light of items 5 and 6, *the Bank of England can mainly swing along i-regime lines only*, even when it attempted a monetarist strategy in the 1980s, and the two-sided Federal Reserve can swing with either of the two orientations.

8. In the light of Friedman's research primarily and items 3 and 4, an M-regime orientation permeates the Friedman system, the experiences the Federal Reserve shares with it, and the Bundesbank orientation.

So what does it mean in specific terms to say that the Federal Reserve can swing both ways? Answers:

1. The Fed can follow an i-regime strategy of relying on the "bank" or "discount" (or closely related "federal funds") rate in its efforts to convey credit ease or tightness when it fails at the targeting of the money aggregate (Figure 3-4).

2. Also, in attempting to target an aggregate of choice it can resort to a variant of the Section 1.4a equation (namely, $\ln M = a_0 + a_1 \ln i_* + a_3 \ln Y$) with attention to M2 dollar balances, interest rates on some short-dated instruments, and the concept of *opportunity cost* (Higgins 1992). It is that the opportunity cost of an action or inaction (say, of acquiring or holding money balances) is the cost foregone from not choosing the alternative (say, of foregoing the yield on bonds by holding money balances). Although the concept is quite generally used in economics, it creeps into Keynesian economics as I state it. Stretching the concept it can also be said to appear in Equation (1) of Section 1.5a, where expected returns from four classes of assets enter. The analytical complication found there, however, is that the Friedman time frames also enter the analysis. (They make a big difference, especially in reference to the virtual impossibility of separating the detailed effects by econometric means which are called for by the short-run orientation.)

3. In addition, the central bank may be in the position of accommodating the deficit spending (or GNP creation) of the central government, as well as the wage and price increases that may arise. The accommodation of the Treasury's deficit financing need not be direct, however, as it was in the Bank of England case during the Keynesian era. Rather, extra growth in bank credit comes about to provide the extra funds to the financial markets.

Finally, in the EMS case, the member European states confront the choice between (a) more modest, M-regime arrangements to achieve its goals; (b) the i-regime arrangements; and (c) the "super-central bank" arrangements combining both sets of arrangements. The questions are: How would one choose in the light of the analyses, and monetary and ideological prospects? Which alternative minimizes the loss of sovereignty and achieves the zero-inflation-rate goal? Are all the matters at hand simply too complicated, sophisticated, and subtle to be achieved via economic discussion, which has all too frequently separated ideas of the real goods economy from those of the monetary economy, and which has separated both of the latter from the polity? Could the political and economic leaders behind the European Monetary System in its early formation simply have underestimated the possibilities of economic and monetary union without first attaining political union?

Other questions bearing on the future of the EMS, to which the future will provide answers, are whether the various member countries will meet the conversion criteria set for the different stages of development; whether Frankfurt or London will be chosen as the location for a new EuroFed bank; whether the ECU will be a so-called "parallel currency" or whether it will come to replace the deutsche mark, the pound, and so on; whether the Bundesbank will impose its self-image and monetarist orientation on the other more Keynesian (say, fiscal policy and interest-rate) oriented central banks (and thereby also Keynesian oriented countries); whether concerns over sovereignty will impede the movement toward "one market and one currency"; whether the economic arguments (economies of scale, reduced transactions costs, reduced uncertainty, etc.) will carry more weight than the political arguments for and against unification; whether the zero-inflation-rate goal will ever by achieved by most European Community countries; and whether the EMS will simply end as one currency block vis-à-vis the dollar and yen blocks.

5.1e The Primary Variable

The primary variable is the money stock and hence the key to the M-regime approach that has the methodological dimensions worked toward since Chapter 1, to Friedman's primary equation, and to the equation I first related to policy and separation-of-effects problems in Section 2.5. Restating the equations, without relabeling the symbols:

$$M/P = f(Y/P, w; \ldots; y) \tag{1}$$

$$
\begin{aligned}
\text{GNP and/or GDP} = {} & a_0 + a_1 \, i + a_2 \, \pounds/\text{DM} + a_3 \, \$/\text{Yen} \\
& + a_4 \, P_{US}/P_{\text{rest of world}} \\
& + a_5 \, \text{fiscal policy (with accommodation)} \\
& + a_6 \, \Delta \dot{M}_{us}/\Delta \dot{M}_{uk} + \ldots
\end{aligned}
\tag{2}
$$

The first enters in the context of a market economy (Frazer 1994a, Section 3.4), the separation-of-effects problem, and the multiple regression and "big models" (fn 4, Chapter 4; and Frazer 1994a, Section 7.4d). It is called a "primary equation" because monetary forces are present that influence many other things such as the inflation, exchange, and interest rates that appear in Equation (2). I can go so far—as the Bundesbank and Milton Friedman do—and consider the control of the nominal stock of money as the most strategic variable in a social market economy, in several senses; namely, there will be no properly functioning/stable market economy without a stable and properly functioning monetary system, the money stock provides the umbrella for voluntary asociation and indirect satisfaction of wants, and the myriad of prices in the market-price system requires stability overall on the monetary side in order to send the proper messages to wage earners and producers (as in Frazer 1994a, Figures 1-2, 3-7, 7-4).

In addition, I link Equation (1) to the bank reserve's accounting control and the previously used symbols, namely, $\pm \Delta \dot{R} \rightarrow \pm \Delta \dot{R}_0 \ (1/r) \rightarrow \pm \Delta \dot{M} \ (Y/M)$. Although Equation (2) is only symbolic of policy and separtion-of-effects problems and is a solution in the context of the "big models,"[2] in a quite formal sense parameters of the equations leading to the solution (Equation [2], e.g.) should be obtainable by working backward from the parameter values of solution equations. So, Equation (2) is really symbolic of a great deal—a lot of interplay of forces; and the way some economists may think. The interplay of forces is of the sort I associate with Equation (1)—the transitory and permanent time frames; the dependence of interest rates, exchange rates, and inflation rates on monetry matters; episodic changes, psychological time, and so on. It is all at odds with attempting to control money aggregates of choice via interest rates ("opportunity cost") and income (or the fiscal policy component of income). To be sure, all the burdens of the selected monetary experiments of the past enter.

As to the way economists may think in reference to the combination of Equation (2) and the mentioned interplay of the forces, I turn to the honorable Governor Leigh-Pemberton. On the one hand, he readily recognizes the absence of any "switches" on the right side of Equation (2) that his office can control to obtain a specified effect on the left side. He may even recognize that the Bank of England controls only a short-term money market rate of interest and hence not the crucial long-term one of Keynes's *General Theory* (1936). But then, on the other hand, the "time honored" method of ceteris paribus returns to the discussion, where the troublesome forces are artificially impounded and with great gusto and precise if unfounded effects and linkages between them appear.

In contrast, the Friedman system of analysis starts with the recognized interplay of forces and the methodological problems confronting an elucidation of them, as well as with the need for simplicity and fruitful hypotheses. The uses of mechanical apparatus and statistical methods are indirect, special time frames enter, psychological forces gain ascendancy (psychological time, expected inflation rates, the definition of money in terms of Keynes, and so on).

5.2   TRADITIONS AND PRACTICES

The main traditions relevant to the banking matters at hand and in the next chapter go back to the last decades of the nineteenth century when the central bank's efforts were directed toward very short-run, liquidity phenomena. They can be dated by the appearance of Walter Bagehot's *Lombard Street* (1873) and the Bank of England's handling of the stress placed on the London's money market in 1891 following the collapse of the firm of Baring Brothers and Company. This posed a threat to the entire banking system, which was handled via the assurance provided for the liquidity of notes traded in the money market.

The Bank of England's technique of intervening in the money market to ensure the purchase of instruments at prices about or above market prices gained acceptance, as did the bank's technique of setting the bank rate as the rate at which it would buy or sell at a discount the money market instruments. Although not exactly open market operations in the strict sense discussed in Section 3.3, OMO is presently seen as a part and possibly even a total part of the practice of ensuring liquidity in the money market in various ways. Notably, the practice can be directed thus: toward ensuring the liquidity of instruments traded in the short run; and as a "defensive operation," and not as a means of ensuring long-run growth in a money aggregate. This matter of ensuring liquidity to the money market is what gave rise to the notion of a "bank rate," a minimum cost borrowing requirement, and a discount (or "rediscount") rate to begin with.

In 1913, when the Federal Reserve was established, the single instrument adopted for dealing with drains on liquidity was the discount rate.[3]   The regional banks of the system were to meet seasonal drains on the liquidity of the member banks by rediscounting "eligible paper" at the discount (or re-discount) rate. It also became the rate at which the Federal Reserve would simply lend its member banks reserves to offset drains on them (FY 1966, 143-145, 156-162). In this sense and in the foregoing Bank of England case, the central banks were lenders of last resort. However, in the United States and in some measure in the United Kingdom case lending was not to be a permanent means of extending liquidity and certainly not growth in reserves, bank credit, and the money stock. Even so, the Keynesian Lord Kaldor came to view the "lender of last resort" function to mean that the central bank would simply supply all the needed reserves to meet loan demand and to see fiscal policy as the instrument for maintaining total spending up to the Keynesian "full-employment" rate.

As noted earlier, the Federal Reserve's approach to the early 1930s drains on liquidity were catastrophic in its effects. Furthermore, the whole interest rate orientation, as it was extended to the commercial banks, was one of loan demand at the commercial banks. The vision in the 1930s was that low interest rates stimulated loan demand by businesses, although interest rates were quite low at the time.   In contrast to what I introduced in connection with psychological time, it was as if a loan rate were placed on the vertical axis of Figure 1-3a and bank loans on the horizontal axis, so that as the interest rate declined, loan demand would increase at the same time via the demand schedule.

Closely allied to their vision was Keynes's money/bond model of the *General Theory* (1936), which later gained ascendancy in academic circles. The rate on the government's long-term bonds appears in the model along with Keynes's "backwardation" view of the interest-rate, control arrangement.   In the shock of the 1930s, when very low interest rates prevailed and little or no loan demand and capital spending came about, the vision can be referred to metaphorically as "pushing on a string." (The loan-demand situation was not too difficult in the United States as late as the 1990-91 recession. Even as the discount rate at the Federal Reserve Bank of New York declined in five steps from 7 to 3.5 percent, and the "prime rate" on short-term bank loans from 10 to 6.5 percent, there was decline in the growth of bank loans.)

Out of the 1930s condition came two divergent strands of thought: (1) the "fiscal policy" emphasis most clearly stated by Kaldor and (2) the "helicopter money" concept as offered by Milton Friedman. In the meantime in the United States, two additional instruments for use in influencing and indeed controlling bank reserves gained legal recognition as a part of the banking acts of 1933 and 1935.   One was changes in the legal reserve requirements of the Federal Reserve's member banks. It was first used to soak up liquidity in the U.S. banking system via a series of increases in 1936 and 1937, with even low interest rates and the 1937-38 recession as a consequence.   The action was tantamount to having the Federal Reserve doubling reserve requirements during the 1990-92 recession at a time when interest rates and growth in bank loans were declining and bank liquidity was rising.

The other central bank instrument to achieve statutory status in the 1933 to 1935 period was open market operations (OMO), which had been discovered at the Federal Reserve Bank of New York. As first pointed out, with OMO comes a means of literally managing reserves (R_o) as they appear in the bank reserve equation.   To be sure, the potential here for the Federal Reserve's Open Market Committee to purchase and sell securities in the open market with the view of controlling R_o, as a substitute for the old gold flows, is radically different from that of the Bank of England's operations in London's money market to ensure liquidity via that market.   Moreover, the bank reserve equation offers an accounting control arrangement that the Bank of England does not have for the U.K.'s banks. As a consequence, the Bank of England is left to simply confront conditions via interest rates and the tone and the feel it has for flows to and from the money market (Staff 1988, 1989). Where it has the potential for OMO of the U.S. variety via its management of the public sector borrowing requirement (PSBR) and via purchases and sales with the select money market firms (Staff 1988), it stops short of reaching for the potential. It would in any case call for accounting control over reserves and changes in traditions governing the Bank of England's management of reserves.

As matters have come about, there are lessons for the Bank of England, and the European Community to be more certain, to be learned from the U.S. experiences, although the great potential of OMO in the United States was not well recognized in even limited circles until the concept of helicopter money was developed. With it, the metaphor whereby the authority could not "push on a string" no longer applied, and, in any case, the Reichsbank achieved money and credit growth under the devastating 1930s conditions without resort to interest rates and efforts to push on a string. Quite realistically, as illustrated first in Section 3.3d, the central banks were in a position to increase reserves (and hence bank credit and the money stock) without borrowers taking the initiative to come to the banks to take out loans.

The lessons to be learned especially by the EC, can be briefly stated. They are, first, that OMO are the only general control over reserves needed to manage the reserves that support bank credit and the money stock, and, second, that OMO and the helicopter money concept are a substitute for the traditional "announcement" effects associated with discount (or bank) rate changes and for fiscal policy. Changes in the discount rate may have some "announcement value" in bringing attention to the central bank's presence, but for the most part they have not been used as a part of the Federal Reserve's general control over reserves. Rather, I see it as simply moving in line with market rates, to avoid being left below market rates when they are rising and above market rates when they are declining.

Further, "announcement effects" can be achieved with OMO as they were at the time of the October 1987 stock market crash in the United States, when Chairman Greenspan met with President Reagan to make such an announcement. Indeed, in mid July 1990, as the Federal Reserve confronted budget-deficit problems in the United States, chairman Greenspan both offered to substitute some monetary ease for a balanced budget, and "announced" Federal Reserve plans for intervention to offset some sign of "credit tightness" at banks, which he combined with a subsequent open market intervention.

The helicopter money concept Friedman offers, the institutional and accounting-control practices underlying it, and the overall analytical system embracing both, provide a substitute set consisting of both central banking prospects and economic analysis. On the one hand, there is the Keynesian/post-Keynesian approach with the arrangements and analytical apparatus illustrated by reference to Lord Kaldor. It is more a part of a collectivist orientation (fiscal policy, the PSBR, funding policy, and the like come to center stage). On the other hand, Friedman's approach points toward only the most general of controls, the substitution of OMO for gold flows in the bank reserve equation, and growth in the money and credit aggregates up to the "natural rate of unemployment." It is markets oriented, and there is voluntary association in markets.

In the Friedman system, the money stock impacts on GNP, although feedback from income to money growth may be involved. Major unanticipated shocks to the economic system aside—such as pointed out in the U.K. case below, where it underwent the privatization of government owned companies in the second half of the 1980s—the money growth can do the job of achieving and sustaining smooth growth in income. As indicated in reference to the government budget constraint, fiscal policy then becomes a means of crowding the private sector in and out of the total economic system rather than a means of sustaining spending. In the 1960s and 1970s, the accommodation of government spending by the central banks of the United States and the United Kindom, along with tax policy, contributed to an increase in government as a percentage of GNP.

In the early 1980s, things changed, as variously discussed—including in reference to monetary accommodation and discipline and inflation rates (Figures 2-1 and 2-2). Among them Ronald Reagan sought to reduce the ratio of government to GNP, in part by using monetary policy to tame inflation and by allowing federal deficits to accumulate in order to maintain pressure on the U.S. Congress to cut government spending (Frazer 1988, Chapter 16). In the United Kingdom, Margaret Thatcher also sought to tame inflation by monetary means, to stimulate economic growth and productivity by tax means, and to privatize government-owned companies. However, the banking and monetary arrangements there were not conducive to this task except in the crudest way, as will be explained. Moreover, in the second half of the 1980s in the United Kingdom changes were ocurring where the government's financing dramatically "crowded in" the private sector.

5.3 "THE BIG U-TURN"

The move away from the banking and Keynesian mode of control, which I label the i-orientation, and along the lines of Friedman's money and credit aggregates means of control, which I label M-orientation, was less successful in the United Kingdom than in the United States in one sense but not in another. In one sense, the United Kingdom did not make the changes needed in the institutional, accounting control operations arrangements (hypotheses H_{CB} and H_{TW}). However, in terms of conducting a highly disciplinary monetary policy, inadvertent or otherwise, the United Kingdom was quite successful.

5.3a The U.K. Case

The impact of Friedman's work extended to the United Kingdom, after research with Anna Schwartz (FS 1982) was broadened in 1966 to include the United Kingdom. Following analyses of data for both the United States and the

United Kingdom for the period 1867 to 1975, a major conclusion was drawn; namely, The two countries have in common the same determinants of money demand. It meant that no conditions special to one country need to be brought into discussion, as far as the important empirical findings were concerned.

However, there was a difficulty connected with basing a change in policy, let alone a change in the policy regime, on these findings. The difficulty was that experiencing the same monetary phenomena did not extend to the presence of the same accounting control and operations arrangements for conducting policy based on the empirical findings. The Bank of England had evolved with different traditions, control, and operational arrangements. The ability to conduct policy along the lines found in the United States depended on the bank reserve equation (Cagan 1965), and a relatively straightforward system of money and credit multipliers (FY 1966, Section 3.3) for relating bank reserves to bank credit and the money stock (Figure 3-7).

Furthermore, in making what I have called "The Big U-Turn," the United Kingdom was faced with the need for far more extreme changes than in the United States. Primary among these was the privatization of the numerous companies that the U.K. government had come to own under socialist governments. In the order of priority found in the move toward less government and free markets, the reform of a banking system to bring about an M-regime policy was of a lower order. In addition, even as privatization got under way in the U.K. in the second half of the 1980s, the impact on household and company spending could not have been forecast by fashionable econometric means. The monetarist means with allowance for episodic change may have worked better, but economists and officials held only the simplest views of monetary control in terms of money and credit aggregates (recall, e.g., Equation [2] in Section 1.4a). Institutional arrangements for implementing a full M-orientation at the Bank of England were not in place, and the U.K. officials were unaware of difficulties that could arise from credit sources extending to building associations and financial intermediaries other than those of the more narrowly defined system of fractional reserve banks (Leigh-Pemberton 1986).

In broad outline, rather immediate effects of privitization are illustrated in Figure 5-1. In particular, as the old merchant banks of the City of London took up the task of floating stock issues in the companies, two significant things happened: (1) income to the government from sales brought budgets into balance and permitted the retirement of some previously accumulated government debt and (2) a broad base of the citizens acquired liquid assets on very favorable terms that they had not previously held (the factor w in Equation [1] of Section 1.5a) and the ratio of holdings of wealth to non-human total wealth, Wnh/W, in the consumption function. The net results were (1) funds of financial institutions were freed up so as to permit the extension of credit to the household and business sectors, (2) the ownership of liquid assets and availability of credit supported strong growth in private sectors spending, and

(3) the growth of government debt was exchanged for the growth of private debt, as shown in Figure 5-1.

In conjunction with the changes that were occuring in private sector saving and in public sector borrowing, the U.K.'s chancellor Nigel Lawson had against Thatcher's knowledge led the Bank of England into attempts to have the U.K. pound mirror the foreign exchange market behavior for the German mark, with the view to entering into the European currency arrangement that appeared in the Delors Report. As a means of doing so he appears to have sought faster economic growth by banking means, but the consequences were complicated by interrelated developments on two other fronts. They were (1) a renewal of inflation in the United States, as shown much earlier in Figure 2-1, at a time when (2) the velocity ratio for the sterling M3 stock of money balances continued downward, as shown in Figure 5-2. Although this velocity behavior would not be normally expected in the presence of rising inflation, it

Figure 5-1
Private Sector Saving and Public Borrowing for the United Kingdom as Percentages of GDP

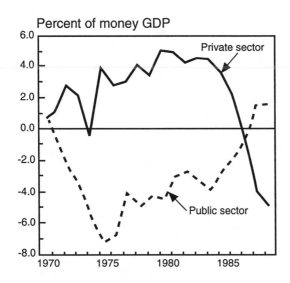

Source: Bank of England

Figure 5-2
**Velocity Ratios for the United Kingdom and the United States, the 1970s
and the 1980s**

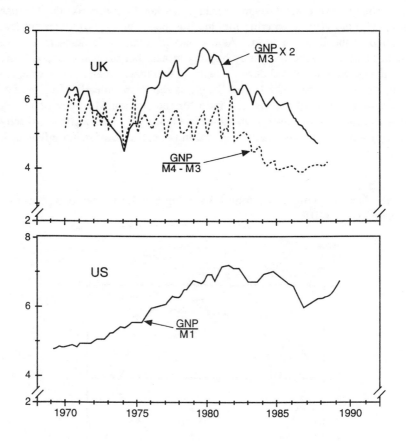

nevertheless appeared in the U.K. setting. The public was expressing a
preference for more sterling M3 balances relative to income (i.e., $-\Delta[Y/M3]$),
even as inflation was reoccuring.

So what happened? The public was relying less on the turnover of M3
balances as a means of making expenditures as credit and the other means of
making transactions on certain classes of assets become available as a result of
the privitization of U.K. companies. This in turn gave support to an increase
in the inflation rate in 1989 (Figure 2-1). An explanation for its doing so goes

back to Friedman's position that households control the real money balances (the primary equation of Section 1.5a). There was a preference for more real sterling M3 in relation to real income (M3/P in relation to Y/P) even as the inflation rate rose for reasons other than reliance on sterling M3 as a means of making transactions. Most notably, there was greater reliance on credit and balances at the building societies.

What occurred in London in this rather unmanageable set of circumstances is a reversion to the older ways of central banking, as balance sheets revealed enormous structural change in the money and financial areas. For the Bank of England's part, the short-term interest rate ("the bank rate") was again pointed to as the principal instrument of policy, and said by its governor, Leigh-Pimberton (1986, 1987), to be the only instrument of policy at its control. Taking up the short-term interest rate as the policy instrument, all the old and mostly static concepts bearing on the defensive strategy and interest rates come back into discussion—the Bank of England operates in the sterling discount market to ensure a balancing out of funds flowing into and out of the market; changes in the interest rate may induce wealth effects, as in the Keynesian, money/bond model; and the Treasury's yield curve (Figure 3-2), may be twisted by the banks operations with the discount houses, which are designated by the Bank of England. As with the ordinary embracement of these static, ceteris paribus based concepts, there is a strenuous separation-of-effects mechanism such as we discussed on variousy.

Further, the view of the United Kingdom as an isolated island dependent on foreign trade and subject to being buffeted by outside forces comes back. Indeed, it appears in the United Kingdom's practice of using the GDP income measure rather than the GNP one,[4] and harks bark to Keynes. In reference to the U.K. and the U.S. economy, he said: "Wide fluctuations which spell unemployment and misery for us, are swamped for them in the general upward movement" (1932d, 233).

The prevalence of this view in the United Kingdom and even the possible "truth content" of it cannot be denied. However, in juxtaposition to the possible "truth content" I point to the FS position (namely, that no contributions special to the United Kingdom needs to be brought into discussions as far as empirical findings for the United States and the United Kingdom are concerned), and to the phenomenon known in the United States as "the chasing of interest rates" (Frazer 1988, 287-298, 567). The phenomenon comes about as open market purchases intended to raise bond prices (and hence lower interest rates) contribute to the inflationary growth of the money and credit aggregates and hence to raises interest rates $[i = i(real) + (1/P)(dP/dt)*]$, and so on. In the U.K. case, there may be variations on the prospect, for example, the effort to support the pound in the foreign exchange through open market purchases of pounds (say, to raise its price, Δ DM/£) with the result that inflation comes about and interest rates rise even as the deutsch mark price of the pound declines (say, $-\Delta$ DM/£).

In any case, looking beyond the Bank of England's traditions, practices, and positions to the larger European community, the concept of a small island economy no longer holds. Anticipating common central banking arrangements for Europe, the size of the new common market would withstand more by way of outside forces—liquidity trade shifts, and all.

5.3b The U.K. Case—Thought Processes

The two relevant equations that illustrate the Bank of England's early efforts at monetarism and the thought processes of its policy makers have been variously introduced. Beyond that, there were references to the Keynesian view of money demand and exchange rates.

The equations, from Sections 1.4a, 2.5, and 4.4, are

$$\ln M = a_0 + a_1 \ln i + a_2 \ln Y \tag{1}$$

and (with some modifications)

$$
\begin{aligned}
\text{GNP and/or GDP} = a_0 &+ a_1 + a_2 \; \$/\text{Index of foreign currencies} \\
&+ a_3 \; \pounds/\text{Index of foreign currencies} \\
&+ a_4 \; (\text{monetary accommodation and discipline}) \\
&+ a_5 \; P_{US}/P_{UK} + \dots
\end{aligned}
\tag{2}
$$

Three features of these expressions are (1) the Keynesian view of controlling the money stock (and its demand via the interest rate), (2) the separation-of-effects problem of analysis, and (3) a very short-run time frame. Further, the equations are not presently viewed along the econometrically fashionable lines in either of two respects: (1) as candidates for the regression of left-hand side variables on the right-side ones (2) nor as functions depicting the officials behavior on the left side as reactions to the right side.[5]

The thought processes involved in the foregoing statements, nevertheless, are mirrored in a combination of the big model approach (Frazer 1994a, Section 7.4) and the long-standing practice of invoking the rather blunt tool of ceteris paribus. This can be seen as the practice of locking up changes ("all other changes," for the most part), while the effects of one variable are considered as being independent of the impounded forces. The practice also gains attention as being a part of forecasting based on the condition or constancy ("impounded," "locked up," "assumed,") of "all other things."[6]

However, in contrast to this practice, the facts of the matter indicate that the policy connected (or right-hand-side) variables of Equation (2) come as a package. This is such that they cannot be separated for control purposes short of the use of force by the state (as in the case of direct price and wage controls).

Indeed, the interdependence of the variables appears on doing the following: recall the dependence of the interest rate (i) on the expected inflation rate, recall the inverse correlation and the trade-off between the inflation rate and the exchange value of the dollar (Figure 4-2a), connect monetary accommodation and discipline to the other variables (or time series) in Section 2.5, and view monetary and fiscal policy as substitutes (including as in Section 3.3e and in the government budget constraint).

So the practice of separating the effects by artificial means comes into focus on an equation, such as Equation (2), which can be called a solution equation (or "reduced form equation," to use the econometric term). In the formal, econometric view, the variables on the right-hand side of an equation such as Equation (2) are viewable as control variables which are exogenous to the system of equations (meaning outside the system in terms of influences etc.) and independent of one another.[7] Even so, no self-respecting officials or staff persons supporting them would view these latter, exogenous/independent prospects as obtainable. I quoted the Bank of England's governor, Leigh-Pemberton (1987), on that earlier.

The officials and support people draw on the thought processes but stop short of the danger zones (the exogenous/independent prospects). They do so by using strong doses of ceteris paribus, especially when attempting to make defensible statements before college audiences and in the press. Taking clues from the Bank of England's "Fact Sheets" and two of Leigh-Pemberton's lectures I see Equation (2) taking some peculiar turns: First, GDP is preferred by Leigh-Pimberton and many U.K. people on the grounds that Britain is very vulnerable to shifts in international finance and trade. As pointed out, they thus net out of GNP the "net foreign investment" category and in that way stress GDP. Second, GNP may be separated as to the product of a price index (P) and real output (Q, or constant price GNP, i.e., GNP/P = Q), so that even the components of the price average can be discussed separately in reference to inflation (i.e., ΔP). Third, a simple price index can be denoted, where in reference to it a decline in the value of the pound (say, in Equation [2] above) can be said to contribute to inflation (ΔP) by raising the price of some of the goods and services entering into the price index via the right-hand member of the price index. This assertion of a source of inflation then becomes possible, even when the decline in the value of the pound may itself be the result of speculation in the foreign exchange markets over the Bank of England and U.K. Treasury resolve to control inflation by monetary means.

In further reference to Equation (2) and the speculation by the participants in the markets, there may even be the prospect that the Bank of England will fund a sizable part of the public sector borrowing requirement and thereby accommodate the inflation. Fourth, the real interest rate (i[rea]), rather arbitrarily defined as the nominal rate (i) less the actual inflation rate (P̣), can be viewed as if the central bank had the capacity to raise and lower it separately from the inflation rate itself, which I deny. Finally, the view can be found that the money stock (M) is being monitored when all of the above are going on, although there is no accounting identity in the U.K. case with which to monitor the reserves that give rise to the money stock (Figure 3-7).

The strange reasoning just described in the five listed points, is made possible by the concept of impounding "all other things" even when doing so is in fact impossible by any known, direct means. To be sure, the discussion as outlined stresses the interdependence of the variables in Equation (2). The money growth may contribute to the prospect of inflation, as encountered in the Bank of England's accommodation of the PSBR, and this in turn may contribute to a decline in the value of the pound, even as the latter is pointed to as the source of the inflation. Further, the interest rate may rise in reference to all of the above (via its dependence on the expected inflation rate). So, the independence of the variables in Equation (2) is not something that abounds in the real world, even as the Bank of England's "Fact Sheets" and the governor's lecture points toward it.

The apparent widespread acceptance of the rather tenuous means of separating effects, and the authority given to pronouncements based on it, has led to the statement I call "the-man-in-the-backroom illusion." [8] Among other things, it alludes to the prospect that the static constructs in economics (even call them partial analysis) can be found in the real world "directly" by known econometric methods (or means known to those people in the backroom); that predictions associated with the ceteris paribus method of impounding other things are tantamount to unconditional predictions (as in the case of some hard sciences); that a variable on the left-hand-side of an equation can be accounted for in terms of a "direct" and adequately detailed treatment of additional right-hand side variables.

The further "escape hatch" found in the Bank of England's "Fact Sheets" is the way interest rates and exchange rates are so confidently said to be determined by supply and demand (as in the old loanable funds theory [Frazer 1994a, Section 7.4a]). This would not be questioned of course, except there are some qualifications that should be pointed to. For one, in the sense of schedules, no economist has ever found loci of points from observations of financial markets that could be called supply or demand schedules. For another qualification, even relying only on the concepts of supply as a schedule and demand likewise, they offer a gamut of prospects. These range from just floating around in response to all sorts of anticipations, to one moving a great deal more than the other when both sides of the market are responding to the prospects.

Using such a limited means of pinning analysis to reality, the "Fact Sheets" offers some interesting conclusions; notably, the yields on "gilt-edged stocks (or gilts)," which are in fact bonds of a long term to maturity (ranging up to thirty years), are determined by supply and demand forces; and the yield on short-dated assets (normally commercial bills of up to three months' maturity) are similarly determined by supply and demand forces. In this context and particularly in reference to the short-dated assets, the Bank of England is said to have considerable influence over the level of interest rates by buying or selling assets. There is little question in the "Fact Sheets" and in the governor's lectures that the Bank of England's influence is on interest rates directly and certainly not via the creation (or extension) of any bank reserves that may support more or less growth in bank credit or the money stock. To be sure, there is even the prospect whereby the Bank of England can "twist" the yield curve, as it varies the quantities offered or withdrawn from the market in very short time frames.

The positions taken separately of the matters concerning the right-side variables in Equation (2) can be made to appear quite plausible on ceteris paribus, a priori reasoning, as the appeal of the traditional reliance on the reasoning would indicate. However, when taken as a whole, the approach is indefensible. There the direct means of separating effects are illusory, even as I see the emphasis on the very short run and the Bank of England's ability to manipulate supply and demand forces at the margin. So, at the base is the man-in-the backroom illusion.

In addition to the traditions, and the absence of accounting controls, some of the Bank of England's failure to adequately move along monetarist lines in the taming of inflation in the early 1980s can be attributed to the excessively simple (even Keynesian) view it held. Both Governor Leigh-Pemberton and his predecessor Gordon Richardson pointed to the control of the interest rates (i) and fiscal policy (say, the government's deficit spending component of Y) as means of controlling M and also thereby of putting the money supply on target (say, ln M of Equation [2]). This came about, even as the Bank of England's advisory and research people and the Governor himself pointed to the instability in the velocity ratio.

Referring to Equation (1), it would consist of the numerator Y and the denominator M. In addition, Equation (1) would be the sort of statistical relation found in the highly visibly work of David Laidler who was pointing to the stability of the money demand relation as the United Kingdom made its control efforts (Frazer 1988, 560-562).

The empirical/policy problem with the finding of stability in the relation between the velocity ratio and the rate of interest (ln [Y/M] = a + b ln i, or alternatively Equation [1]), is mainly threefold, from the Friedman system perspective. It is that it failed to give attention to the four classes of assets with expected rates of return, and not just rates on debt type assets; it failed to take into account the time frames Friedman brought to hear on the analysis of time series; and it failed to take note of Friedman's search for a stable phenomena, and not simply a stable, direct statistical regression (Frazer 1988, 76-77, 79). Friedman allowed for the impact of episodes on the time series, and made adjustments in his data for some of them. One such episode, already mentioned, would be the privatization of government-owned companies in the United Kingdom in the second half of the 1980s. Another, taken up shortly, would be the deregulation of banks in the United States in the early 1980s and the inclusion of new, interest-bearing deposits at that time in the category for the narrowly defined money stock (dollars M1) in the early 1980s (Frazer 1988, 656-658).

When the composition of a time series changes, it should be obvious that an episode has impacted on it to alter a prior, possibly stable relation. Furthermore, as noted earlier in discussion of Figures 3-1, 3-3, a stable velocity/interest-rate relation was altered when the two variables drifted apart as the United States moved into the inflationary era of the 1960s and 1970s. In the case of Figure 3-3, and the early 1960s to mid-1980s period, the interest rate was being driven by the level for the expected inflation rate [$i = i[\text{real}] + \dot{P}^e$] when spending on capital goods was being driven more closely by changes in the expected inflation rate. Also, uncertainty in the forecast can enter, and it makes no sense to simply allow for these foregoing prospects by adding terms to regression equations ordinarily viewed. The numerous reasons include that: (1) the variables being treated are all interdependent, (2) the forces in operation are nonrepetitive, (3) retaining the variables when they no longer operate yields rather meaningless coefficients, and (4) inflation (or deflation) can have one effect when it proceeds from a zero rate and quite another when it builds on a situation that is already socially disruptive.

Drawing on the prospects just reviewed, there are means of obtaining a stable money demand relation through allowance for episodic changes via methods suggested by Friedman. Proceeding from a known stable relation between two variables and the theoretic prospects I note, the approach calls for adjustments in the time series for the episodes. In some instances, such as that for deregulation in the United States in the early 1980s and the series for dollars M1, the approach is quite simple; namely, take the prior, known stable relation between the logarithmically transformed adjusted money base (ln AMB) and the money aggregate (ln M1) and use the stable relation to reproduce the episodically altered segment of the time series that leads the series to depart from its prior stable position. The new time series—reconstituted with the estimated segment—can then be used to reestimate a stable relation and the difference between the estimated segment and the original, episodically altered series can be attributed to the known episode.

5.3c The U.S. Case

The operations problem of controlling money and credit aggregates and taming inflation by monetary means was far less difficult in the period of Ronald Reagan's presidency in the United States than in Margaret Thatcher's United Kingdom. This was partly because the U.K. situation had deteriorated more, and partly because the Bank of England lacked the accounting control and operations means for controlling money and credit aggregates. As variously pointed out, the United States had a fairly direct means of accounting for bank reserves (the R_0 in Figure 3-7 and the bank reserve equation; OMO in the New York money market had become a means of supplying and controlling reserves; direct links, via credit and money multipliers, were possible; and measures such as the money base (or R_0) and the main money aggregates (M1, M2, . . .) were relatively well identified.

Nevertheless, the foregoing measures and accounting arrangements are subject to shocks, often imposed by government itself. One example, mentioned elsewhere in the U.S. case (Frazer 1988, 656-659), came in the early 1980s, when new types of interest bearing accounts were included in the narrowly measured M1 money supply. These new accounts were called NOW accounts (negotiable order of withdrawal accounts), MMDAs (money market deposit accounts), and Super NOW accounts. Further, the old NOWs became Super NOWs (essential old NOWs but without regulated interest rates). Restricted to individuals, governmental units, and certain nonprofit institutions, these became effective in January 1983. The special problems of controlling the current M1 then arose for what may be an obvious reason, notably, the new presence of an interest rate can cause switching to M1 from money-market assets, but there is no longer the same inducement for switching out of the M1 category when an interest-yielding asset is included in the measure for M1. In any case, the institutional changes and growth in M1 beyond the original target range of 4.0 to 8.0 percent led the Fed at mid year to reset its goal for 1983, both by changing the base rate and by setting the range at 5.0 to 9.0 percent. This, called "base drift," is shown in Figure 5-3 for the M1 aggregate for 1983.

These statistical difficulties need not be mentioned further, except to note two things: (1) the Federal Reserve suspended the targeting of M1 and switched to other money aggregates (such as M2 or the money base) in their presence, and (2) the suspension was consequently not so much a change in policy as the recognition that a non-repetitive (or "episodic") change had occurred to alter the meaning of targeting M1. The switch to another aggregate for targeting in 1983 could be termed simply a recognition that an episode had altered the M1 series and that the targeting of another aggregate was simply a means of recognizing this.

5.3d The U-Turn, and EMS-member and Non-member Countries

The EMS came into being in 1979, just as the "U-Turn" changes from the 1970s to the 1980s were occurring. It did so in part with German leadership, with initial prospects for symmetry as to power and participation but with what is see nlater as Bundesbank dominance. The coincidence of the timing for the EMS and the "U-Turn" changes I associated mainly with the United States, the United Kingdom, and to some extent the Federal Republic of Germany as a

Figure 5-3
The U.S. M1 Target Ranges, 1983

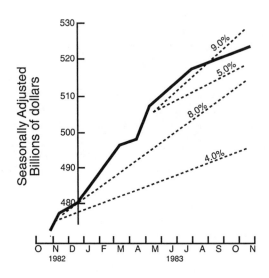

"strong" Fed/Friedman/monetarist institution, has led some economists to see the EMS as a positive 1980s force for disinflation.

Combining these notions, and drawing on Fratianni and von Hagan (1990, 87, 93-95), recalls three of the hypotheses first cited in Section 1.1, namely:

H_{FTL}. *Follow the leader (FTL)*. Following Bundesbank and German leadership, the EMS Member countries find credibility for inflation-control commitments by virtue of membership in the EMS.

H_{PA}. *Policy autonomy (PA)*. EMS Member countries are attracted to the democratic, flexible arrangements offered by the EMS for voting, the prospects for realigning exchange rates, and hence by autonomy in the policy sphere.

$H_{U\text{-}Turn}$. *The "U-Turn."* The main non-Asian Western trading countries of the 1970s and 1980s were led for the most part by Keynesian ideas in the 1970s and—following crises in the United Kingdom, the United States, and to some extent elsewhere—monetary/disciplinary and markets/oriented ideas for much of the 1980s.

Statistical results for the United States, the United Kingdom and the Federal Republic of Germany have been reported in terms of trends and changes in direction. In addition, Fratianni and von Hagen show inflation-rate data for the

Federal Republic of Germany and six other EMS countries, and for nine non-member countries. What they report is that inflation for the EMS and non-EMS countries—and for the United States and the United Kingdom, separately—reached peaks in 1980. Inflation rates then dramatically declined for the groups involved and for the United States and the United Kingdom separately. In addition, most of the countries experienced peak inflation rates in 1980; most moved toward considerable lower rates through 1987; and as inflation rates declined, the standard deviations for the inflation rates in the EMS and non-EMS countries also declined.

These results support the H_{FLT} (or follow-the-mark) and $H_{U\text{-}Turn}$ (or shared-ideas) hypotheses, and offer no evidence that countries were autonomous in following monetary and inflation-rate goals. Fratianni and von Hagan conclude that the first hypothesis is impossible to test separately from the shared-ideas one because the observations to support the two are equivalent, but rather I see that the results do not lead to rejecting H_{FLT}. Fratianui and von Hagan provide some weight for the German dominance thesis by pointing to FRG's role in "the group of five" major countries and to the fact that the Germans did not impose on the EMS a strategy of pegging to the dollar.

5.4   AN OVERVIEW

Overall, the United Kingdom attempted to control the money aggregate sterling M3 as a means of taming inflation in the early 1980s. Indeed, the Bank of England under Governor Richardson had moved since the mid 1970s toward the possible targeting of money aggregates. However, as noted, the U.K. efforts to control the money stock, narrowly defined (sterling M3), by using interest rates and fiscal policy. These appear more as a Keynesian, i-orientation way of doing things than the M-orientation alternative Friedman offered. Moreover, I have noted some very special impediments to the Bank of England's implementation of a monetary policy—the traditions and past practices and the absence of accounting control arrangements comparable to those in the United States. Said differently, the U.K. government never restructured the Bank of England's operations and arrangements for the undertaking of a Friedman monetarist policy.

Along this line, the Bundesbank did not need any restructuring. Coming later in time as a central bank, the Bundesbank took on a federalist structure and adopted the instruments found at the U.S. Federal Reserve. Moreover, it was committed early to a regulation of the money supply. This was such that it did not require major changes in its control arrangement and approach as it adopted the idea of targeting a money aggregate of choice along the Friedman/monetarist line. I see it thus in terms of M-orientation.

Table 5-1

Summary of Selected i- and M-regime Features

i-regime	M-regime
1. Raising and lowering interest rates (the bank rates), above or below what it would be exclusive of intentional policy change from ordinary pattern. There is the prospect expressed by Governor Leigh-Pemberton that the money aggregate is not ignored by any means. But this enters via a relation such as $\ln M = a_0 + a_1 \ln i + a_2 \ln Y$, which we relate to Figure 1-2, as opposed to the regime symbolized by $M/P = f(Y/P, w; ...; u)$.	1. Accelerating and decelerating money growth (interest rate determined in the market, where agents form inflationary expectations and adjust rates accordingly); long-run concept of inflationary expectations, $i = i(\text{real}) + (1/P)(dP/dt)^*$; but structure underlying the formation of expectations may change such that previously long-run prospects become short-run, and vice versa; plus uncertainty in the prospect $Pb[(1/P)(dP/dt)^*]$ may enter to yield $i = i(\text{real}) \, Pb[(1/P)(dP/dt)^*] (1/P)(dP/dt)^*$.
2. Concept of two-asset model (causation; interest induced wealth effect; expected inflation rate constant, as a given condition for purpose of policy execution; short run). See Figure 1-2.	2. Concept of four-asset model (inflationary prospects taken as revealed by the market; inflation rate prospects tied to money and credit growth; proceeding from zero inflation, inflationary prospect moves rate of return on real capital in a positive direction, accelerates growth in real capital until adjustment in the asset structure complete, raises interest rates and yields just the reverse effect on the growth in real capital from that of the interest induced wealth effect under the i-regime). Note also time paths illustrated in Figures 1-4.
3. Twisting the yield curve (supply-demand-quantity mechanism comes into play in the short run).	3. Yield curve influenced by inflationary prospects as under item 1 above [except specific long-run time horizon (pull effect toward

Table 5-1 (continued)

i-regime	M-regime
	normality) and short-run horizon for short rate]. A supply-demand-quantity mechanism may come into play in the long run.
4. Separation of effects; direct methods; ceteris paribus; short run (inflationary expectations constant for purposes of ascertaining effects of policy--i.e., credit ease or tightness as depicted by interest rate).	4. Indirect method (analysis of a few variables at a time before proceeding otherwise); mutatis mutandis; time frames as depicted in Figure 1-4 [plus structure underlying formation of inflationary expectations may change as in item 1 above; monetary authority influences nominal (not real) interest rates and nominal stock of money such that inflationary expectations not constant for policy purposes].
5. Fiscal policy and monetary policy [as indicated by credit conditions and more accurately referred to as "credit policy" (i.e., credit "ease" or "tightness")] both enter into determination of income.	5. Monetary policy as a substitute for fiscal policy; government budget constraint such that fiscal policy simply crowds private sector in and out as percent of GNP.
6. No microeconomic (price theoretic) foundations as ordinarily understood, except in post-Keynesian variant the theories of market structure may explain inflation rather than growth in money and credit aggregates (Frazer 1994a, Section 7.3b).	6. Price theory and Keynesian statics as statement of position, plus price theoretic foundations via Friedman's tying of Marshall's and compensated demand curves to price index and quantity-theoretic expression $M = k(. . .) PQ$.

Table 5-2

Central Bank Operations: The U.K.'s Bank of England and the U.S. Federal Reserve

U.K.'s Bank of England	U.S. Federal Reserve
1. Banker to the government. This activity is the same as in the U.S., with two exceptions. One is that the Bank of England is itself an operating bank. The other is that the Bank may transfer funds to the U.K. Treasury's account which represents the assumption of some of the public sector borrowing requirement (PSBR) by the Bank.	1. Banker to the government. Treasury checks are drawn against accounts at the operating regional banks of the Federal Reserve System. Payments to the Treasury in taxes get transferred from private-sector accounts to the operating arms of the Federal Reserve.
2. The Bank assumes direct support of the U.K. Treasury's financing. It does so by taking responsibility for the PSBR and by assuming the financing for some, all, or an excess of the PSBR. Of significance here is the fact that the assumption of the financing is equivalent in its bank-reserve creating capacity to the open market operations (OMO) under item 3 for the Federal Reserve. In addition, as we addressed earlier in section 3-3 under Keynesian (or Kaldor) causation, the counterpart to OMO in the U.S. is set in motion by the U.K. Treasury's PSBR and the Bank of England's funding policy.	2. No direct support of Treasury financing.
3. Dealings with discount houses in the London market by buying or selling commercial and Treasury bills at the bank rate. This activity is directed toward facilitating the clearance of the money market for	3. Open market operations (OMO). Direct dealing is done with a select group of government securities dealers (London's equivalent to the discount houses under item 3), but with a major

Table 5-2 (continued)

U.K.'s Bank of England	U.S. Federal Reserve

commercial bills in the short run. Consequently, in contrast to item 3 on the Fed's side, consideration of the permanent impact from these dealings on growth in the money and credit aggregates is ambiguous.

exception, no rate of interest such as a discount or bank rate is set). OMO constitute the only major and permanent means for the Federal Reserve to expand the reserves of the non-central bank, in part since the discount windows are only temporary means of obtaining reserves. This activity is set in motion via monetary policy (and not PSBR or deficit financing by the government, as under item 2 for the Bank of England).

4. Lending in the inter-bank market. Here and in close relation to item 3 above, the Bank of England sets the discount rate (or bank rate, or bank dealing rate, all without much difference as to meaning). A rate is set at which the Bank advances funds to the market. Whether the rate is below market rates determines the extent of the Bank's purchases of bills and extension of funds to discount houses. In the context of meeting temporary liquidity needs of the London discount market, however, the lending in the interbank market stops short of being seen as the Bank's main means of supplying reserves to the system (depending also, of course, on matters surrounding the PSBR, under item 2 above).

4. Lending in the inter-bank market for bank reserves. This lending is said to take place through the Fed's discount windows. The discount rates are set at the initiative of the operating arms of the central governing board in Washington, D.C. Usually they are set in unison, so we speak of the discount rate (the price for borrowing reserves). It follows market interest rates upward and downward very closely, and rarely appears as a means for controlling reserves. The so-called discount window is viewed as a temporary source of bank reserves for the purpose of facilitating adjustments in reserves at non-central bank, banking units. Moreover, the latter banks trade in reserves with one another on very short-term bases. The market is called the federal funds market.

Table 5-2 (continued)

U.K.'s Bank of England	U.S. Federal Reserve
5. Conducts open market operations in foreign exchange markets. This activity is the same as on the Federal Reserve side. In the years since 1971, when the U.S. closed the gold window (i.e., no longer offered gold at $35.00 per ounce in exchange for dollars held abroad and by foreign central banks) and moved toward floating exchange rates, the private-sector, foreign exchange operations have grown. By the same token, private capital, which moves about the world freely, has grown in abundance. All of this is thought to have weakened any power central banks may have had to influence the rates (the prices, i.e., at which one currency exchanges for another).	5. Conducts open market operations in foreign exchange markets. These may be via the use of a pool of accumulated currencies or via outright purchase of a currency ("phase 3," Section 4.1a), as in the open market purchase of securities under item 3 above. In the latter case, the activity is more or less a substitute for OMO ordinarily viewed. It may be self-defeating as a means of supporting a currency since all the problems of expected inflation may come about, which led to a weak currency to begin with.

The immediately foregoing theme of the i- and M-orientations has been present since Chapter 1. Elements comprising it are pulled together in Table 5-1. The elements making up the additional theme of theory choice, bank operations, traditions, and practices are pulled together in Table 5-2, where special attention is given to the Bank of England and the Federal Reserve.

Two main conclusions follow from the present treatment of the alternative approaches, institutional arrangements, traditions, and practices. One is that the Bank of England never fully moved to an M-regime approach to monetary policy. The second is that the Bank of England was precluded from doing so by the presence of a rather Keynesian view of controlling the money stock and by the inadequacy of the accounting controls and the institutional, market arrangements it inherited from its more distant and successful past.

The "rather Keynesian view" extends to the prospects for doing several things—controlling the money stock via the use of interest rates and fiscal policy; finding a "flat out" stable relation between the interest rates, the fiscal policy, and the money stock, rather than one allowing for the impact of episodes; and the separation of the effects of variables, which appear interrelated and hence inseparable in the alternative approach. Central among these interrelated variables are interest rates, inflation rates, and exchange rates.

The second conclusion also suggests that the appropriate accounting control and market-intervention arrangements are necessary for the execution of an M-regime approach to the conduct and implementation of monetary policy. Anticipating new central banking prospects for a nucleus of EC Member states, I conclude that the new arrangements to be put in place are related to the choice of the policy to be implemented. This choice of policy may be along Keynesian, i-orientation lines or Friedman, M-orientation lines. The former set gives attention to fiscal policy that some EC Member countries may wish to retain control over as a right of the member state and as a part of national sovereignty. The latter set is an alternative to the Keynesian arrangements. It offers the greatest sovereignty to the member states.

Moreover, the failures of operations and the execution of policy in the United Kingdom and elsewhere do not bring into question the theoretic/empirical economics Friedman offered other than in relation to operations, policy execution, and the analysis of the time series for a monetary economy. Rather this failure does two things: (1) it shifts some renewed attention to interest rates, exclusive of the attention to interest rates and fiscal policy as means of controlling money demand in a Keynesian context, and (2) it elevates the importance of episodes, structural changes underlying the formation of inflationary expectations (expectations generally, psychological time, and so on). This place for episodes (exogeneous matters and like) and non-repetitive change (perhaps even with regard for the place of repetition in psychological time) has long been a focus of central bankers—the center of the idea of crisis management as it relates to money matters (traditionally, the money market as the market for the most liquid of assets, but extending in the United States in more recent times to the stock market and confidence in the banking and financial systems). In relation to the money, capital, and credit markets, the interest rate as the price of credit and the indicator of credit conditions gains high visibility and the prices of the instruments traded show great volatility.

Given such behavior and its future prospect, I ask: (1) Why do those in the print media and central bankers other than those exceptional ones at the Bundesbank prefer to give so much attention to interest rates over that given to the targeting of money and credit aggregates? (2) What are the lessons to be learned from the theoretic/empirical approach Friedman set on course and from the central banking experiences with it? As Leigh-Pemberton said about the experiences with controlling inflation: "The slowdown in inflation, though starting earlier in the UK and from a higher level, has been accompanied by a similar development in other major countries. . . . Other countries, too, . . . relied heavily on monetary policy to contain their rates of inflation" (Leigh-Pemberton 1986).

To answer the first question, I go back to Section 1.4b and turn again to Leigh-Pemberton, and point to the following: the ready availability of interest rate data; the fact that they reflect the processing of masses of information on the part of market participants; and the ease with which significant but complicating information can be surpressed via a Keynesian/central-bank emphasis on interest rates. Such misleading discussion of interest rates (such as for interest rates in the 1930s and the 1990-92 recession) routinely appears in textbooks and media reporting as if the central bank can be viewed as simply raising and lowering the rates by direct means (say, via a rise or decline in the "bank" or "discount" rate, or via simply a purchase or sale of securities for the Federal Reserve's open market account). Leigh-Pemberton said quite simply:

In the high-inflation environment of the time [the outgrowth of the 1970s], . . . oversimplification served a useful purpose, adding credibility to the authorities' counter-inflationary resolve. Subsequently, frequent redefinition of the targeted aggregate and upward revision of the target range—often missed even so—resulted in public confusion rather than confidence, and it was for this reason that we have not set a broad money target for this year. (Leigh-Pemberton 1987)

To answer the second question, I again turn to the Bank of England's governor: "The absence of a £M3 target emphatically does not mean that the behaviour of broad money and credit is regarded as of any less importance than before. We continue trying to understand, and to explain publicly, the influences on broad money and their implications for policy" (Leigh-Pemberton 1987).

So, where do we stand on interest rates? In brief:

1. For much of U.S. history, as Friedman reported it, decelerated money growth ($-\Delta M$) led to the downturn in business conditions (and in the coinciding interest rates), and accelerated money growth led the upturn.

2. The procyclical behavior of the interest rate (actually "the price of credit") in the U.S. history means "credit" tightness in the expansion phase of business conditions, and the reverse in recession, when the condition of "tightness" or "ease" is measured by the interest rate. This remains true, although bank credit (Figure 3-6) may be accelerating during much of a boom (credit "tightness" by the i-rate standard) and decelerating in much of a recession (credit "ease" by the i-rate standard).

3. In the history of business conditions—before the special efforts at manipulation by government—there are parallel movement in interest rates and income velocity (Figure 3-1), where "actual" money balances exceed

"desired" during booms and where the inequality reverses itself during recession.

4. Against the background of features 1 and 2, I encounter the meaning of the term *credit crunch,* namely: bank credit decelerates approaching a peak in business conditions, even as the demand for it continues until the peak in business conditions and thereby contributes to a "crunch" (or liquidity-decline) condition between the peak in the money aggregate and the peak in business conditions.

5. Inflationary (deflationary) expectations translate into higher (lower) interest rates after the lags in time, which Friedman addressed, before an acknowledged change in the structure underlying the formation of inflationary expectations which he dated as beginning in the mid-1960s. Afterward, the sensitivity in the formation of inflationary expectations on the part of market participants was greater.

6. Viewing control of the bank (or "discount") rate as an instrument for manipulation of the structure of interest rates (in either the short time to maturity segment of the market, the long time, or both), ceteris paribus, results in wealth effects. An example would be the interest-induced wealth effect encountered in the Keynes/Keynesian money and bond model (the C/CV inequality) when interest rates are lowered. However, I have been rather critical of the prospect of attaining such effects after the allowance for (a) a broader range of assets, (b) market sensitivity in the formation of inflationary expectations, and (c) psychological time. Rather, in reviewing the positions of the Bundesbank, I come to a Bundesbank effect (Figure 1-1) whereby reductions in the discount and lombard rates can lead to a rise in the long-term bond rate (i_L), which is the significant rate in terms of attaining national economic goals. Via the idea of managing liquidity to achieve money targets, a lowering of the price of credit at the discount window can quite possible be interpreted as inflationary. Hence, the long rate rises, $\Delta \dot{P}^e \rightarrow \Delta i_L$, as in $i = i(real) + \Delta \dot{P}^e$.

7. In the immediately foregoing, short-run, ceteris paribus context is also the unbelievable prospect of twisting the yield curve in a fairly short-run time frame (Δi_S and $-\Delta i_L$, Figure 3-2), via some supply-demand-quantity mechanism, although such market fundamentals may come about in the long run. Of course, the long rate may be lowered in the short run, but that would more likely come about from a combination of a rise in the short rate and a reversal of the Bundesbank effect and not simply that of some supply-demand-quantity mechanism.

8. In the presence of great sensitivity in the formation of expectations regarding central bank actions and inactions and debt monetization prospects, I note an unusual development in the United States. Notably, in the evolution of fiscal policy in Section 3.5 there is the experience where a deficit reduction policy has meritorous effect as a fiscal stimulus by way of

reducing the long term bond rate in terms of $i = i(\text{real}) + \dot{P}^e$ and not by way of an expenditure, fiscal-stimulus effect.

9. When the sea is relatively tranquil—as may be implied by Leigh-Pemberton's (1987) comment on the taming of inflation in the early to mid 1980s, and by the long expansion of business conditions in the United States following the November 1982 trough—the errors and difficulties in targeting and achieving values for a given monetary aggregate may be disproportionately large in relation to any clear and discernable need to tame the inflation. As the clear and discernable need diminishes, the central banker's historical preoccupation with short-term interest rates may take over, although I do not see that prospect in the Bundesbank's case (nor that Bundesbank president Hans Tietmeyer will alter it).

The precision in the interest rate data and their ready availability may make references to them very appealing, along with the additional fact that from a central banker's and market participant's point of view, the interest rates (and exchange rates, and commodity prices, and stock- and bond-indexed futures) contain a good bit of processed information about the outlook for the real-goods economy. The central bank's use of this information may be important in connection with the view to achieving a favorable outlook, and, indeed, I used long-term bond rates as surrogates for monetary accommodation and discipline.

Episodes calling for the presence of central bankers—such as those that the markets reacted to with vehemence and sensitivity in the second half of the 1980s—are unlikely to depart the economic scene entirely. Prominent ones include the October 1987 stock market crash in the United States, the ten days in September of 1992, and the privatization of previously owned government industries in the United Kingdom in the 1985-88.

Finally—in the context of these happenings, and given (a) that interest rates and exchange rates embody a great amount of processed information about an economy and (b) that interest rates are quite important—there is no monetary policy matter bearing on them ("announcement effects" and all) that cannot be handled by way of open market operations exclusive of fiscal policy and discount and lombard rates. Open market operations of the special sort found in the United States are the only instrument needed by a "one-money/one market," EuroFed central bank from a Thatcher/monetarist/sovereignty perspective, although there may be some advantage to giving banks access to borrowed funds through the discount windows on a temporary basis. To dispense with any illusion about the control of interest rates in such a case, the discount and lombard rates may be tied to other short-term rates. The movements in the "bank rates," as it were, appear to move with short-term market rates in the United States and in the Federal Republic of Germany in any case.

NOTES

1. Actually each regional bank of the Federal Reserve System could set its own rate, and still can, but the practice became one of following the New York bank for the most part. And because of this practice, one rate can be discussed.

2. Early stages of the "big model" approach and solutions to them (reduced form equtions, and so on) are covered in Frazer (1973, Chapter 14). But refer also to note 10 of Chapter 4.

3. In its operations in the discount market mostly in commercial and Treasury bills, the Bank of England deals directly with a select group of discount houses (Staff 1988, 1990). This is not unlike the direct dealing between the Fed in New York and its own select group of money market firms. The major differences between the Bank of England's operations and the Fed's open market operations are three: (1) the Bank of England holds deposits from the banking system to meet financial obligations at the end of each business day, more like a check-clearing operation; (2) the opertions are "defensive," smoothing operations rather than a means of influencing bank reserves as a way of achieving targeted growth in the money and credit aggregates; and (3) the banking system's deposits at the Bank of England are not the system's main reserve component.

4. Gross national product (GNP) represents the total of expenditures for consumption, government, and private investment in real capital, as well as foreign expenditures for net exports of goods and services (a minus when imports exceed exports). Gross domestic product (GDP) is GNP adjusted for the net export of goods and services.

5. Functions depicting the reactions of the policy-making authorities, as indicated by some policy variable (say, M) to a list of other variables (say, the income and inflation and unemployment rates) became common in the 1960s, as the modern computer came on the scene. There is an extensive literature (Frazer 1973, 196-198).

6. On conditional and unconditional forecasts see (Frazer 1988, 117-118).

7. Confer Section 3.3d, note 8 of Chapter 3.

8. Compare Chapter 4, note 12.

Chapter 6

The European Monetary System, Money and Markets, and Lessons Regarding Transition

6.1 INTRODUCTION

The initial moves that established the European Monetary System in 1979 were formidable enough, but pale by comparison with the enormity of the steps called for in the Delors Report of 1989 to achieve a common currency, a EuroFed, and a zero-inflation rate for EMS Member countries. That elected politicians would later at Maastricht endorse a treaty committing to the move toward one money and a common market is even more beyond ordinary belief, even though some may have seen the prospects differently from others and the Germans may have assured themselves that careful scrutiny of the matters at stake would favor their highly successful Bundesbank. Whatever these refinements, the Report and the actions at Maastricht raised the visibility of the undertakings regarding a new central bank and called attention to the need for greater understanding of a super-national money, as will be pointed out. Taking the matters set on track overall, there are lessons to be learned from the conflicts at hand, including lessons that may be used by societies seeking market economies that require monetary arrangements of the sort discussed in regard to the EMS and transition to a condition I call "one money and a common market."[1]

This chapter concludes the book by way of a review of central banking and the European developments. There is a sketch of the plan and prospects that appeared to be on track as a result of the Maastricht treaty, a review of the sovereignty issue, an outline of an alternative to the Delors Report and the Maastricht treaty approach, and an assessment of the foregoing with respect to the lessons to be learned.

6.2 CENTRAL BANKING AND THE EUROPEAN MONETARY SYSTEM

Viewed in terms of the overall period from the time of Bagehot's *Lombard Street* (1873) through the early post-World War II period, the two major central banks of the world were the Bank of England and the Federal Reserve in the United States. Probably because of the Bank of England's historical role and London's location in relation to the rest of Europe, London emerged (and has remained) the largest financial center in Europe, although the Deutsche Bundesbank emerges as the most significant of the central banks in Europe. Modeled in part after England's bank, the Federal Reserve entered on the scene at the outset of World War I. Its beginnings were not auspicious (Frazer 1988, 424-425, 686), but its federalist structure with regional operating arms and a central governing arrangement was unique for its time. It came about in the United States out of a fear of central power and some historical regard for the sovereignty of the states making up the union.

Thus, as a nucleus of European states and the United Kingdom moved toward more integrated trading and currency arrangements at the close of the 1980s, it appears natural that attention turned to U.S. Federal Reserve and to the Federal Republic of Germany's Bundesbank, because of the federalist structure of both the central banks and because of the Bundesbank's success in monetary matters within the context of German law. In addition, the respective U.S. and FRG institutions have gone through many experiences in money and banking that are relevant to plans for Europe. Most notably, (1) the United States' went through the experience of achieving a "common currency," beginning with the National Banking Act of 1863; (2) open market operations (OMO) with the money and credit creating powers of the sort outlined in Section 3.3 were discovered; and (3) M. Friedman's part of the monetary revolution of this century began in the United States and had impact extending to Britain and other countries. Indeed, in the light of the Bundesbank's success with the deutsche mark, the United Kingdom's experience with Friedman's monetarism, the greater awareness of institutional arrangements for monitoring and controlling money and credit aggregates broadens the options governments face for new central banks.

Even though the term "currency" enters widely into discussions, such as those at hand, it does so ambiguously. The term can be used simply to mean paper notes and coins, even as I introduce world trading in currencies, by which I mean trading in the money stocks of the various countries and especially in check and electronically transferable deposits. To be sure, the present reference to a "common currency" is actually to a common money supply consisting of currency notes and coins and transferable deposits at banking institutions. In Hjalmar Schacht's *The Magic of Money* the term "currency policy" is used to mean "monetary policy" (1967, 113-118).

The reference to "currency" in general is of historical origins, but has peculiar connotations that can be misleading. These arise when fractional reserve banking is introduced, the roles of creating bank credit (loans and investments comprising the assets of banks) and money balances (the transferable deposits comprising bank liabilities) are extended to banking systems, and "the government budget constraint" is discussed.

As the U.S. situation evolved, the central bank authority drifted toward the center in Washington, D.C.; OMO became the principal (and only necessary) instrument for controlling the growth of bank reserves (and hence, in a fractional reserve system, bank credit and the money supply); and the central policy-making body became the Federal Open Market Committee. It came to meet periodically and to comprise some members who do not reside in the Washington area or operate from there. This is a point not to be overlooked in the establishment of a governing board such as the Bundesbank's Central Bank Council.

There is much detail to the history part of the foregoing introduction to how the world worked and to post-World War II reconstruction; to the establishment of the International Monetary Fund (IMF); to the establishment of the Bundesbank in 1957, with roots in the earlier period of allied occupation of the Federal Republic of Germany; to the United States's closing of the gold window in 1971; and to the partial floating of exchange rates since the 1971-73 period. However, through all of this, three major, operational, policy-significant matters stand out. These are: (1) the discovery of the effects of open market operations of the sort I illustrate and find upper-most in the Friedman system; (2) the shift in the 1970s in the United States from the use of interest rates in reporting policy (say, the i-regime) to the use of money and credit aggregates for reporting policy (say, the M-regime); and (3) similar moves on the part of the Bundesbank and the Bank of England, among others. For its part, the Bundesbank has been the most successful in targeting money aggregates as well as in controlling inflation. For the Bank of England's part, there were only small successes in targeting money aggregates, and none of much significance in containing and reducing inflation by monetary means before Margaret Thatcher became the U.K. prime minister.

The early effort on the Thatcher government's part is especially instructive in any consideration of a common money supply for the EMS. Operational problems, additional to those experienced in the United States, arose in the United Kingdom because of the following: the absence of any clear measure of bank reserves of a homogeneous quality; because the composition of the money stock measure it targeted for control (sterling M3) bore no relatively clear relation to the central bank's instruments for controlling bank reserves (Frazer 1988, 552-558, 626-627); and because of the absence of any accounting equation comparable to the "bank reserve equation" in the United States. Present also at the U.K. Treasury and at the Bank of England was the idea that the effects of a number of control variables could be separated along the lines of Equation (2) from Sections 5.1e and 5.3b.

In essence, the Bundesbank and the United States moved toward the control of money aggregates in the mid 1970s. The Bundesbank did so as early as December 1974, and a 1975 congressional resolution was written into the Federal Reserve Act. It mandated the Fed to report policy plans periodically for one year in advance in terms of a money stock measure (most visibly M1 for the United States at the time). However, contrary to much public discussion, the choice of the measure and the statistical problems of sticking to one aggregate are secondary to the intent in the United States which was to stabilize the Federal Reserve's erratic behavior as revealed in a phenomenon referred to as "the chasing of interest rates" (Frazer 1988, 212-213, 297-298, 448-449, 545, 567, 652, 653, 746, 809). As with Friedman's rule, the objective was more one of stabilizing the central bank's contribution to bank reserves than of putting any one measure on target, especially when the measure is subject to statistical discrepancy such as arises when new type accounts are included under a single targeted measure.

Parallel to these operational and policy-significant matters are some economic, policy-significant ideas that interplay with operations/policy matters. As do features of banking under the Bundesbank in the Federal Republic of Germany and the Federal Reserve in the United States, all of this bears in important ways on efforts to move toward one money and one market (as in "common market"). I draw on these, Neils Thygesen's early commentary (1988), and the changes that came after Nigel Lawson resigned and after Thatcher's removal from leadership.[2] I proceed to develop the central ideas and anticipate possible misperceptions, before commenting directly on proposals, organizational prospects, perceptions found in the Delors Report, and plans for European monetary arrangements.

Suggestions leading toward new monetary arrangements for Europe follow. As startling as it may seem, following Lawson's resignation and Thatcher's removal from leadership, the Bank of England's governor came to support U.K. plans similar to those Thatcher opposed in the Delors Report. I touch on these, the official course, and a rather strictly academic exercise; namely, I offer a distinctive M-orientation approach—not i-regime; no fiscal-monetary arrangement for Europe; and no combination of the three. As an academic matter mainly, the M-orientation approach offers the attainment of a main objective for any unified trading area (namely, a common currency and, at the same time, an elimination of bothersome and costly interstate exchanges of currencies). It does so while impinging in a minimal way on the national sovereignty of the respective member states. There are some positive notions about changing from one set of monetary arrangements to another. As the Bank of England reported (Staff 1991), "there is more to setting up a monetary union than agreeing [to] the *constitution of a central bank* and the *tools of monetary management*."

In events since—and running through the ten crises days of September 1992—I wonder, as some others have, whether moves toward political union should not have accompanied or preceded the efforts at monetary union. The guidance offered by economists toward union was not too helpful, possibly because in the main tradition of economics itself there has not been much by way of a union of the real goods and monetary sectors and the policy emphasis Keynes and Friedman saw for economics. Mostly what has abounded is traditional Keynesian economics (including that with a post-Keynesian flair), the remarkable Bundesbank record, and only parts of the Friedman system I develop.

In the economic, monetary, social, and political unification of the two Germanies beginning in the July to October 1990, there was a leap in the dark of sorts, but not to the same extent as set on a course for EMS Member countries by the Delors Report and the Maastricht treaty. In the German case, there was less prospect for cultural shock as a result of opening up and intermingling than for a broader array of European countries. Some cite the People's Republic of China as a state in gradual transition to a market economy, but here the maintenance of central control is a major ingredient (Dorn and Xi 1990). Mostly what has occurred with respect to transition—as in the former Soviet Union, Poland, Slovakia, and the Czech Republic—simply followed the breakup of former states, the emergence of underground/off-the-record markets, and unplanned and unresearched efforts at transition.

6.3 ANALYSIS AND CENTRAL BANKING

Central banking in its heyday of the nineteenth century was shrouded in mystery. It so appeared in J. M. Keynes's day and still does in some quarters, and in practices at the Bank of England. As mentioned in Section 5.3b, the Bank reverts entirely to the older positions of central banking and to the havens of the short-run, highly static methods of economic analysis, although such positions appear to have been avoided entirely by the highly successful Bundesbank.

The positions encountered at the Bank of England are that the bank controls only the short-term rate of interest (i.e., literally raises and lowers it); that interest rates are important [which no one would deny, $i = i(real) + (1/P)(dP/dt)^*$, and so on]; that the yield curve can be twisted (at the short end, at least); that interest induced wealth effects are possible and obtainable (as in the two-asset, money-bond model; and, at the bottom (albeit largely hidden), that the static supply-demand-quantity mechanism comes into play along with the false prospects for separating effects by direct means (via interest rates, exchange rates, inflation rates, and so on).

6.3a Monetary Analysis

As variously stated, J. M. Keynes gave special prominence in his famous
1936 work to the prevailing banking view of interest rates, which is still found
at the Bank of England and embodied in hypotheses H_{CB} and H_{TW}. Drawing on
Wicksell, he offered the idea of "the rate of interest" (later viewed as a
structure of rates) that could be raised or lowered at will in relation to the
marginal efficiency of capital. It was, quite formally, the rate of return for
relating an expected stream of net earnings (net at all costs except the cost of
capital as borrowed funds) to a given cost (or supply price) for real capital
(productive facilities, and so on). This stream could be highly volatile as
treated in Keynes's work because of the dependence on long-term expectations,
which could reflect inflationary expectations in his famous work. However, he
was unyielding in denying the entry of an inflation premium into the rate of
interest (Keynes 1936, 141-142), although Friedman fully recognized it as did
the Bundesbank (1989, 82-84, 97-103). Said differently, "the rate of interest"
was a directly controlled variable for Keynes. In his adamancy, he was
reacting to Irving Fisher's 1896 statement of the nominal rate of interest as the
sum of the real rate and the expected inflation rate $[i = i(real) + (1/P)(dP/dt)^*]$.

Along the way with perception and analysis bearing on the rate of interest,
several things happened over the period from the early 1930s through the
United States's greatest peacetime inflation. First, in Keynes's flawed analysis
concerning the interest rate, increasing (decreasing) the money stock lowers
(raises) the interest rate, and at low rates money balances may go into a "trap"
where they have no effect on interest rates. Parallel to this, even a lowering
of the interest rate may have no effect on real capital outlays (say, via the
inequality following from Wicksell). The flaws in the analysis gave support to
the concept of a fiscal (deficit-spending) policy. It was ushered into the world
by Keynes's great work to become a part of the analysis behind the
management of total domestic demand for the current output of goods and
service.

Second, as Milton Friedman's research (with Anna Schwartz) on *Monetary
Trends in the United States and the United Kingdom* (1982) got under way in
the 1960s, two very relevant things come about. One is the concept of
"helicopter money," and the other is empirical research relating the nominal
interest rate to the expected inflation rate. In the very broad sweep of history
also, there have been some other relevant occurrences: expectations about the
future of economic activity and policy have likely become more sensitive; rapid
communication of news and events has become more evident; and the
deliberations of boards governing public policy have become more open to
public scrutiny and hence political control.

The "helicopter money" concept harks back to the significance of OMO and
control over spending by the general public via money and credit aggregates

rather than via interest rates. It is closely related to Friedman's empirically based monetary research and to Friedman's "monetary rule." The rule is a guide in the conduct of monetary policy by central banks or treasuries (depending on where the authority lies). The attention is on central bank control over money and credit aggregates and changes in income velocity (and not interest rates). Here also, a government budget constraint on fiscal policy enters (defined, say, in terms of the public sector borrowing requirement and "funding policy" in the United Kingdom). With it, under the M-regime orientation, monetary policy is a substitute for fiscal policy. And, indeed, the entire analytical approach I attribute to Friedman is a substitute for that with interest rates and fiscal policy at the center. A main thing fiscal policy as a deficit can do is to crowd in and out the private sector (external or foreign financing aside, such as appeared in the United States in the 1980s [Frazer 1988, 218, 271-272, 689]), although there was the unusual case in the United States, where deficit reduction had the stimulating effect of reducing the long-term bond rate by way of $i = i(real) + \dot{P}^e$. This is very much a 180-degree departure from the early demand management view of fiscal policy.

Further, as the dependence of the nominal interest rate on the expected rate of inflation suggests, the central bank controls the nominal rate (not the real rate). When price level stability and a zero-inflation rate are offered explicitly as goals of monetary policy, as in the Delors Report (Report 1989; and Thygesen 1989), the door is closed on what the central banks as an authority can do with interest rates. A question of setting the real rate of interest arises (say, as defined by the rate at which goods today exchange for goods one year hence). Even so, this rate depends more on the interplay of the saving-to-income ratio, the rate of growth in production, and tax authority rather than on monetary authority (also Frazer 1988, 212-213, 815-817).

6.3b Analysis and Policy

OMO in conjunction with the concept "helicopter money" means that the growth in money and credit aggregates can occur until the "actual money stock" in nominal terms exceeds the "desired stock," and spending occurs. It calls for action by the central bank, as under the conditions of inadequate total demand in the 1930s (Frazer 1973, Chapter 11). The initiative to expand bank credit does not lie with borrowers nor depend on the i-regime inequality Keynes offered, as was imagined in the 1930s. Further, at the full employment (non-inflationary) state of production, fiscal policy is not needed for the management of total spending. Where deficit spending may occur on the part of the state (dependence on out-of-country sources aside), its effect on total spending depends on the monetary authority. If the authority accommodates the deficit (say, purchases the PSBR) the effect on money and credit growth is the same as with expansive OMO. Otherwise, the financing of the deficit takes funds and hence resources that would be available to the private sector. There is "crowding out."

I recall that Friedman's rule (Bundesbank 1989, 97-98) is that the central authority's contribution to bank reserves should grow at a constant rate (hence support for growth in the money and credit aggregates), depending on production potential and estimated, sustainable growth in real output and the velocity ratio. The growth rate may be altered, depending on the secular (or trend) changes in the turnover (or spending) of money balances, and the Bundesbank may even attempt more by way of stabilization. However, Friedman was inclined to limit the change in policy (i.e., the money or reserve growth) to the secular changes in the turnover of balances because the effects of monetary acceleration (deceleration) are immediate, powerful, and cumulative. As a consequence of the immediate, powerful, and cumulative effects, short-term departures stood to destabilize business and credit conditions, if the use of monetary policy was careless or misguided, which he found to be the case in the past history of the Federal Reserve. Moreover, as I have pointed out, there are complex measurement and data-quality problems in monitoring and refining monetary accommodation and discipline in empirical terms. Even the Bundesbank takes a rather ad hoc approach at the operations if not the thought-process level.

Others have recognized a role for the central bank to counter the effects of destabilizing shocks to the economy, including when drawing on its role as a lender of last resort (Frazer 1978a). There are prospects for what the Bundesbank may regard as liquidity management and for offsetting the effects of happenings that may impinge on the demand for liquid balances and thus on destabilizing prospects. Also, along similar lines, there are such prospects whereby the Federal Reserve and the White House may commit to supplying needed reserves to the banking system when shock-induced demand arises.[3]

To be sure, I focus on liquidity and money and credit aggregates, but I do not escape from interest rates. Section 2.2 viewed long-term bond rates as surrogates for monetary policy in money-stock terms, but with a reversal of the spin usually placed on them when central banks are viewed as raising and lowering rates directly. As presently viewed, high and/or rising rates are more likely a reflection of present and prospective monetary accommodation than changes in real rates $[i_L = i(real) + \dot{P}^e]$. And, similarly, low and/or declining rates are more likely a reflection of present and anticipated monetary discipline since monetary matters have become more subject to scrutiny by bond trades and since the consequences and roles of money stocks and income velocity have become better known. Especially, the prospects for the monetization of government deficits and debt may enter, as may the reverse which occurred in the United Kingdom in the second half of the 1980s. The potential for debt monetization may be less great in the case of a highly independent central bank, such as the Bundesbank, but it need not be confined there. Nevertheless, an independent monetary authority has the power to nullify the fiscal-policy and spending effects of governing bodies, where politics enters, as FRG officials apparently learned (Kennedy 1991, 33, 53, 63).[4]

Although less than in the case with the Federal Republic of Germany and the Bundesbank, the U.S. Congress and/or presidents have gotten their way with the Federal Reserve in the post-World War years when they wanted it, even though it is cited as an independent central bank. In the post-World War II years, the Fed responded to the wishes of the Treasury for quite some time, until money matters became disruptive; retained independence in the Eisenhower years as he supported its backing away from the Treasury; chased interest rates upward as they rose gradually in the 1960s; accommodated the wishes of Congress in the Arthur Burns years, as he interpreted them; acted as Jimmy Carter directed, following the removal of Arthur Burns; and carried out very much the monetarist policies Ronald Reagan wanted (Frazer 1988, Chapter 16).

As Milton Friedman came to perceive correctly, the Federal Reserve was cloaked in the myth of independence but was highly political in reality. The Bundesbank, on the other hand, has been more able to maintain independence, but then—even more than in the U.S. case—the Deutsche Bundesbank Act of 1957 was written with that independence in mind.

In the U.S. case, the reality and the placing of responsibility for its actions has been made more obscure by the Federal Reserve's alleged independence. This political role is made more evident in the M-regime orientation because central bank policy is potentially more measurable and obvious. The moves to validate expansive fiscal policy by accommodating it or to nullify its effects are more obvious and less deceptive than those connected to claims implying direct control over interest rates. In such important matters Friedman came to see the need for putting the Federal Reserve under the Treasury, with the view that the public would place responsibility more clearly for swings in inflation and unemployment rates. Quite bluntly, in the Bundesbank case, the targeting of the preferred money aggregate, its attainment, and the matters of money demand hold primary positions in relation to what may be called the Bundesbank's interest rate policy (1989, 51-56, 81-109).

Times change but analysis does not lose its relevance, as in the move from the i-regime orientation to the M-regime orientation. The two approaches to the conduct of policy are simply at odds, and not possible as compromises, which fundamentalists, committees, and politicians may prefer. In the end, the lack of a unified, single-authority view—free of political overtones and all—will weigh heavily on the outcomes for the European Monetary System. As Otto Pöhl pointed out at the December 1990 meeting of ministers, the EMS Member countries will be confronted with two choices, and therein lies the prospect for getting the EMS off its three-stage course. The choices are between (1) a real Eurofed that looks and acts like the Bundesbank and (2) a compromise (an amalgamation of European central banks) that negates everything the Bundesbank has stood for.[5] The latter will not work and it will be unacceptable to the Germans.

6.4 SOVEREIGNTY AND THE THATCHER ENIGMA

The Delors Report came from an EEC committee charged with studying and reporting on the means of achieving an economic and monetary union. The enlargement of the mandate to the committee to consider both aspects of union came from the insistence of Margaret Thatcher. She had strong monetarist leanings early (Frazer 1988, Chapter 15) and, no doubt in part as a consequence, perceived the broad social, political, and economic significance of monetary union. To be sure, she experienced the relevance of monetary policy to other changes she sought to bring about in in the United Kingdom.

In the light of this beginning, and Thatcher biographer Hugo Young's final chapter titles "Into the Vortex" and "Herself Alone," I may wonder why Margaret Thatcher was not more positive in her leadership with respect to one money and a EuroFed institution for the EMS Member countries. She was aware of Roy Jenkins labor party and the French socialist connections to the founding of the EMS. She furthermore correctly saw some loss of sovereignty in what the Delors Report of 1989 had been quite explicit about (namely, the control of fiscal policy). Quite clearly a Keynesian-oriented central bank was envisioned in the Delors Report. There was to be control over fiscal policy as a means of executing a non-inflationary monetary policy. Her own Bank of England could have been the model for the report.

Could it be that she missed out for one, all, or some combination of the following reasons: (1) because those ministers who opposed her had the Bank-of-England orientation (including in combination with support for the fixed exchange rate mechanism); (2) because advisors such as Alan Walters and Professor Friedman had been too adamant in opposition to the exchange rate mechanisms, and/or (3) because no clear vision of a Bundesbank-dominated EMS with minimum loss of sovereignty was put before her in 1989 and 1990.

Why did Thatcher not proceed to modernize the Bank of England in her own years in office (to redo it in the image of the Bundesbank). Clearly there are fundamental flaws in the i-regime orientation—that the crucial long-term rate can be raised and lowered at will by the central bank (within any neighborhood of action that makes a difference, psychological time, and so on), that the rate has the effects on capital spending attributed to it (Frazer 1994a, Section 5.4c), that monetary and fiscal policy can be separated as if the expenditure effects of fiscal policy were independent, and that the stock of money and money demand can be controlled by interest rates and fiscal policy. Moreover, the problems of analysis and perception are not that a fiscal-policy-dominated central bank does not work in its fashion, however poorly. Rather the public problem is that the i-regime bank unwarrantably separates the attention given to monetary policy. It perpetuates the idea in the public's mind of an independent "fiscal stimulus" as an effective means of demand management directed at improved economic performance irregardless of monetary policy. In other words, it does not aid in understanding who is responsible, which was Friedman's reason for wanting to put the Federal Reserve under the Treasury in the United States following his problems with his friend Arthur Burns in the 1970s (Frazer 1988, Chapter 8).

Also, no small matter, the i-regime view perpetuates the public's and the media's view of raising and lowering interest rates by way of the IS-LM model. The point is not that the public embraces an economic model, as economists do. Rather, as Friedman noted years ago, a player in the game of pool does not need to know the higher mathematics behind the game to play. Rather, the interest-rate orientation perpetuates simple and even false arguments that appeal to economists and to the print media when they seek to communicate in the simplest of terms.

Further, why did Thatcher not place on her public agenda the prospect of overhauling the Bank of England in view of her monetarist leanings and the Bank's stances on the use of fiscal policy and interest rates to control the money stock and money demand? Could it simply be a British addiction for tradition? Possibly, in the heat of political action, the matter never came up. Possibly by the time of the Delors Report, changes of a more sweeping sort were on the agenda. Possibly, as Richard Nixon summarized on entering his 1968-72 term (Frazer 1988, 231-240), economic issues were not good for Republicans. (But that was before the Tory's Thatcher and Ronald Reagan.)

One can even comment on the fiscal policy restrictions and other aspects of the forced conformity found in the EMS moves toward fulfilling Delors-Report/Maastricht-Treaty conditions. Notably:

The rationale for setting limits, as done in the Treaty, on the public deficits that can be run by national governments in a monetary union does not arise from a belief in the potency of fiscal policy or a desire to control fiscal policy at the "federal" level, but rather from the risk that excessive deficits, through their effects on financial systems, may jeopardize the objective of monetary stability.[6]

But of course, I question this because it misses the points (1) about monetary accommodation of deficits and (2) about the actual practice of some central banks such as those of the Bank of England and the Bank of Italy. Added overlapping points missed by this comment are: about the hypotheses H_{CB} and H_{TW}; (4) about the i- and M-regime distinctions; (5) about the fiscal policy and monetary policy as substitute approaches, and (6) about the EMS Member choices with respect to a real EuroFed that looks and acts like the Bundesbank and a compromise that negates everything the Bundesbank has stood for.

The Keynesian orientation toward central banking and the European matters is alive and well. It appears in numerous places other than in textbooks and the other economics literature (e.g., Emerson et al. 1992, 178-179, 189-190). For example, U.S. officials have attributed to central banks the power to raise and lower interest rates (meaning i_L) by direct means such as are seen in the IS-LM context, and they publically critized the Bundesbank for maintaining high rates, in the early 1990s setting, despite its 1970s and 1980s history of having low rates by U.S. and European standards.[7]

Addressing the possible need for realignments in the exchange rate mechanism in 1992, *The Economist* viewed realignments as "an alternative to changes in fiscal policy or interest-rate policy, which manifestly impinges on domestic policies." Also, it says: "The finance ministries and central banks . . . should make a more serious commitment to reaching a consensus on appropriate exchange rates [$\$/£$, $£/DM$, . . .], interest rates [$i_{L,FRG}$, $i_{L,UK}$], and fiscal policies." And, again: "A multilateral consensus on the appropriateness of exchange rates, interest rates and fiscal policy is needed if there is to be genuine solidarity during crises."

Of course, a part of the rub is that once matters are set on a zero-inflation goal, all the other rates fall in line. There are no known statistical means for separating the effects. To be sure, in the foregoing examples from the economics literature, official positions, and journalistic writing, the same variables that are a part of the separation-of-effects problem are encountered. In the symbolic equations I use, they are:

$$\ln M = a_0 + a_1 \ln i + a_2 \ln Y$$

$$\begin{aligned} GDP = \ &a_0 + a_1 \, i_L + a_2 \, £/DM \\ &+ a_3 \text{ fiscal policy (PSBR adjusted for funding policy)} \\ &+ a_4 \, M_{UK}/M_{FRG} + \ . \ . \ . \end{aligned}$$

6.5 THE DELORS REPORT AND REPORT/TREATY PROSPECTS

The Delors Report set forth objectives for the EMS and, as noted, it was followed by controversy, then the U.K. entry into the EMS in October 1990, and then a statement of a three-stage British plan in early 1991. By December 1991 the Maastricht Treaty provided added impetus to the three-stage plan I presently discuss as the Delors-Report/Maastricht-Treaty track. Two distinguishing features of it and developments observed in the EC are forced "harmonization" with respect to EMS Member countries and uncertainty over the outcome. A journalist labeled the final stages of the Report/Treaty track a "leap in the dark."

Along the foregoing line, I offer more background, mention the U.K. plan, and outline the stages of the Report/Treaty track. To highlight these matters and provide further perspective, Section 6.6 offers an exercise in what may have been possible with a minimum loss of sovereignty.

6.5a Background

As indicated by Thygesen, who was an expert member appointed to the Delors Committee, the Report sought to outline what the ultimate stage of an EEC union would look like, and to indicate stages for arriving there (1989, 638). In Thygesen's comments, the Report was said to meet the requirements of a system of fixed exchange rates, but the language "fixed exchange rates" suggests the exchange of different currencies, and not a common currency (i.e., a common money supply). With any system of exchange rates, there are transactions costs that leave the economic system short of the complete integration. So the final stage is in fact a stage with a single currency and without exchange rates.

Thygesen went on to say, "the locking of parities and the freedom of capital movements do imply that only one monetary policy will be feasible" (1989, 639). But this is indeed not so in terms of any past, known system. The systems of fixed exchange rates under the auspices of the 1920s conditions and later under the International Monetary Fund (IMF) in the post-World War II years were country-leader oriented and did not bring common monetary policies in any well-timed or coordinated way. Price levels in the respective EMS member countries would still have to adjust fully to ensure the workings of fixed exchange rates on the scale of the European Community.

The imposition of a system for "macroeconomic policy coordination, including binding rules for national budgetary policies," such as Thygesen mentioned would have been highly authoritative, including on the part of the governing body of the EC. It calls for forced compliance to be imposed on free governments. When combined with some sort of majority voting arrangement at the governing board, it would impose a majority rule over the minority. As Thygesen stated, the prospect of yielding to a common "budgetary authority" was the most controversial with respect to the Delors Report (1989, 639).

What I see here is a profound matter—even a workable monetary arrangement with fixed exchange rates calls on a country to give up control of its fiscal (or domestic deficit) policy. This would probably be no problem for Germany and the countries aligned with it, but going back to the government budget constraints, the EEC's governing board would have had power over the sovereignty of the member countries to "crowd in" and "crowd out" the private sector. With the history of ideological conflict that has existed in Europe, this was very unlikely to come about.

Thygesen went on to address the question "Why a supranational budgetary authority?" and to consider the central banking system (1989, 639-640). In addressing the question, he noted the requirement of achieving "a proper balance between monetary and fiscal policy." The fact is, he is dealing with substitute and not complementary policies and the decisions about the mix boil down to the ideology of a larger or smaller government sector and to the control and containment of inflation rates.[8]

The central banking system called for in the Report is called the European System of Central Banks (ESCB). There is a central institution with the separate, national central banks. This amounts to policy authority residing in a central body with separate, operating banks as in the case of the regional banks in the U.S. central banking system and that of the Federal Republic of Germany. As in the long history of central banking and monetary analysis, emphasis is placed on the goal of stability in a price level. Perhaps not surprising in the light of the Bundesbank's success, the proposal for a governing body for the ESCB made the body "independent of instructions from national governments" (Thygesen 1989, 641).

The approach to the union proposed by the Delors Committee was set out in three stages. They were seen as a single package to which member states would commit themselves at the first stage, and then move toward a final "hard union."

Even so, in the sequence of happenings, the United Kingdom entered the EMS in October 1990, and the Bank of England's governor Leigh-Pemberton was supporting the United Kingdom's favored approach to monetary union. Not unlike the Delors Report, it offered three stages. They were reviewed by Leigh-Pemberton (Staff 1991) as follows: Stage 1—The exchange rate mechanism (ERM) by which EMS countries tied the price of their currencies to the deutsche mark; Stage 2—Strengthening the mechanism of the ERM by moving toward the mobility of labor and capital across the frontiers of the EC; Stage 3—The establishment of an institution with the real operational functions. It would be the basis of a European System for Central Banks.

This stage 3 institution was to be a European Monetary Fund (EMF), analogous to the IMF which functioned in the post-World War II years until the closing of the gold window in 1971. It would issue and manage a new "common currency," the "Hard Ecu," which however would circulate along with existing national currencies. The idea was that the EMF could build on the credibility and legitimacy of the Deutsche Bundesbank and at the same time familiarize people with the idea of a "super-national money" along the way.

6.5b Leap I, the Report/Treaty Track

At the summit meeting in Maastricht, Netherlands, in December 1991, the EC nations tentatively agreed to set up a common central bank and to begin using a single currency no later than 1999. At this landmark summit, an escape route was left, as discussed in Section 4.4. Britain and Spain were said to have imposed roadblocks to a quest for a political federation of the twelve-nation European Community. In any case, the three stages following the Maastricht meeting are:

Stage I. Stage I begins with the exchange rate mechanism and the linking of currencies to the deutsche mark. There is asymmetry of power in that one particular central bank acts as de facto leader.

Stage II. Stage II begins in 1994, depending on the ratification of the Maastricht Treaty. If the treaty is ratified, a European Monetary Institute (EMI) falls in place. Under the plans, the EMI consists of the committee of central bank governors. It would become a council with a president appointed by EC heads of government. There would be more cooperation by EMS member countries as procedures would be put in place for stage III.

Stage III. Stage III would be the "leap in the dark." Under the lock-steps it would begin as early as 1997 and no later than January 1, 1999, with the "one money" and EuroFed of the Delors Report. As suggested under the leap designation, member states will have been brought into conformity with respect to the Maastricht conditions for balanced budgets, interest rates, and public sector debt.

On a less visible agenda, one is led to expect harmonization in growth and wage rates. The possible social costs of adjustments without harmonization of these rates starts to surface. Where the system is left only partly harmonized, the prospects enter for Germans to come to Britain and change the nature of the state, and so on.

The harmonization and/or loss of cultural identity loom larger as the public gains understanding of what a super-national money entails. First, I see this in taking note of broad support for a "common currency" in Britain in 1989 and 1990 when Thatcher lost party leadership over the issue, in the weakening of support for the EMS since, and in the attention given to the need for the public to gain familiarity with what a common currency means in social, cultural, and political terms.

Next, I see the need for added enlightenment when comparing the early French and German leadership roles regarding the plan with Otto Pöhl's remarks in December 1990 about two choices (a real central bank like the Bundesbank and a compromise that negates what Germany has stood for in monetary policy). By the early months of 1993, *The Economist* could report the German's position thus: "The only kind of monetary union attractive to them [the Germans] is one in which a D-mark zone managed by them is gradually extended to the Benelux countries [comprising Belgium, the Netherlands, and Luxembourg], Austria and perhaps France." *The Economist* continues to say, "But there's the rub. The attraction of EMU to France is to have an equal say with the Germans in managing European monetary policy, instead of having slavishly to follow them, as at present."

Possible outcomes are a German/Bundesbank dominated one and some amalgamation of central bank theories and operations that fails to achieve the Delors Report's goals.

6.6 LEAP IN THE DARK II: ANOTHER VIEW

J. M. Keynes wrote of money balances as the most liquid of assets (1936, Chapter 17). They yield little or no return, except in the form of the security and convenience provided by their liquidity, as I have indicated. It—the liquidity—extends a protean quality to money. As Hjalmar Schacht said of money in this regard:

Money may . . . be converted into other goods, . . . properties, or . . . but the reverse is not true. The magic of money lies in its protean nature, which enables it to be used at all times, in all directions and for all purposes. (Schacht 1967, 7)

Indeed, in accounting practice, assets are classified and ranked according to the descending order of their liquidity, for example,

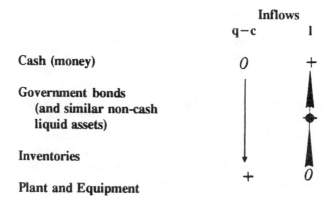

	Inflows	
	$q-c$	l
Cash (money)	*0*	**+**
Government bonds **(and similar non-cash** **liquid assets)**		
Inventories		
Plant and Equipment	**+**	*0*

Here $q-c$, yield less carrying cost, denotes the tangible or dollar component making up the rate of return, where as l denotes the liquidity (security and convenience) and hence an intangible component.

However, in the evolution of money various goods have served as money, and gold especially entered in the emergence of fractional reserve banking. Paper notes could be issued against a reserve base and in time even deposits at banks grew in importance relative to the note issue. Before the Civil War in the United States, when the note issue and metallic coins predominated as circulating media, some note issues around the country traded at a discount and hence were not fully substitutable. That is to say, there was a system of exchange rates internal to the national state.

After the passage of the Banking Act of 1863—and the establishment of a system of national, federally chartered banks—a unified currency system evolved (FY, 1966, Section 7.4). Said differently, the exchange rates vanished. And the acceptance of deposits at banks dramatically increased to substitute freely for currency notes and metallic coins. The money supply shared by the public in the states of the union came to consist of the sum of transferable deposits, currency notes, and coins. The early post-World War II years, the accounting for the money stock included assets near to money (M2, and so on) as well as the category M1. However, maintaining a category that can be called money, and that can include simply balances on books reckoned by the unit of account, requires that the assets in question serve as the substance of liquidity (ease of disposal, without loss of principal and purchasing power).

Against such background, organizational arrangements called for in establishing a European monetary system with EC countries sharing a common money supply could have proceeded along two lines, which comprise "leap II." These are the policy, managed, money-supply line and the banking, and operations line where the common money supply appears. To be sure, currency (i.e., paper notes and coins), money supply, and control mechanisms would be called for. Complicated transitional plans would have been called for.

This view is leap II, not because the monetary system that results is uncertain, as in the case of the Report/Treaty track. Rather it is a leap in the dark because harmonization proceeds from voluntary association rather than forced compliance. It is the end results in terms of cultural impact, and costs that are uncertain. In other words, one may ask what happens when labor is free to seek its best employment opportunities. What happens in cultural and budget terms if states compete for plants? What happens if some states offer vast social programs and others rather limited programs? In these outcomes lie uncertainty.

Although leap II is also uncertain in its way, it may be what comes about if some EC member countries ultimately enter the final stages of monetary integration. Such a prospect may loom for the U.K., for example, as in the case of Parliament's voting to ratify the Maastrich treaty on John Major's promise that ratification does not force the U.K. to join the EMS's exchange rate mechanism.

6.6a Policy and the Managed Financial System

The present central banks of the respective EC countries (or some subset of them) should become the operating arms of a board analogous to the Bundesbank's Central Bank Council (CBC). It will be the policy making body, provided with a staff and headquarters in Frankfurt. Except for auditing arrangements to ensure the execution of policies and compliance by the operating arms, no operations or supervisory authority is needed by the governing board or committee.

The membership on the committee could be comprised of no more than one voting member from each sovereign state, after some passage of time, because initially the Bundesbank should be disproportionally represented. Ultimately, the votes may be weighted to reflect the size of member country economies in some way. One would be the member country's gross national product in constant-price terms as a percentage of the total, constant-price GNP for the participating countries.

There should be economic argument and debate at the central governing committee meetings. A policy directive should be passed along to the officer in charge of OMO. What can be directed should be circumscribed by rules passed along in the establishment of the central authority to begin with. The rule may be stated in zero inflation terms or it may be a Friedman/Bundesbank monetarist rule.

The OMO would best be based in the largest financial center, which would be London. Those staff people working at the trading desk in London would be responsible to, and carry out the instructions provided by, the manager of the account. The trading desk would have direct ties to the trading desks at selected investment banks operating in the private financial markets of the member countries. There should always be the objective of trading on the best terms available in issues of minimal and comparable risk. And, finally, each member country will share in a proportion of the earnings made through OMO. The sharing will be on the same basis as the voting at EMC meetings, after a small take by the EMC to support the staff and operation of the central authority.

As in the United States, all sovereign states will retain the rights not preempted by their being a part of the currency union. There is no reason in theory or practice for the sovereign states to give up any freedom in formulating budgets, engaging in financing, and setting taxes. In the United States most states prohibit budget deficits and some do not, some states have income taxes and others do not. And, of course, the respective states may attempt to ensure business patrons of good labor markets, a friendly environment for business, and so on.

These immediately foregoing matters are apparently not problems with the prospective currency union countries. Neils Thygesen himself reported three areas found in the Delors Report where economic changes were well on their way to realization. These are "(1) a single market within which persons, goods, services, and capital can move freely; (2) competitive policy, and other measures aimed at strengthening market mechanisms; (3) common policies aimed at structural change and regional development." (1989, 639)

Ultimately to achieve a common "money supply," prices in the EMS member countries would be denominated in terms of the single bookkeeping unit. This final change—as would be called for to achieve a "super-national money"—would be analogous to changing from driving on the left side of the road to driving on the right. Signs and signals would all have to be put in place and the change made on a given night or weekend.

6.6b Bank Operations and the Money Supply

In the common currency case (meaning common money supply), a new class of reserves would be established (called R_o below). All checks issued for open market purchases would be recorded in this new account as they cleared through the operating arms of the central monetary authority. The commercial or private sector banks could even trade in this new class of reserves. A multiplier can be stated limiting the extent to which a given bank could leverage loans and investments based on the new category of reserves. This—in combination with the elimination of all other means of creating bank reserves on the part of the participating central banks—would ensure in time the elevation of this important class of reserves (R_o, below), and ultimately in effect the elimination of all other classes as to their being of any importance.

As the credit granting banks extend credit, deposits are created, and any of the check transferable deposits should be freely substitutable for "new" notes denominated in ECUs (as bookkeeping units). These would be obtained as the private banks exchange the new reserves for the "new" notes, and hence there would be a drain on reserves as the public sought to add to its holdings of paper notes and coins.

As in "currency reform," all the old notes and coins could be exchanged for new ones. With the past history of growth in output and the further prospect for it, the addition to the notes and coins in circulation should, on balance, always be positive. The record keeping on this component of the money supply would combine with that for the existing stock of notes and coins. Since this measure too would become precise, the result would be an aggregate measure for the stock of notes and coins. Further, the new category of reserves would bear a clear, multiplier relation to bank credit (the multiplier B_c/R_o), and in a short time this would be clear for the links between both reserves, bank credit, and the stock of check transferable deposits that results from the "homogeneous reserve account" (R_o). To this check (electronic) transferable class of deposits are added the notes and coins aggregate to get a targetable measure for a money supply aggregate. Thus, the needed set of money and credit aggregates are in place—the reserve category, the bank credit bearing a multiple relation to it, the check transferable deposits, and the sum of the latter plus the notes and coins in circulation.

This latter aggregate could be viewed as the policy variable and its turnover monitored by the authority to ensure zero inflation. In the transition period of arriving at this position, the policy authority would simply stabilize its activity and allow non-inflationary growth in the "new" category of reserves, the homogeneous reserve account.

At the time EMS member countries enter on the new arrangement for central banking, they would do so depending on their exchange rates (1) against the deutsche mark or (2) against the ECU. These entry rates would be those at which accountants and computers would start denominating in ECU units rather than in pounds, francs, liras, guilders, krones, and so on. The bookkeeping would be analogous to currency reform. The records would yield precise aggregates, as has been stated. With these there is a common money supply. There would be no more exchange rates internal to the participating countries. They vanish.

6.6c An Aside on Reserve Requirements

The analytical system--with the aforementioned multipliers and use of a minimum reserve requirement as a part of a monetary control arrangement--has its roots in U.S. developments, as I have pointed out (Section 3.2). The United Kingdom has no such legal minimum requirement, but I do encounter it at the Bundesbank (Section 3.4), along with some familiar criticism of the practice. Referring again to the German economist and central banker Hjalmar Schacht (1967, 153-154; and Section 3.4), he offers the following remarks on reserves:

The minimum reserve thus owes its origin to the need to safeguard the client. It was never intended to be a means of regulating the circulation of money. In the history of German currency, too, the minimum reserve had no part to play until the banking law of 1934. Naturally the Reichsbank expected that each client who enjoyed the privilege of having a transfer account with it--and that in itself was always a business recommendation--would maintain a credit balance on his account with the bank. But the reason was more a question of covering costs than one of general monetary policy [as was indeed the case when open market operations came about at the Fed of New York]. . . . It was not until the banking law of 1934, which was passed as an aftermath of the bank crash of July, 1931, that the banks were obliged to maintain a cash reserve. And even then it was intended only as a safeguard against losses, and thus conceived in terms of ability to pay. (Schacht 1967, 153-154)

Continuing Schacht said,

The cash reserve makes sense as a means of securing the bank's obligations where its banknotes and investments are concerned. As a means of maintaining liquidity it is by and large superfluous. There are other short-term assets capably of serving this end. The only real reserve of liquidity is the central bank with its banknote printing process.

So, turning to the EuroFed prospects and going back to Schacht's time, I agree and disagree with some observations about reserve requirements. First, I must distinguish between the use of simply varying legal reserve requirements, and the existence of a minimum fixed requirement which I see as fundamental to the evolution of central banking.

Second, I confront Schacht about reserves being mainly a means of protecting depositors, which they do not in the absence of some place for a "lender of last resort." In any case, the lender-of-last-resort function gained its place in central banking lore following the Bank of England's handling of the stress placed on London's money market in 1891, following the collapse of Baring Brothers and Company. The three main reactions to the position Schacht represents are: one, the discount window(s) provide a means for individual banks to meet such drains temporarily; two, the requirements need not be met every day and instant, as opposed to an average over a period of time; and, three, they do provide the basis for a system of money and credit multipliers with the added means that system offers for control over money and credit aggregates, as I have indicated.

Although I have cited Schacht on fundamentals, such as the variant of a "real bills" and "currency policy" orientation, I see him as very dated in two main respects and possibly three. They are: (1) his view on the minimum reserve requirement; (2) the absence of any sense of open market operations of the special sort I point to (Section 3.3), including in connection with the bank reserve equation; and (3) the minor reference to the use of the discount rate as a means of checking an inflation (Section 3.4, note 15).

6.6d Some Further Asides

Further asides come with respect to the following: the definition of inflation as a rise in the price index; the zero inflation rate goal; and the tie I make by way of Milton Friedman to the terms of a price index and the substitution and income effects of a price change Section 1.5a). As regards the definition, I see no need for an exception which Hjalmar Schacht takes into account, as have numerous others. It is namely (Schacht 1967, 163), that a rise in some prices comprising the index (and thus a rise in the index, unless some prices adjust downward) may be justified in terms of quality improvements in goods and services and not as a consequence viewable as inflation. The responses to this are several. First, quality may decline as well as rise and be difficult to measure in any refined way.[9] Such occurrences are unlikely to be short run in the time frame of Keynes (Section 1.3), to be sure. If they do occur—and I may cite numerous instances in selected areas--and if they are not offset by losses in quality elsewhere--then so what. The implicit decline in the price index, as where quality is occurring and being recognized, may contribute to a decline in the velocity of money via the holding of greater stock of money balances which makes transactions with money balances more efficient and convenient. The long-run process, where slow and gradual changes appear, would make little difference on business conditions anyway in monetary policy terms.

What is most crucial to the functioning of the price system is the functioning of relative prices (Frazer 1994a, Section 3.2) and the avoidance of distortions to them that come in periods of inflation rate swings, such as I point to for the 1970s (Section 2.2).

As many have pointed out, the functioning of the price system entails details that go beyond the reaches of those who wish to identify and regulate even small changes in the price system (Frazer 1988, Chapter 8).

Simplicity and directness are called for in discussing the price system where possible, including at the price of abstracting from some detail. And, finally, as the 1990s history of the European Monetary System suggests, public and even expert understanding of complicated economic processes does not come easily. Indeed, policy and the goals of policy (say, the zero inflation rate) need to be kept as straight-forward as possible in order to facilitate public understanding.

6.7 A 1994 FASHION OF TARGETING SHORT-TERM RATES AND BUNDESBANK DOMINANCE

In offering leaps in the dark I and II and throughout I have drawn distinctions between an essentially i-regime and an M-regime approach (Tables 5-1 and 5-2) with roots in Keynes's work and Friedman's respectively (Sections 1.4 and 1.5). In this interest-rate orientation, however, "the interest rate" is the long-term rate (i_L), although short-rate control arrangements enter into the Keynes/Keynesian liquidity preference and investment blocks (Figures 1-2 and 1-3). As envisioned these control arrangements are such that direct control by the central bank over the short rate can impact changes in the same direction to the long-term rate (i_L). It is seen as significant for control over expenditures and hence such ultimate goals as income growth and stability and low-to-zero inflation rate goals.

In such a context as the foregoing, a matter of expediency on the part of operating officials appears with respect to the envisioned arrangements because of central bank traditions and practices (hypothesis H_{CB}, Sections 1.1 and 5.1b). They are such that attention drifted to control over the short rates because the central banks were thought to control such rates and because institutional complexities made the attainment of money aggregates difficult. I came to do two things--to question why the institutions were not changed to accommodate control of money aggregates, and to see the Bundesbank as a preferred model for a new and possibly only a hypothetical European central bank.

In contrast to this questioning, however, a variant of the i-regime orientation has gained some attention. It appears in a Federal Reserve publication by Stuart Weiner (1992) and in lesser measure in comments by Greenspan (Section 3.2d), and the failure of the Federal Reserve to come within the target range for dollars M2 in 1992 (Figure 3-4). So, in closing with "leaps in the dark," I turn to the Weiner analysis, assess it from a Friedman system perspective, and close with comments by Friedman (1993).

6.7a Weiner's Account

In his account Weiner pleads for an open mind. He says, "there is no inherent reason why a central bank need target the money stock." Even though, I believe that history and a host of facts enter, as opposed to "no inherent reason," I proceed with Weiner's exposition. He says:

It could be the case that another intermediate target, say, a medium-term interest rate, is deemed to be more closely related to the ultimate goal variables. If so, monetary control can be deemphasized or even abandoned, in which case reserve requirements again become irrelevant as a vehicle for directly controlling the money stock. (Weiner 1992, 55)

In the argument advanced by Weiner, the distinction is made between an "interest rate operating procedure" and the "reserve operating procedure" which I sketch in Section 3.3 and extend to the Bundesbank in Section 3.4. Weiner embraces these distinctions as Friedman intended when he said, "Direct control of the monetary base is an alternative to fiscal policy and interest rates as a means of controlling monetary growth" (Section 3.5). Although not touching on fiscal policy at all, Weiner says (1992, 56)—along the lines of H_{CB} (Section 1.1 and 1.5b)—"institutional structure within a country . . . may still have an important role to play" (meaning in the public choice between the interest rate and reserve requirements operating procedures).

Weiner's case for a short-rate orientation proceeds with time series for "effective" reserve ratios and the money multipliers that go with them in fractional reserve banking systems (Sections 3.3c and 4.2). United States, Canadian, and German series appear. They show downward trends for the effective reserve ratios from the early 1970s to 1992 and upward trends in the corresponding money multipliers. The United States and Canadian multipliers are more upward than the German one.

In connection with the trends in the reserves and the multipliers, Weiner points out that lower requirements (and higher multipliers) have the effect of magnifying the errors in the targeting of the liabilities for depository institutions. The smaller the reserve requirements (and the larger the money and credit multipliers) "the greater the overshoot [or error in falling within the target ranges, e.g., Figure 3-4]." In terms of earlier symbols Sections 3.3c and 4.2): (1) open market operations enter the bank reserve equation at R, $R_o = G + R - Cs + . . .$; (2) federal reserve credit enters via R to impact on R_o (or $R_o + C_s$ to get "base money"); and (3) R_o links to the money stock (M) by way of the multiplier $(1/r)$.

Overall, in growth rate terms, $\Delta \dot{R}_o (1/r) \rightarrow \Delta \dot{M}$, so an error made in putting R_o on target gets magnified by the amount of the multiplier $(1/r)$ as it enters the growth rate for the money stock $(\dot{M})$.

Also, in Weiner's analysis, the reserves for the United States, Canada, and the Federal Republic of Germany pay no interest. For Weiner, this means that reserve requirements call for the depository institutions to forego interest income. The reasons he offers for the reserve-requirement declines are:

1. the obvious income loss from requiring reserves (plus, I add, lower total earnings from bank credit when requirements restrict credit expansion)

2. the Federal Reserve is cited for a 1992 reduction that was directed at strengthening balance sheets of depository institutions

3. the Bundesbank acknowledged "competitive bias" against German depository institutions as opposed to European competitors

4. deregulations and innovations, where financial institutions have a strong incentive to avoid reserve requirements.

Of course, in making such changes in reserve ratios (as in adding new accounts to data series, and so on, Section 3.2d) central bankers in some measure contribute to their own difficulties with respect to errors in targeting money aggregates.

In any event, Weiner goes back to what I see as earlier stages of the Keynesian orientation (Teigen 1965) to come up with ordinary supply and demand functions for the money stock, with the view of also dealing with the unlikely prospects of actually identifying the respective functions. For the monetary approach I associate with Friedman, this problem of the identification of supply and demand relations is dealt with by viewing money demand in terms of velocity, by treating households as determining the real money stock (M/P, in Equation [1], Section 1.5) and by having the central bank determine the nominal money stock (Frazer 1988, 210, 543, 743, and note 69, 776). The behavior of the households and central bank is thought to be different, hence identification.[10]

Weiner offers a money/interest-rate (M-i) plane with M on the horizontal axis and with i(short term) on the vertical axis, which I show in Figure 6-1.[11] A downward sloping demand curve and an upward sloping supply curve are imposed on the plane. They intersect at the "effective money supply" line (M_s, effective). The intersection is a solution (equilibrium, or balance) point [point $A(M^*, i^*)$]. Growth conditions such as I stress in Sections 1.5, 2.2 and throughout are possible in that the static money supply and demand curves (M_s and M_d) may move about and outward as growth occurs. The idea, under the conditions of change is that point A moves along the path for the effective money supply (M_s effective). A money supply line with lower reserve requirements appears ($M_{s,lrr}$). It intersects at point A, and rotates downward as reserve requirements are lowered. The downward rotation also reflects the potentially greater impact of short-term interest rate changes on the quality of

Figure 6-1
A Hypothetical Interest Rate Operating Procedure

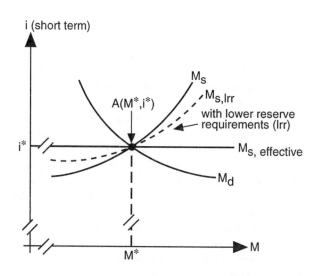

money (the M-axis), but that variable is insignificant to the analysis. It just comes about and appears as the effective money supply.

The money stock comes about when the short-term market rate (i*) is set by the central bank. Weiner says (1992, 54), the central bank focuses on achieving the market interest rate (i*) rather than providing reserves and relying on the link between reserves and the money supply. The implication is that the market interest rate known as the "federal funds rate" may be used to target a real rate of interest (and hence a zero inflation rate goal). Weiner says, "A crucial implication is that the level of reserve requirements is now irrelevant i.e., requirements no longer play a direct role in monetary control."

In taking up a changing role for reserve requirements, he says (1993, 45): "Reserve requirements are no longer seen as a vehicle to directly control the money stock but rather as a vehicle to facilitate control over short-term interest rates." Going further, he says, "depending on a country's institutional framework, there may be scope for reducing or even eliminating reserve requirements."

Of course, changes in reserve requirements per se are no unusual thing, nor need they be seen as a means of controlling reserves (or "base money" defined as reserves plus currency and coins in circulation). In the context of the bank reserve equation, as stated on various occasions (Sections 3.3b and 4.2), the Federal Reserve may readily intervene with open market operations to counter the reserve-requirement change and continue to control the growth of reserves (or "base money") irrespective of the legally required level for reserves. From a money-aggregates control perspective, nothing really changes but possibly the "effective" money and bank-credit multipliers.

6.7b Factual and Analytical Difficulties

There are crucial factual and analytical difficulties with the view of setting monetary policy in terms of a short-term interest rate such as the federal funds rate in the United States. *First*, it is misleading to say, as Weiner does (1992, 55), that the Bundesbank has made a choice to target the money stock via "an interest rate operating procedure" or to target some variable other than the money supply with the view to attaining German economic goals for income and inflation rates. Citing the Bundesbank's own text (1989), and drawing on Kennedy (1991) and other print media, the view of the Bundesbank's management of liability to set a money-stock variable within a target range (Section 3.4) is more accurate than the Weiner position. Moreover, even Weiner vacillates on the matter saying "German monetary policy" is "geared somewhat more toward traditional monetary control considerations." In addition, in Weiner's reference to Dudler (1986), Weiner also says Dudler characterizes the Bundesbank as not following a "pure 'interest rate' strategy" and as stressing that short-run procedures are not based on a rigorous 'money multiplier' approach." (Weiner 1992, note 17).

Quite clearly, where central banks commit themselves to offsetting the effects of destabilizing episodes and liquidity shifts such as appears initially in money and financial markets, there is unlikely to be any pure reserve and money-multiplier approach. Shifts toward liquidity such as coincide with the 1937-38 recession in the United States or even 1990-91 in the United States (Sections 3.2a and 3.2d) need to be met by monetary policy when possible if it is to be stabilizing.

In the context of deficit reduction, stabilization was not possible in the 1990-93 period in the United States. And in more general terms, the difficulty with United States policy is that it has too often been destabilizing in connection with the interest-rate orientation (Sections 3.2a and 3.2b).

Second, the rationale for the upward slopping money supply curve in Figure 6-1 is as follows: "The money supply curve slopes upward because increases in the market interest rate encourage borrowing [on the part of the non-central bank] and discourage excess reserves, boosting the money supply."

Even though this may be the rationale, I see it as being based on observations which are that banks and households draw down on liquidity as booms progress and market interest rates rise. At such times, banks borrow reserves more aggressively to support the growth of loan and investment portfolios. So, it is not the interest rates that encourage borrowing but rather the boom state. Inflationary expectations may enter, where not held in check, so a rise in interest rates is possible [$i = i(\text{real}) + \dot{P}$].

Third, the money demand curve slopes downward on the Keynesian rationale (Section 1.4). Stated on a priori grounds by Weiner, it is that when interest rates are low "the opportunity cost of holding money also declines, reducing the incentive for households and businesses to economize on money holdings." Now, this too is at odds with the evidence on the behavior of interest rate and liquidity shifts by households and firms, namely: (1) shifts into liquidity on the part of banks coincide with low interest rates (as in the 1937-38 recession, Section 3.2a), "pushing on a string" and all); (2) the velocity of money too declines in tandem with low interest rates (Figures 3-1 and 3-3); and (3) there is no evidence that the central banks raise and lower long-term interest rates exclusive of their control over inflation. Indeed, considering the interest-rate and inflation-rate data in Figures 2-1 and 2-2 respectively, I see that interest rates trend upward with monetary accommodation and rising inflation and downward with monetary deceleration and declining inflation rates. Further, I see that the Federal Republic of Germany had the lowest interest rates of the three countries shown, as well as the lowest inflation rates.

Fourth, mentioning numerous analysts, Weiner says the Bundesbank seeks "to closely influence longer term money market rates" (1992, note 22). However, in opposition to this I quote the Bundesbank's position:

[T]he Bundesbank decided after much deliberation to make its intentions in stabilization policy clear to the public in advance by announcing an annual monetary growth target. The Bundesbank still regards this as a most *valuable intermediate target*. (Bundesbank, 1989, 82)

Longer-term rates in the capital market in particular are likely to change spontaneously with fluctuations in the price climate, without any action by the central bank, i.e., to contain "inflation premiums" which are very hard to measure. The "ambivalent" nature of interest rate movements makes market rates an unsuitable intermediate goal for a monetary policy directed towards price stability. (Bundesbank, 1989, 83)

[T]he close empirical connection which exists over the longer term between the movement of the money stock and the movement of prices also suggests that the most suitable intermediate target to show the effects of the Bundesbank's stabilization policy is to be found in the range of aggregates relating to the volume of money. (Bundesbank 1989, 84)

Fifth, drawing on what Weiner regards as "most analysts," he distinguishes between sources of shocks (or I say, episodic impacts) on the data series. On the one hand, he says:

An economy subject to frequent shocks in money demand emanating from portfolio shifts, for example, is best served by an interest rate intermediate target. Such an approach insulates the real economy from unwanted fluctuations, and while the money stock may increase or decrease unexpectedly, such movements have no effect on the inflation rate.

On the other hand, Weiner says:

An economy subject to frequent shocks in money demand emanating from unexpected changes in consumer or business spending . . . is best served by a money stock intermediate target. By allowing interest rates to adjust, a money stock target prevents large fluctuations in real growth and at the same time keeps inflation close to its desired level. (Weiner 1992, 56)

But the analytical difficulty here is that most significant episodes are indistinguishable in their impacts on financial markets and household spending in the real goods sector.[12] To be sure adjustments to impacts appear first in the markets for the most liquid assets and may even be reversed in the minor instances before the effects appear in the real-goods sector. Yet, all of this, does not separate the money and financial markets from the real goods and service markets where I observe the spread of events to production growth, employment, and inflation rates. A major effect of Friedman's extensions of analysis to transitory and trend time frame and to the 4-asset model (Section 1.5) was the link between the monetary and real goods sectors. To repeat an earlier position: If there are changes in the underlying conditions (say, a change toward the prospect of a decline in prices), then there would be an increase in the demand for money in connection with its store of value function of money demand (note 4, Chapter 1). This means a decline in demand in product-market terms, such as I show in Figure 6-2, namely: A positive (negative) shift in the community's demand to hold money gives rise to a decline (rise) in velocity and output as illustrated in Figure 6-2 (the move from point A to B). If output adjust faster than prices, as when recession occurs, I end at an unemployment level of output (q_u). On the other hand, if and when supply conditions (and wages as a special price) adjust to the demand-shift condition I end at point C and full employment output (q_f).

So Weiner is straining to separate effects that should not be separated and likely cannot be separated by known statistical means over time frames that matter for the economy. The ultimate goals for the central bank and the state, or the G-5 and G-7, appear in respect to the real goods sector. The monetary role is that of a vehicle for arriving there.

6.7c Friedman and the Short-Rate View

In connection with a trend at the Federal Reserve to target a federal-funds rate (the rate on the interbank borrowing of reserves), Milton Friedman reacts thus:

Figure 6-2
A Strengthened Preference for Money Balance with and without Wage (Cost) Adjustments

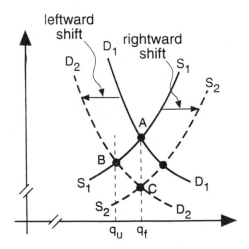

[P]egging the federal-funds rate is strictly peripheral to the Fed's real task, which is to ensure that the quantity of money behaves in such a way as to produce a stable price level.

In my opinion, the Fed should not be concerned with the federal-funds rate at all. It should stick to controlling the base (currency plus deposits at the Fed), the only nominal magnitude that it can directly control over any short or long period—and that no market forces can prevent it from controlling. By contrast, it if tries to peg the federal-funds rate at the "wrong" level, it will sooner or later fail. In the interim, it will do much harm—as was demonstrated so dramatically in the 1970s [confer earlier Section 5.2].

Continuing, Friedman said: "The Fed can peg the federal-funds rate over short periods and therefore give the illusion of performing successfully, even when it is doing a poor job at its real function, as unfortunately it has over the greater part of its history." (Friedman 1993)

6.8 TIME SERIES, OPERATIONS AND POLICY

Conjuring up changes in the relationships between European central banks brings up some reflections on lessons from the past. These come about when I recall components of information contained in time series; relate the components to a Friedman/Bundesbank-type rule, bank operations, and policy; recall some old functions of central banks, which were largely "defensive" in nature (countering seasonable drains on reserves and smoothing the effects of disruptive flows of funds to and from the money markets and among them); and take account of the need to extend the notion of a new, unified central bank to encompass such operational and policy-related functions as the monitoring and interpretation of time series data and information of an essentially episodic (news and events, non-repetitive) nature.

In the first instance, the kind of time series information central banks and economic policy authorities have traditionally been interested in has included (1) seasonal changes; (2) credit and business conditions, or cyclical changes; and (3) secular trends (or growth paths). There is awareness of the potential presence of news and information impacts on all of the foregoing, ranging from day-to-day happenings to secular-trend shifts. These are such as may occur in the income velocity of money, when the public's habits, and technological or other changes occur with respect to the payments mechanism. In the orientations of those who gave speeches and wrote in the mid-twentieth century decades, countering, smoothing, or eliminating the cycle was thought to be of high priority, as was providing an environment conducive to sustained growth in output (and possibly even increasing it).

The Friedman system, with its statistical underpinning, has borne on these foregoing changes, the time frames, and episodic changes. However, it focused on "transitory change" (the label for cycles), and "permanent magnitudes" (the secular trends) and episodic changes mainly in reference to shifts in the trends, but there was also the prospect for changes in relation to seasonal and defensive responses to disruptive flows in the money markets. This focus was oriented toward the formation of expectations by the players in the markets, and it bore on the way I state the Friedman/Bundesbank-type rule. Friedman himself took a lot for granted on the operations side, and conceded little to short-run responses on the part of the authorities. On the other hand, the Bundesbank would surely confront short-run disturbances and that can be expected.

6.8a Defensive Operations and Secular and Episodic Changes

On the money-supply side, the central bank provides a money stock, and on the demand side, there is the velocity (or turnover) of the money stock variously measured (e.g., the ratio of income to the money stock or even the ratio of income to bank reserves). In the control over bank reserves and other money aggregates is the idea that the main objective in supplying the money stock is to interface it with demand so as to ensure the attainment of desirable economic goals (zero inflation appearing among them, to be sure). The Friedman/Bundesbank-type rule as I have stated it, enters into this, but I presently invoke it only after recognizing a place for "defensive operations," as they were once called. Quite likely, with the expanded scope of the financial markets brought about by closer economic integration, the private sector will have the opportunity to develop means for making its own adjustments to potentially disruptive financial movements of funds. Further, some sort of limited operations in foreign exchange markets may be called for by the new arrangements, as mentioned shortly. Recall, however, that exchange rates, interest rates, and inflation rates are interrelated. They come as a package. Attempts to treat them as if each can be independently controlled (e.g., to target an exchange rate, as if the inflation rate were separate) can be regarded as potentially very dangerous.

Anticipating subsequent accounting for a category of bank reserves, I offer the bank reserve equation (actually an accounting identity), which has been routinely reported in Federal Reserve records. There is one category of reserves (R_o)—such as I propose under new arrangements—as the left-handed member of an equation. On the other side, is the sum of categories reflecting gold-flows before the U.S. closing of the gold window and other international monetary reserves (G), central bank credit (R), the public's holding of currency (a currency drain, say C), and a residual of very secondary accounts. To be sure, the central bank must have the capability of monitoring and anticipating changes in some components on the right-hand side so as to set central bank credit (R) in order to meet the desired target for reserves (R_o). The source of the central bank's extension of credit on any permanent basis should be OMO.

All of the preceeding matters bearing on time series enter here as well as for the other major time series. I have mentioned defensive operations and others, but a present and subsequent point is that there is a well-defined category for reserves (R_o). It should turn out, too, to be a highly homogeneous category of reserves, which the new central organization takes responsibility for controlling. It will be, specifically, reserves on deposit at the operating arms of the newly arranged organization.

6.8b The Delors Report and Bank Operations

Amazingly in what it sought, the Delors Report said nothing about accounting controls, bank operations, traditions, and practices. This is very much in contrast to the attention given here to bank operations and accounting controls, to the traditions and practices at the Bundesbank, and to the Bank of England's and the U.K. government's inability to make a switch to an M-regime orientation.

Questions avoided by the Delors Report may be as follows: How would bank reserves be defined, measured by accounting practice, and controlled? Would there in fact be a common measure for bank reserves and any relatively homogeneous categories for the bank liabilities entering into the aggregate for the money stock (say, for M1, M2, . . . and so on)?

One may prefer not to dwell on the Bank of England and the Federal Reserve, except for the reasons of their past prominence. However, operational problems bearing on Europe and the prospect of a monetary union appear in a comparison of the respective operations and the reasons for the United Kingdom's departing from efforts to target money and credit aggregates with the results reported in Chapter 5. These were rising inflation and interest rates and a declining exchange rate against the DM in the 1988-89 period.

The United States prospects for targeting money and credit aggregates, and for accounting for the Federal Reserve's behavior, are relatively simple by comparison with those for the United Kingdom. First, in the accounting for bank reserves, there is the bank reserve identity; in addition, the category "bank reserves" (R_o) means only the sum of vault cash (coins and notes) and deposits at the Federal Reserve's operating regional banks. (For a time, the category meant only the deposits of member commercial banks at the Federal Reserve banks.) Second, until bollixed up by such statistical matters as including new categories of deposits (e.g., NOW accounts) in the Fed's M1 measure of the money stock (Frazer 1988, 654-659), the money aggregate categories had distinct meanings. Even then, the matter of allowing for such changes was more statistical than a displacement of the measure as a monetary target.

In contrast in the United Kingdom, there was a different past and a different banking tradition and practices coming from it. Allowing for the prospect that changing habits and practices may be more difficult than reverting to the past, there should be no surprise that the Bank of England under U.K. Treasury auspices departed from its earlier efforts at accounting for and targeting money and credit aggregates.

Now, extrapolating from the prospects in the U.K. case to all of the EC member banking traditions, the complexity of achieving a common currency (meaning a common money supply) for Europe is compounded. It is even further compounded by the recognition that the forces of politics and bureaucratic inertia may even be stronger at the operations levels of central banking than at the policy/organizational levels confronted in the Delors Report and at Maastricht. As M. Friedman concluded from his experiences, there is a law of bureaucratic inertia at the operations level. It says: "Every large bureaucracy . . . is certain that the way it conducts its affairs is the only way they can be conducted" (Frazer 1988, 505). Herein lies an explanation of why the Delors Report and the Maastricht meeting avoided the operations dimensions.

Picking up on the intent and the omissions of the Delors Report, I seek a common money supply for Europe through a twofold arrangement. It consists of (1) simple accounting and control procedures that provide for the conduct of policy along M-regime lines and (2) procedures that interfere least during the transition and in the long run with the existing banking systems. A key to the implementation of a Friedman/Bundesbank-type rule is that by all means the central governing committee's contribution to bank reserves must be measurable and easily understood as a part of a "managed money" system. The central banking people themselves must forgo the days when mystery surrounded what they did—the way gold worked in vaults, the dealings in the money market, the idea of raising interest rates via inflationary components to attract foreign capital, and so on.

6.8c Currency Swaps and OMO in Foreign Exchange

The EC member countries may wish to extend some authority in foreign exchange matters external to the new arrangements for a proposed European committee. But the extension of this authority may also be very limited. In brief, note the two kinds of operations—one is relatively innocent and benign, the other redundant in the overall strategy of monetary policy. In the benign case, the central authority maintains a pool of foreign currencies (meaning, access to foreign money supplies) for the rainy day. Let the pool consist of dollars and yens, for example. In such a case, an increase in the ECU price of yens may be countered in some minor, short-run way by using the yens to buy ECUs. There is a swapping of currencies.

In the redundant and surely self-defeating case, the central authority may purchase its own currency (the ECU) in the open market with a check drawn on itself. Here, the clearing of the check contributes to accelerated growth in bank reserves and hence, via credit and money multipliers, to accelerated growth in bank credit and the money stock. These effects are the same as OMO in the securities markets. Along the dynamic lines I am following (acceleration and not simply an increase), the end results are a further rise in the inflation rate and the ECU price for yens. Since the latter authority is redundant, there is no EC need for it.[13]

6.9 AN OVERVIEW

Among other things the Delors Report on European Economic and Monetary Union called for a layering of a complex administrative European bureaucracy on the existing governments and central banks and interference of a fairly direct sort in the budgetary matters of sovereign states. It drew on ideas associated with the IMF system of fixed exchange rates and on the methods used by the IMF in the post-World War II days of fixed exchange rates to ensure the functioning of the fixed rate system (FY, 1966, Chapters 22, 23). To be sure, the Delors Report comes to the point of proposing a super, IMF/central-bank system. However, its proposals did not come to the point of achieving a common currency with vanishing exchange rates. Rather, the Report and the later Maastricht Treaty arrangements ended with a system of such overwhelming power as to eliminate the need for any adjustments in exchange rates.

This forced compliance and other factors foretell that full realization of the steps along the Report/Treaty track will not be realized on the Treaty's schedule. The other factors include the recognized need for more public understanding of a super-national bank and a common money, and likely hesitancy on the part of officials to accept the Bundesbank model.

A more likely outcome, once Germany settles into unification and until a more distance future arrives, is a two-speed Europe. Germany and those states most likely to line up behind the deutsche mark will be the fast track for some time. Britain, Italy, Greece, Spain, and others will hobble along for a time.

The ERM which Thatcher dreaded in 1989, which then emerged with U.K. support, and from which the United Kingdom withdrew in September 1992, may appear troublesome. The ultimate outcome may further vindicate Thatcher in some measure.

A move toward a European monetary system with a "super-national money" and a minimum loss of sovereignty would require giving up two illusions on the part of central bankers and the immediate support personnel. One is that monetary and fiscal policies are complementary, whereas in fact they are substitutes for one another. The other has perhaps more ancient roots in central banking lore. It is that by some means central banks and governments can move to control separately, and by fairly direct means, the interest rate, the inflation rate, and the exchange rate. The fact is that rising (declining) interest rates, declining (rising) exchange rates, and rising (declining) inflation rates come as a package. Short of the use of direct force by the state authority, there is no known statistical means of separating out the control of one variable from the others.

The two analytical matters involve (1) the government budget constraint, and (2) the related fact that a central bank purchase of a country's securities (say the PSBR) has the same effect on money and credit creation as an open market purchase of securities of the same magnitude. Indeed, apart from "crowding out," the purchase of the PSBR depends on monetary policy to get its effect on the total demand for goods and services.

Some technical credit and money multiplier matters are involved in relation to parts of the policy-oriented presentation. The statement of a Friedman/Bundesbank-type of rule gives attention to the central bank's contribution to what Bundesbank officials call "liquidity management" as well as to bank reserves and bank credit and monetary growth. The reserve aggregate and a credit multiplier for it should be easily set apart for all the banking institutions where check transferable deposits appear for the member countries sharing what I have called "the common European money supply." A link would be clearly established between the new category of reserves and the deposits arising with respect to them from either an inflow of paper notes and coins or the creation of new money balances arising from the extensions of bank credit. The control authority may wish to target the "money stock" category as a policy variable, and also to monitor its turnover. In any case, the establishment of well-defined links between the new reserve category and bank credit and the money stock should be helpful to the authority in the conduct of monetary policy.

NOTES

1.   For those societies functioning under the most disruptive conditions, the Reichsbank's 1934 to 1939 efforts may be relevant. On the transition to markets in less developed countries, see also Frazer (1988, 339-341) and Friedman's *Money and Economic Development* (1973).

2.   The last chapters of Hugo Young's biography of Margaret Thatcher are titled "Into the Vortex" and "Herself Alone" (1991, 542-624). They address developments surrounding Nigel Lawson's actions and resignation, and Thatcher with regard to the European Monetary System. See also Lawson (1993, 917-971) and Thatcher (1993, 688-815).

Taking up inadequacies at the Bank of England, for dealing with unstable monetary prospects, there is a noticeable absence of recommendations on the part of Thatcher's principal economic/financial advisors to move the operations at the Bank of England more along the modern lines of the Bundesbank and/or toward what I call "open market operations of a special sort." In the stressful days concerning the U.K. entry into the EMS, Alan Walters was content to take up Friedman-type views on exchange rates (phase 5, sect. 4.1a) and Lawson was content to view the EMS's ERM of the early 1990s as harboring "a central part of the necessary financial discipline for the United Kingdom" (Lawson 1993, 970) that the United Kingdom could not impose on itself. He accepted the traditions, practices, and i-orientation at the Bank of England, even as he aspired to be its governor.

However, anticipating future governments, Lawson did at one time propose making the Bank of England "independent" but still responsible to Parliament (1993, 867-870) as a means of giving assurances to the financial markets. In hindsight he repeats this position:

The lesson of history is that the new-found enthusiasm for a floating pound will not last. Meanwhile, however, the Government needs to do everything possible to reinforce the credibility of Britain's lasting anti-inflation commitment. An independent but accountable Bank of England, under a new statutory framework, would in any case be desirable for the reasons I advanced in 1988 and recount . . . It is double so following sterling's inglorious departure from the ERM. (Lawson 1993, xi)

Even given the Lawson position, there is no hint of reforming the means of monetary operations to better control the money stock and/or of moving to "open market operations of a special sort." (On central bank independence, see Sections 3.2d and 3.4; note 14, Chapter 3; and note 4 below.)

3.   An announcement such as this arose at the time of the stock market crash of October 1987 (Frazer 1988, 686). The effect of such an announcement is expected to occur through its influence on the outlook of the market participants. To have the desired effect, however, the official or agency making the announcement must have credibility (Hass and Frazer 1979). In central banking lore "announcement effects" have most often been related to discount rate changes, even when the action did nothing

more than bring the discount rate in line with short-term market rates of interest. Along much more substantial lines, note the joint announcement of Alan Greenspan and Ronald Reagan on the occasion of the stock market crash of 1987.

4. In the highly regarded Volcker/Gyohten, reflections/memoirs book (VG 1992), Volcker gets caught in the web of his own remarks about the independence of the Federal Reserve when he turns to the political and policy changes that came with the Reagan presidency and the Treasury of that period (confer notes 4 and 11 in Chapter 3; and see Volcker in VG 1992, 1974-1975). First, in his own account, Volcker looked for no "misunderstanding ... about the importance of an independent central bank" before taking the appointment as chairman, but then yielded to White House concerns to use the Fed in efforts to control consumer credit in early 1980 (Volcker in VG 1992, 164, and 171-172). Second, Volcker notes support from Arthur Burns in countering the influence of Friedman, Friedman led monetarists, and some others to compromise the Fed's independence by subordinating it to the Treasury (in VG 1992, 173-174), when in fact Burns had seen the Fed as subordinate to the Congress in monetary-policy matters (Section 3.2d).

5. The idea of an amalgamation existed well before the Delors Report of 1989 appeared. Referring simply to the Delors proposals as of 1985, Eizenga (1987, 20) offers an interesting paragraph:

Like the Deutsche Bundesbank, The Nederlandsche Bank objects to the Delors proposals. For instance, Mr. A.F.P. Bakker, Chief of the Bank's International Affairs Department, called these proposals disappointing because "the objective of an economic and monetary union, with one central bank and one central currency, is not incorporated into the Treaty [of Rome], even though all Member States are agreed on it." And he continues: "The purpose of the EMS, to promote monetary stability, is endangered if the checks and balances now existing at the national levels between central banks and governments are disrupted without being replaced by similar arrangements."

6. The quotation is from peer-review comments on an unpublished paper titled "A European Monetary System with Minimum Loss of Sovereignty."

7. In addition to the rate patterns shown in the earlier Figure 2-1, Howe and Pigott (1992) report on some long-term interest rates for several industrial countries using quarterly data covering the period 1975 through 1990. The nominal yields they report are for ten-year government bonds, except in the case of Germany, where the term is four years or longer. In the case of the nominal rates, the FRG yields are most consistently well below the U.S. rates and certainly below those for the United Kingdom and France. For the period covered, the FRG rates tend to be more in line with the Japanese rates.

Howe and Pigott also report on the nominal yields less inflation rates of the past three years. They refer to these results as "real rates," which would be very much at odds with $i(real) = i - Pb[\dot{P}^e]\ \dot{P}^e$ and analysis regarding the real rate.

Although quite different from the real rates I discuss (Section 1.5d) the so-called long-term, real rates Howe and Pigott report move together, except for the 1983-85 period when the United States moved aggressively toward controlling inflation under Reagan's leadership.

The analytical problems with the Howe and Pigott measurement of so-called real rates center about the omission I indicate. I would even weight the expected inflation rate by the probability of its outcome, $Pb[\dot{P}^e]$, to get $i_L = i(real) + Pb[\dot{P}^e]\ \dot{P}^e$. Along this line of analysis are all the crucial issues of central bank credibility, central banks bailing out governments, and the dynamics of bond market behavior.

8. This latter statement is drawn on the analyses in Section 3.3e and 3.3f, which in turn are the basis for Friedman's law (Frazer 1988, 650-651, 731); namely, inflation is always and everywhere a monetary phenomenon.

9. There are even added dimensions that flow from this concept of quality changes. A quite early one goes back to the recognition of small changes in the differentiation of products, such as I encounter in the theories of imperfect and monopolistic competition, and the "purpose" of the economic theory to begin with (Frazer 1994a, Chapter 3). At this point I encounter the still further matters concerning the truth of axioms and passing truth forward (as in modus ponens) and the purpose as prediction (or passing error backward, as in modus tollins or reverse logic).

Still further dimensions arises when the term "quality" applies to the quality of life, welfare gains or losses, and environmental matters. Here I get into the adverse effects of production on third parties and phenomena referred to by the technical term "externalities" (meaning external to the ordinary workings of the interactions of firms and households in ordinary market channels).

10. In connection with the use of the economist's mechanical apparatus, Friedman made much of the possibility of dealing with the identification problem indirectly (i.e., other than by attempting to find points along static [or zero time] schedules such as depicted by the ordinary supply/demand relations [e.g., Figures 6-1 and 6-2]).

11. Shown and discussed in reference to Figure 6-1, the Weiner idea is similar in its interest rate control prospects to those found in the work of the Swedish economists Knut Wicksell (1851-1926) who also is said to have influenced Keynes. The Wicksell view (as found in Frazer 1994a, Section 6.4c) is that the central bank sets a rate of interest called a "market rate" that leads to inflation (deflation) when set below (above) the "real rate" of interest (or the "natural rate" to use Wicksell's term). So, overall, there is the idea from Wicksell that the central bank could set a "market" rate in relation to the "real rate" and thereby achieve a zero or other inflation goal. Presumably, as in Weiner's case, some money stock would arise (call it "the effective money stock"). However recalling that the interest rate is the price of credit (Chapter 3, note 12), I say (as in the loanable funds theory of interest, Frazer 1994a, Section 7.4a) that the demand for funds and not money balances is what Wicksell had in mind.

12. A list of some more and less significant episodes that impact time series may be brought forward from the *Legacy* (1994a, Section 3.5). Confined to the 1970s and 1980s decades and impacts on U.S. and U.K. data, it is as follows:

Viewing episodes as a problem with respect to the analysis of the time series and even confining ourselves to the decades of the 1970s and 1980s as I will at times, I may list some for those episodes. In general terms, I see the 1970s as Keynesian dominated, the 1980s as a Thatcher/Reagan decade with a different policy orientation, and the U-Turn as separating the two. In more detailed terms there were: (1) the efforts at "direct" control over prices in the 1970s, first by Richard Nixon and then by Jimmy Carter, (2) Richard Nixon's decision to close the gold window in 1971, (3) oil cartel pricing which first appeared in 1973, (4) the Iranian crisis of 1979 and the Iraqi invasion of Kuwait in 1990, (5) Margaret Thatcher's privatizing of British industries in the second half of the 1980s, (6) pronouncements by a U.S. Treasury secretary to the effect that the dollar will be allowed to decline (say in lieu of further declines in the U.S. inflation rate), (7) Reagan's and Greenspan's assurance at the time of the 1987 stock market crash that the Federal Reserve would not repeat the mistakes of the past, (8) the breaching of the Berlin Wall in the fall of 1989, (9) news about the balancing of the U.S. federal budget in the fall of 1990, (10) the closely related matter of whether the U.S. Congress would force cuts in spending on the part of the government, and a strong increase in the holdings of U.S. currency (a sizable component of the U.S.'s "money base") by foreign nationals in 1990 and 1991. The latter occurred at a time when the U.S. dollar appeared to become a currency of choice under the new conditions confronted by "agents" in Eastern European countries.

U.S. dollars also circulate in Cuba. There are some prospects that they will be made "legal tender" in Cuba.

13.   Using the terms, "sterilized" and "unsterilized" the U.S.'s career, exchange-market official Paul Volcker offers parallels to what I label "benign" and "redundant." Drawing on a 1982-83 international study, he says, "intervention is 'sterilized' if the initial purchase of foreign currency is offset by the central bank by the sale of another asset, say a Treasury bill, so that monetary reserves and monetary policy remain unchanged." (Volcker in VG 1992, 236) Continuing in reference to practicing central bankers and "unsterilized intervention," he says,

I can testify to an important fact: Central bankers don't ordinarily think that way in conducting their operations. Almost every central bank has its own objectives for monetary policy, and they are not framed in terms of the amount of its foreign exchange intervention. If that intervention either enlarges or contracts the monetary base, the natural instinct is to offset it by domestic monetary actions. In other words, they automatically sterilize intervention to the extent they can.

Defining "unsterilized intervention," in any case, Volcker says, it "means that a central bank, when buying or selling a foreign currency, permits the resulting change in its assets to work its way through to a change in the money supply and interest rates" (Volcker in VG 1992, 236). Continuing with a textbook view, and invoking "ceteris paribus," Volcker says:

Just as the textbooks say, if the Fed created dollars to buy marks, those dollars would, like any open market purchase, increase bank reserves and ultimately the amount of money in circulation by some multiple of that reserve increase; interest rates would tend to decline, other things being equal [ceteris paribus] (Volcker in VG 1992, 236).

This textbook view of the interest rate and its reliance on ceteris paribus is of course just what I question for the years since markets have become more sensitive in processing information and forming expectations (Section 1.5b and 3.3d). Indeed, even on Governor Greenspan's account the interest rate outcome via inflationary expectations is stressed (Section 1.2b).

References

Avery, Robert B., Elliehauser, Gregory E., Kenickell, Arthur B., and Sprindt, Paul A. 1986. "The Use of Cash and Transactions Accounts by American Families." *Federal Reserve Bulletin* 72 (February): 87-108.

Bagehot, Walter. 1873 (original data). *Lombard Street*. Fourteenth edition, London: Reprinted by John Murray.

Barro, Robert J. 1976. "Rational Expectations and the Role of Monetary Policy." *Journal of Monetary Economics* 2 (January): 1-32.

___. 1977. "Unanticipated Money Growth and Unemployment in the U.S.? *American Economic Review* 67 (March): 101-115.

___. 1981. *Money, Expectations, and Business Cycles: Essays in Macroeconomics*. New York: Academic Press.

___. 1984. *Macroeconomics*. New York: John Wiley & Sons.

___, and Grossman, Hershell. 1971. "A General Disequilibrium Model of Income and Employment." *American Economic Review* 61 (March): 82-83.

Bigman, David, and Taya, Teizo. 1984. *Floating Exchange Rates and the State of World Trade Payments*. Cambridge, Mass.: Bollinger Publishing.

Bundesbank. 1989. *The Deutsche Bundesbank: Its Monetary Policy Instruments and Functions*. Deutsche Bundesbank Special Series, no. 7 (July).

Burns, Arthur. 1988. *The Ongoing Revolution in American Banking*. Washington, D.C.: American Enterprise Institute for Public Policy Research.

Cagan, Phillip. 1965. *Determinants and Effects of Changes in the Stock of Money, 1875-1960*. New York: Columbia University Press for the National Bureau of Economic Research.

Carlson, John B., and Samolyk, Katherine A. 1992. "The M2 Slowdown and Deposit Intermediation: Implications for Monetary Policy." *Economic Commentary*, Federal Reserve Bank of Cleveland, September 15.

Chandler, Lester V. 1958. *Benjamin Strong, Central Banker*. Washington, D.C.: The Brookings Institution.

Classen, Wolfgang-Dieter. 1987. "Schacht, Horace Greeley Hjalmar" In Eatwell, John, Milgate, Murray, and Newman, Peter, eds. *The New Palgrave*, vol. 4. London: Macmillan Press.

Commons. 1980. *Memoranda on Monetary Policy*, House of Commons, Treasury and Civil Service Committee, Session 1978-1980. London: Her Majesty's Stationary Office.

Conference. 1984. *The International Monetary System: Forth Years after Bretton Woods*. Proceeds of a Conference Sponsored by the Federal Reserve Bank of Boston.

De Grauwe, Paul, and Papademos, Lucas, eds. 1990. *The European Monetary System in the 1990s*. London: Longman.

Domar, E. D. 1946. "Capital Expansion, Rate of Growth, and Employment." *Econometrica* 14 (April): 137-147.

Dormael, Armand Van. 1978. *Bretton Woods: Birth of a Monetary System*. New York: Holmes & Meier Publishers.

Dorn, James A., and Xi, Wang, eds. 1990. *Economic Reform in China*. Chicago: University of Chicago Press.

Dudler, Hermann-Josef. 1986. "Changes in Money-Market Instruments and Procedures in Germany." In *Changes in Money-Market Instruments and Procedures: Objectives and Implications*. Basle, Switzerland: Bank for International Settlements.

Eizenga, Wietze. 1987. "The Independence of the Deutsche Bundesbank and the Nederlandsche Bank with Regard to Monetary Policy: A Comparative Study." *SUERF Papers on Monetary Policy and Financial Systems*, no. 2.

___. 1990. "The Banque de France and Monetary Policy," *SUERF Papers on Monetary Policy and Financial Systems*, no. 8.

___. 1991. "The Bank of England and Monetary Policy," *SUERF Papers on Monetary Policy and Financial Systems*, no. 10.

Emerson, Michael, Gros, Daniel, Italianer, Alexander, Pisani-Ferry, Jean and Reichenback, Horst. 1992. *One Market, One Money*. Oxford: Oxford University Press for Commission of the European Communities.

___, eds. 1980. *Rational Expectations and Economic Policy*. Chicago: University of Chicago Press for the National Bureau of Economic Research.

Evans, Michael K. 1983. *The Truth About Supply-Side Economics*. New York: Basic Books.

Fratianni, Michele, and von Hagen, Jürgen. 1990. "Asymmetries and Realignments in the EMS." In de Grauwe, Paul, and Papademos, Lucas. eds. *The European Monetary System in the 1990s*. London: Longman.

Frazer, William. 1967a. "The Demand for Money, Statistical Results, and Monetary Policy." *Schweizerische Zeitschrift für Volkswirtschaft and Statistik* 103 (no. 1): 11-29.

___. 1967b. *The Demand for Money*. Cleveland, Ohio: The World Publishing.

___. 1968. "Statement on Monetary Policy Guidelines." In *Compendium on Monetary Policy Guidelines and Federal Reserve Structure*. Washington, D.C.: U.S. Government Printing Office (December): 166-203.

___. 1973. *Crisis in Economic Theory*. Gainesville: University of Florida Press.

___. 1978a. "Evolutionary Economics, Rational Expectations, and Monetary Policy." *Journal of Economic Issues* 12 (June): 343-372.

___. 1978b. "The Government Budget Constraint." *Public Finance Quarterly* 6 (July): 381-387.

___. 1980. *Expectations, Forecasting and Control: A Provisional Textbook of Macroeconomics*, 2 volumes. University Press of America.

___. 1983. "Lord Kaldor, Friedman and Pertinent Episodes." *Wall Street Review of Books* 12 (no. 4): 261-284.

___. 1984. "*The Economics of Supply and Demand* and Friedman." *Economic Notes* 13 (no. 3): 47-71.

___. 1988. *Power and Ideas: Milton Friedman and the Big U-Turn*, two volumes. Volume I, *Background*, and Volume II, *The Big U-Turn*. Gainesville, Fl: The Gulf-Atlantic Publishing Company.

___. 1994a. *The Legacy of Keynes and Friedman: Economic Analysis, Money, and Ideology*. Westport, Conn.: Praeger Publishers.

___. 1994b. "Exogenous/Endogenous Money Supply Theory." *Journal of Economic Issues* 28 (December).

Frazer, William, and Yohe, William (FY). 1966. *Introduction to the Analytics and Institutions of Money and Banking*. Princeton, N.J.: D. Van Nostrand.

Frazer, William, and Sawyer, Kim, eds. 1984. *Taped Discussion on Some Uses of Statistical Methods with Milton Friedman*, June 25, Las Vegas, Nevada.

Friedman, Milton. 1949. "The Marshallian Demand Curve." *Journal of Political Economy* 57 (December): 463-495. Reprinted in Friedman's 1953 collection of essays.

___. 1951. "Test of Econometric Model." In *Conference on Business Cycles*. New York: National Bureau of Economic Research.

___. 1953. "The Case for Flexible Exchange Rates." In *Essays in Positive Economics*. Chicago: University of Chicago Press.

___. 1957. *A Theory of The Consumption Function*. Princeton, N.J.: Princeton University Press for the National Bureau of Economic Research.

___. 1962. "The Interpolation of Time Series by Related Series." Technical Paper No. 16, National Bureau of Economic Research.

___. 1969. *The Optimum Quantity of Money and Other Essays*. Chicago: Aldin.

___. 1973. *Money and Economic Development: The Horowitz Lectures of 1972*. New York: Praeger.

___. 1974. "A Theoretical Framework for Monetary Analysis." In Robert J. Gordon, ed., *Milton Friedman's Monetary Framework*. Chicago: University of Chicago Press.

___. 1983. "The Keynes Centenary: A Monetarist Reflects." *The Economist* 287 (June 4): 17-19.

___. 1991. "A Cautionary Tale about Multiple Regressions." *American Economic Review* 81 (March): 48-49.

___. 1993. "End the Fed's Fine-Tuning." *Wall Street Journal* 222 (Sept. 15): A-22.

Friedman, Milton, and Roosa, Robert V. 1967. *The Balance of Payments: Free versus Fixed Exchange Rates*. Washington, D.C.: American Enterprise Institutes for Public Policy Research.

Friedman, Milton, and Schwartz, Anna J. (FS). 1963. *A Monetary History of the United States, 1867-1960*. Princeton, N.J.: Princeton University Press for National Bureau of Economic Research.

___. 1982. *Monetary Trends in the United States and the United Kingdom: Their Relation to Income, Prices and Interest Rates, 1867-1975*. Chicago: University of Chicago Press for National Bureau of Eeconomic Research.

___. 1991. "Alternative Approaches to Analyzing Economic Data." *American Economic Review* 81 (March): 39-49.

Giavazzi, Francesco, Micossi, Stephana, and Miller, Marcus, eds. 1988. *The European Monetary System*. Cambridge: Cambridge University Press.

Giovannini, Alberto, and Mayer, Colin, eds. 1991. *European Financial Integration*. Cambridge: Cambridge University Press.

Goodhart, Charles. 1988. *The Evolution of Central Banks*. Cambridge, Mass.: MIT Press.

Gowa, Joanne. 1983. *Closing the Gold Window: Domestic Politics and the End of Bretton Woods*. Ithaca, N.Y.: Cornell University Press.

Greenspan, Alan. 1993a. "Statement before the Committee on Banking, Housing and Urban Affairs, U.S. Senate, February 19, 1993." *Federal Reserve Bulletin* 79 (April): 292-302.

___. 1993b. "Statement before the Committee on the Budget, U.S. House of Representatives, February 24, 1993." *Federal Reserve Bulletin* 79 (April): 302-307.

Halcrow, Morrison. 1989. *Keith Joseph: A Single Mind*. London: Macmillan.

Hass, Jane W., and Frazer, William. 1979. "The Political Business Cycle: Adjustments through Persuasion Techniques." *Economic Notes* 8 (no. 2): 113-133.

Hicks, J. R. 1974. *The Crisis in Keynesian Economics*. New York: Basic Books.

___. 1983. "The Keynes Centenary." *The Economist* 287 (June 18): 17-19.

Higgins, Bryan. 1992. "Policy Implications of Recent M2 Behavior." *Economic Review*, Federal Reserve Bank of Kansas City 77 (no. 3): 21-36.

Hotelling, Harold. 1929. "Stability and Competition." *Economic Journal* 39 (Spring): 41-57.

Howe, Howard, and Pigott, Charles. 1992. "Determinants of Long-Term Interest Rates: An Empirical Study of Several Industrial Study of Several Industrial Countries." *Quarterly Review*, Federal Reserve Bank of New York, 16 (no. 4): 12-28.

Joint Economic Committee. 1977. *Employment Act of 1945, as Amended, with Related Laws (annotated) and Rules of the Joint Economic Committee, Congress of the United States*. Washington, D.C.: U.S. Government Printing Office.

Judd, John P., and Scadding, John L. 1982. "The Search for a Stable Money Demand Function: A Survey of the Post-1073 Literature." *Journal of Economic Literature* 20 (September).

Kahn, George A., and Jacobson, Katrina (KJ). 1989. "Lessons from West German Monetary Policy." *Economic Review*, Federal Reserve Bank of Kansas City (April): 18-35.

Kaldor, Lord (Nicholas). 1980. "Memorandum by Professor Lord Kaldor." *Memoranda on Monetary Policy*, House of Commons, Treasury and Civil Service Committee, Session 1979-1980. London: Her Majesty's Stationary Office.

___. 1982. *The Scourge of Monetarism*. Oxford: Oxford University Press.

Karlick, John R. 1977. "Some Questions and Brief Answers about the Eurodollar Market," A Staff Study Prepared for the Use of the Joint Economic Committee,

Congress of the United States. Washington, D.C.: U.S. Government Printing Office.

Kemp, Donald S. 1975. "Balance-of-Payments Concepts—What Do They Really Mean?" *Review*, Federal Reserve Bank of St. Louis 57 (July): 14-23.

Kennedy, Ellen. 1991. *The Bundesbank: Germany's Central Bank in the International Monetary System*. London: Pinter Publishers for the Royal Institute of International Affairs.

Keynes, John M. 1920. *The Economic Consequences of the Peace*. New York: Harcourt, Brace and Howe.

___. 1923. *A Tract on Monetary Reform*. London: Macmillan.

___. 1925. "The Economic Consequence of Mr. Churchill." Reprinted in J. M. Keynes. 1932. *Essays in Persuasian*. New York: Harcourt, Brace and Company, 244-270.

___. 1932a. "The Consequence to the Banks of the Collapse of Money Values (Aug, 1931)." Reprinted in J. M. Keynes. 1932. *Essays in Persuasion*. New York: Harcourt, Brace and Company, 168-178.

___. 1932b. "The Return to the Gold Standard." Reprinted in J. M. Keynes. 1932 *Essays in Persuasion*. New York: Harcourt, Brace and Company, 179-294.

___. 1936. *The General Theory of Employment, Interest and Money*. New York: Harcourt, Brace and Company.

Klamer, Argo. 1984. *Conversations with Economists*. Totowa, N.J.: Rowman and Allanheld.

Kloptstock, Fred H. 1949. "Monetary Reform in Western Germany." *Journal of Political Economy* 57 (August): 277-292.

Knight, Frank H. 1921. *Risk, Uncertainty and Profit*. Boston, Mass.: Houghton Mifflin Company.

Kubarych, Roger M. 1978. *Foreign Exchange Markets in the United States*. New York: Federal Reserve Bank of New York.

Lawson, Nigel. 1993. *The View from No. 11: Memoirs of a Tory Radical*. London: Corgi Books, Tranworld Publishers Ltd.

Leamer, Edward E. 1978. *Specification Searches*. New York: John Wiley & Sons.

___. 1983. "Let's Take the Con Out of Econometrics." *American Economic Review* 73 (March): 31-43.

___. 1985. "Sensitivity Analysis Would Help." *American Economic Review* 75 (June): 308-313.

Leigh-Pemberton, Robin. 1986. "Financial Change and Broad Money," Lecture delivered at Loughborough University Banking Center, 22 October.

___. 1987. "The Instruments of Monetary Policy," Mais Lecture given at City University Business School, 13 May.

Lucas, Robert E., Jr. 1981. *Studies in Business-Cycle Theory*. Cambridge, Mass.: MIT Press.

Lucas, Robert E., Jr. and Rapping, Leonard A. 1969. "Real Wages, Employment and Inflation." *Journal of Political Economy* 77 (September): 721-754.

Lucas, Robert E., Jr. and Sargent, Thomas J., eds. 1981. *Rational Expectations and Econometric Practice*, vols. 1 and 2. Minneapolis: University of Minnesota Press.

Ludlow, Peter. 1982. *Making of the European Monetary System: A Case Study of the Politics of the European Community*. London: Butterworth Scientific.

McAleer, M., Pagan, A. R., and Volker, P. A. 19785. "What Will Take The Con Out of Econometrics?" *American Economic Review* 75 (June): 293-307.

Melamed, Leo, ed. 1988. *The Merits of Flexible Exchange Rates, with an Introduction by Milton Friedman*. Fairfax, Va.: George Mason University Press.

Michaelson, Jacob B. 1973. *The Term Structure of Interest Rates: Financial Intermediaries and Debt Management*. New York: Intext Educational Publishers.

Miron, Jeffrey, A. 1989. "The Founding of the Fed and the destabilization of the post-1914 US Economy." In De Cecco, Marcello, and Giovannini, Alberto, eds. *A European Central Bank?* Cambridge: Cambridge University Press.

Morris, Frank E., and Little, James S. 1974. "The Role of the Eurodollar." In Prochnow, Herbert V., and Prochnow, Herbert V., Jr., eds. *The Changing World of Banking* New York: Harper & Row.

Muth, John. 1961. "Rational Expectations and the Theory of Price Movements." *Econometrica* 29 (July): 315-335.

Pippenger, John. 1973. "Balance of Payments Deficits: Measurement and Interpretation." *Review*, Federal Reserve Bank of St. Louis (November).

Polyani, Karl. 1944. *The Great Transformation*. New York: Rinehart and Company.

Report. 1975. *First Report on the Conduct on Monetary Policy*, from the Committee on Banking, Housing and Urban Affairs, United States Senate. A Report filed Pursuant to House Concurrent Resolution 133. Washington, D.C.: U.S. Government Printing Office.

Report, Delors. 1989. *Report on Economic and Monetary Union in the European Community*. Luxembourg-Bruxelles: European Documents.

Santoni, G.L. 1984. "A Private Central Bank: Some Olde English Lessons." *Review*, Federal Reserve Bank of St. Louis 66 (April): 12-22.

___. 1986. "The Employment Act of 1946: Some History Notes." *Review*, Federal Reserve Bank of St. Louis 68 (November): 5-16.

Sargent, Thomas J. 1987. *Macroeconomic Theory*, 2nd ed. Orlando, Fla: Harcourt Brace Jovanovich.

Sargent, Thomas J. and Wallace, Neil. 1976a. *Rational Expectations and the Theory of Economic Policy*. Studies in Monetary Economics 2, Federal Reserve Bank of Minneapolis.

___. 1976b. *Rational Expectations and the Theory of Economic Policy, Part II: Arguments and Evidence*. Studies in Monetary Economics 2, Federal Reserve Bank of Minneapolis.

Scaperlanda, Anthony. 1977. "Hansen's Secular Stagnation Thesis Again." *Journal of Economic Issues* 11 (June): 223-243.

Schacht, Hjalmar. 1927. *The Stabilization of the Mark*. New York: The Adelphi Company, English translation by Mr. Ralph Butler.

___. 1931. *The End of Reparations*. New York: Jonathan Cape & Harrison Smith, English translation by Lewis Gannett.

___. 1964. "'Money and Currency'—A Historical Perspective." Lecture translated and published by the University of Wisconsin's Bureau of Business Research & Service, vol. 2 (no. 1).

___. 1967. *The Magic of Money*. London: Oldbourne. English translation by Paul Ernskine.

Schwartz, Anna J. 1990. "Monetarism and Monetary Policy," a paper prepared for Southern Economic Association Session, November 1980.

Silk, Leonard. 1985. "Protectionist Mood: Mounting Pressure." *New York Times* 134 (September 17): 29, 36.

Slesinger, Reuben E. 1968. *National Economic Policy: The Presidential Reports.* Princeton, N.J.: D. Van Nostrand.

Solomon, Robert. 1977. *The International Monetary System, 1945-1976, An Insider's View.* New York: Harper & Row.

Staff. 1988. "Bank of England Operations in the Sterling Money Market." Bank of England, October.

___. 1989. "Why peg the pound?" *Economist* (November 4): 111.

___. 1990a. "Bank of England Fact Sheets." Bank of England, Information Office.

___. 1990b. "The European Monetary System." *Fact Sheet*, Bank of England, November.

___. 1991. "The World Economy and Europe: A synopsis of remarks by Leigh-Pemberton." *Bank Briefing*, Bank of England, February.

___. 1992. "Commission of the European Communities." *One Market, One Money.* New York: Oxford University Press, for the Commission of the European Communities.

Subcommittee on International Economics of the Joint Economic Committee, Congress of the United States, Report. 1974. *Making Floating Part of a Reformed Monetary System.* Washington, D.C.: U.S. Government Printing Office.

Sunt, Chris. 1989. *Legal Aspects of the ECU.* London: Butterworths.

Supplement, Proposed Second Amendment. 1976. *Summary Proceedings of the Thirty-First Annual Meeting of the Board of Governors.* Washington, D.C.: International Monetary Fund.

Teigen, Ronald L. 1965. "The Demand for and Supply of Money." In Warren L. Smith and Teigen, *Readings in Money, National Income, and Stabilization Policy.* Homewood, Il: Richard D. Irwin, Inc.

Terrell, William T., and Frazer, William. 1972. "Interest Rates, Portfolio Behavior, and Marketable Government Securities." *Journal of Finance* 27 (March): 1-35.

Thatcher, Margaret. 1993. *The Downing Street Years.* New York: Harper Collins Publishers, Inc.

Thygesen, Neils. 1988. "Introduction." In Giavazzi, Francesco, Stefana, Micossi, and Miller, Marcus, eds. *The European Monetary System.* Cambridge: Cambridge University Press, 1-20.

___. 1989. "The Delors Report and European Economic and Monetary Union." *International Affairs* 65 (August): 637-652.

Triffin, Robert. 1961. *Gold and the Dollar Crisis*, rev. ed. New Haven, Conn.: Yale University Press.

Vogel, Thomas T. 1993. "Bond Rally Rolls On As Inflation Fears Recede; Yield on 30-Year Treasury Issues Falls to 6.73%." *Wall Street Journal* 221 (March 5): C1 and C17.

Vogel, Thomas T., Jr., and Wassel, David. 1993. "Arcane World Is Guide and Beacon to a Populist President." *Wall Street Journal* 221 (February 25): 1 and 4.

Volcker, Paul, and Gyohten, Toyoo. 1992. *Changing Fortunes: The World's Money and the Threat to American Leadership.* New York: Random House, Inc.

Walras, Leon. 1954. (English translation of W. Jaffé). *Elements of Pure Economics.* London: 1st ed., Lousanne, 1874, final definitive ed., 1926.

Weiner, Stuart E. 1992. "The Changing Role of Reserve Requirements in Monetary Policy." *Economic Review*, Federal Reserve Bank of Kansas City 77 (fourth quarter): 45-63.

Weinninger, John, and Parlan, John. 1992. "Small Time Deposits and the Recent Weakness in M2." *Quarterly Review*, Federal Reserve Bank of New York 17 (Spring): 21-35.

Wood, John Cunningham, and Woods, Ronald N., eds. 1990. *Milton Friedman: Critical Assessments*, 4 vols. London: Routledge.

Young, Hugo. 1991. *One of Us: A Biography of Margaret Thatcher*. London: Macmillan.

Index

About the Author

WILLIAM FRAZER is a Professor in the Department of Economics, College of Business Administration, University of Florida. His publications include *Power and Ideas: Milton Friedman and the Big U-Turn* (two volumes), *Expectations, Forecasting and Control: A Provisional Textbook on Macroeconomics* (two volumes), *Crisis in Economic Theory*, and *The Demand for Money*. He was co-author with William P. Yohe of *The Analytics and Institutions of Money and Banking*.

ISBN 0-275-94732-7

9 780275 947323

HARDCOVER BAR CODE